D0985036

THE TRANSITION TO
STATEHOOD IN THE
NEW WORLD

NEW DIRECTIONS IN ARCHAEOLOGY

THE TRANSITION TO STATEHOOD IN THE NEW WORLD

Edited by

GRANT D. JONES
Hamilton College

ROBERT R. KAUTZ
Hamilton College

CAMBRIDGE UNIVERSITY PRESS

CAMBRIDGE
LONDON   NEW YORK   NEW ROCHELLE
MELBOURNE   SYDNEY

Published by the Press Syndicate of the University of Cambridge
The Pitt Building, Trumpington Street, Cambridge CB2 1RP
32 East 57th Street, New York, NY 10022, USA
296 Beaconsfield Parade, Middle Park, Melbourne 3206, Australia

First published 1981

Printed in the United States of America

Library of Congress Cataloging in Publication Data
Main entry under title:
The Transition to Statehood in the New World.
(New directions in archaeology)
Based on papers presented at a conference held at Hamilton College,
Clinton, N.Y., Jan 19–21, 1979.
Includes bibliographical references and index.
1. Indians–Tribal government–Congresses.
2. Indians–-History–Congresses. 3. Government,
Primitive–America–Congresses. I. Jones, Grant D.,
1941– II. Kautz, Robert. III. Series.
E59.T75T7 970.01'1 81-2569
ISBN 0 521 24075 1 AACR2

Contents

Preface

The chapters of this volume are the final outcome of a conference entitled, "The Transition to Statehood in the New World: Toward a Synthesis," held at Hamilton College, January 19–21, 1979. This conference was organized by us, with the financial assistance of The Winslow Lectureship, an endowed fund of Hamilton College. Each author of the contributions that follow presented his interpretations to an audience consisting of both fellow specialists and nonspecialists. The extensive discussion of the issues presented took place in this public forum, often with comments and questions from observers. This was an unusual and stimulating setting for a conference on such a broad and controversial subject.

As evidenced by the degree of change in several of the papers presented at the conference, compared to the chapters in this volume, this meeting of minds had its desired effect – to stimulate new ideas and to move beyond earlier issues. Most of us realized during the final sessions that only a portion of the knowledge shared and the ideas generated had stemmed from the papers themselves, in light of which each author would be forced to reevaluate his ideas. These chapters, in essence, then, represent the continuing impact of the conference discussions upon the authors' original contributions.

The phrase "transition to statehood" reflected our concern as organizers of the conference that the discussion should be directed primarily toward the prehistoric conditions and processes that stimulated the development of the first state level societies in Mesoamerica and Peru. That is, we hoped that participants would address, in particular, those problems that archaeologists must face in their direct analysis of physical remains of the past. Although ethnohistorical and ethnographic analogies have long been regarded – and rightly so – as essential to the study of prehistoric processes, their uncritical application to the special phenomena characterizing "pristine" state development has its problems. A primary concern is with the "paradigm lag" (Leone 1972:16) that can result from the dependence in archaeology upon old ethnographic models; such dependence can even take the form of unwittingly withholding new and readily apparent archaeological insights from the model-building enterprise.

An equally significant problem is a frequent lack of awareness of changes in social anthropological and ethnohistorical thinking that might cast doubts on older analogies. Such issues were frequently addressed during the conference. Although they were not always broached specifically, the contributors appear to recognize a growing need for better archaeological solutions to the state origin problem and for more sensitivity to the problems as well as to the possibilities of ethnographic analogy.

A glance at the Works Cited section informs the reader of the remarkable growth of the anthropological literature concerning state origins. The references are worldwide in scope, theoretically diversified, and varying in their emphasis upon particular aspects of state origins. Thus it was no surprise, given the diverse points of view of the contributors, that whereas some perspectives were fully agreed upon, others were subjects of lively debate. Points of consensus included an antidiffusion bias (inherent, perhaps, in the conference title itself), an acceptance of an evolutionary framework, and a general–(although not totally shared)–suspicion of universally applied monocausal theories of state origins.

One source of debate centered around definitions of "the state," because such definitions are generally derived from varying and often conflicting theoretical positions. Several participants disliked the emphasis placed by others upon "stages" rather than upon processual development. Some intense disagreements were due to varying theoretical biases. This was anticipated, both in the selection of participants and in the organization of the three-day conference into one-day sessions, emphasizing, respectively, ideological, sociopolitical, and environmental factors in the explanation of state origins. With certain shifts this framework has been maintained in this book, and the reader will discover how the lines of argument are drawn.

Robert L. Carneiro, who had been assigned the difficult task of serving as synthesizer for the conference, did so with balance and tact, at the same time infusing his overview with a summary of his insights on the subject. Carneiro's ideas are expanded in the chapter on chiefdoms, situated squarely within the context of a political explanation of the evolution of the centralization of power.

President J. Martin Carovano of Hamilton College, Alice Maxfield, who at that time was Assistant to the President, and Assistant Dean Carol D. Locke provided valuable assistance and support in the planning and execution of the conference, which led to the preparation of this volume. We are grateful for their help and encouragement. We also wish to thank C. Duncan Rice, Dean of the College since 1979, for his continuing support of our efforts to see this work through to publication. Our departmental colleagues Douglas A. Raybeck, Henry J. Rutz, and Michele Teitelbaum who were enthusiastic supporters of the project, made our task easier by their encouragement and advice. Various Hamilton colleagues, especially those of the Government Department, offered valuable suggestions on the ideas presented in Chapter 1. Most of all we owe an immense debt to the contributors of this volume for their patience, their tolerance, and the intellectual stimulation that they brought to the entire project.

Grant D. Jones
Robert R. Kautz

PART I

Introduction

1

Issues in the study of New World state formation

GRANT D. JONES AND ROBERT R. KAUTZ

The aim of this chapter is to identify the principal issues, problems, and common themes that we regard as central to the contributions of this volume and to consider their implications for future studies of the transition to statehood in the New World. Although we attempt to move beyond the particulars of such issues in the later sections of this chapter, the problems that we have chosen to address appear to be inherent in the discussion and polemic, which the contributions themselves are likely to generate. Despite the particular differences among the authors of this volume, we sense an expanding common ground of methodological and theoretical agreement. In our methodological comments we attempt to pinpoint the problems that nevertheless continue to hamper the progress of comparative research in this area; we tentatively suggest how some of these problems might be resolved. Our closing comments are directed toward issues of a more theoretical nature and may well be regarded by some as more divisive than synthetic in their net effect. The aim of these comments, however, is to attempt to demonstrate that a synthesis of divergent perspectives is an appropriate strategy at this point and that in fact the differences among authors may be less significant than generally supposed.

We provide at the outset an overview of the volume as a whole, discussing each chapter as an aspect of the larger organizational themes. This is followed by a discussion of certain definitional problems that still plague the archaeology of state formation, concluding, perhaps unfashionably, that definitions should be as fully grounded empirically as they are logically constructed from theoretical premises. We then consider some of the methodological problems inherent in studying the archaeologically ephemeral but historically necessary processes of development that must have led to state level societies. We conclude with a set of exploratory remarks on the study of the ideology of power in the context of state formation. Our remarks are in no sense intended as a full review of the literature; however, the volume as a whole may be considered as a first step toward such a review.

An overview

During the planning stages of the conference we indicated that it would be useful to categorize the various approaches to the processes of state formation in terms of their respective emphasis upon sociopolitical, environmental, or ideological factors. Individuals were asked to focus upon one of these, although they were in no sense led to believe that the conference organizers thought that knowledge or theories could be so neatly pigeonholed. As Jones remarked during the introduction to the conference,

> Just as anthropologists tend to see the state holistically as a type of central leadership, we find it most useful to regard processes of social and cultural change as a systematic phenomenon including continuous and shifting interactions among social and political institutions, ideological phenomena or systems of belief, and physical processes of interaction with the environment. Any attempt to cast particular weight to any of these phenomena is thus only a matter of emphasis reflecting varying theoretical persuasions on the nature of the particular questions being asked of the data.

It is therefore of no surprise that the following papers tend to view the principal questions at hand from a broad and synthetic rather than from a narrow and strictly empirical perspective. Likewise, the general subject areas into which the chapters fall, even though reflecting the main themes of these chapters, appear to function primarily as guideposts. Although the subject matter has often been a matter of intense, polemic debate, these chapters – with some exceptions – seem to search for a resolution of conflicting theoretical positions and for an increased degree of cooperation in the discovery and analysis of data.

Part II, "Sociopolitical Factors in State Formation," addresses two principal issues: the nature and role of the chiefdom in the process leading up to state formation and the nature of the evidence for "class conflict" in the early New World states. Both chapters emphasize their authors' belief that conflict was a pervasive feature in both the process of state formation and the further consolidation or institutionalization of state control. Such conflict, they maintain, appears to intensify and widen over time, becoming increasingly pervasive with the establishment and maintenance of mature state organizations. Whereas one of these authors – Haas – would clearly identify himself solidly in a camp of "conflict theorists," the other –

Carneiro – is perhaps not so easily categorized. Their approaches differ in important ways, even though they both recognize that a study of relatively rapid systemic changes at the social and political levels *must* be based upon assumptions regarding the importance of conflict.

Carneiro (Chapter 2) develops a set of ideas that formed the core of his conference presentation; that is, the formation of the state is but the culmination of earlier processes of increasing scale in the size and, more especially, the scope of the political unit. In Carneiro's view there is a direct relationship between increasing degrees of political hierarchy and an increasing "transcending of local autonomy." The chiefdom – "an autonomous political unit comprising a number of villages or communities under the *permanent* control of a paramount chief" – represents, then, an ideal type, the first political system based upon "permanent," potentially hereditary control over a multicommunity unit. Although social stratification is a feature of chiefdoms, he considers it to be epiphenomenal to the political process. In this sense his theoretical approach differs significantly from that of Haas, for whom social stratification is the central feature of the process of state formation. In this regard it is important to point out that Carneiro is not explicitly concerned with the early state itself, as is Haas, but, rather, with its predecessor as an ideal type. Also, unlike Haas, who seeks to describe the role of conflict in the maintenance of the early state, Carneiro is concerned more with the evolutionary processes in which conflict serves ultimately to consolidate centralized leadership.

Carneiro presents a valuable synthesis of the history of the concept of the chiefdom, crediting the modern coinage of the term to Oberg (1955) but the modern origin of the concept to Steward (1948). The evidence for the chiefdom as defined by Carneiro is primarily ethnohistorical, and it is likewise ethnohistory that informs his minimal/typical/maximal chiefdom classification. Yet we find that Carneiro's own intellectual roots reach down to the logical rather than to the empirical categories of Herbert Spencer, whose "doubly compound" society conforms to Carneiro's multicommunity chiefdom concept. We wonder if parallel intellectual genealogies could not be reconstructed from other nineteenth-century evolutionary writers as well; this would certainly be the case if an attempt were made to account for Steward's important concept of levels of sociocultural integration (Steward 1955), an idea central to the notion of additive process in sociopolitical evolution.

Challenging other writers who do not share his view of the universal importance of the chiefdom as a stage in state formation, Carneiro criticizes as well the diagnostic criteria that most archaeologists have applied in seeking to identify prehistoric chiefdoms. His solution to the latter problem would be systematic surveys, the results of which would be comparative plottings of size versus frequency of sites. Such surveys, however, might better be regarded as tests of the bimodal curve/chiefdom versus the trimodal curve/state model rather than as independent confirmation of the sociopolitical phenomenon itself. Finally, Carneiro seeks to establish a unitary theory of the origin of chiefdoms and, by extension, of the state itself. This theory is an elaboration of his earlier statement (Carneiro 1970) on the evolutionary role of warfare in situations of environmental circumscription, but in this case the argument is more explicitly extended to apply to the chiefdom as well as to its logical successor – the state. Population pressure and a large potential territorial scale are considered as additional necessary conditions for the growth of three-tiered polities (potential states) that possess, in addition, the power to draft an army, tax its citizens, and enforce laws (true states). Warfare in the sense of territorial conquest is a prime mover in this process; class conflict, although perhaps an inevitable result, is nonetheless epiphenomenal in Carneiro's theory of the origins of political stratification. We see that the state is the mature expression of the process of warfare and territorial consolidation – a process through which the two-tiered chiefdoms were passed and superseded somewhere along the way. The model is thus elegantly simple and, of course, the subject is of considerable controversy.

Haas's chapter (3) is based on the premise that "the state developed primarily as a coercive mechanism to resolve internal conflict that arises between economically stratified classes within a society." Such a premise would, as Haas argues, be opposed to one that views the role of the state as "an integrative mechanism to coordinate and regulate the different parts of complex societies." The aim of the chapter is not, however, to argue the relative merits of these two positions on conceptual grounds but, rather, to demonstrate empirically the superiority of the conflict premise. This demonstration is solidly grounded in Fried's (1967:186) focus upon stratification (differential access to basic resources) as the sine qua non of the state. Because the presence of stratification must in such a model rapidly lead the short-lived chiefdom to the state proper, through the mechanism of class conflict, we find Haas focusing more upon the early state than upon its evolutionary predecessors or the processes that led to its emergence (see Friedman and Rowlands 1978 for a contrasting neo-Marxist approach to this problem). Similarly, he dismisses the problem of distinguishing the characteristics of pristine and secondary states (Price 1978) on the grounds that early states in general will manifest similar characteristics, regardless of their historical status (a position taken to considerable extremes by Claessen and Skalnik 1978).

With such methodological dilemmas left in abeyance, Haas proceeds to explore the evidence in Andean and Mesoamerican early states for the differential distribution of three types of "resources that can be considered basic in all societies." He examines, in particular, evidence for differential access to food, the tools used to produce and prepare food, and the items used defensively against the physical environment and an antagonistic social environment. In a valuable synthesis of heretofore scattered data Haas presents, on the basis of such evidence, a strong case for the presence of economic stratification in early New World states. He then goes on to examine in an original fashion the archaeological evidence for "internal conflict and centralized application of force" in such prehistoric societies. Such conflict would, in contrast to the system-expanding, transformational warfare cited by Carneiro, appear to be primarily system-maintaining or system-reinforcing – that is, a necessary condition for the maintenance of economic stratification but not a sufficient condition for the emergence of such stratification. It must therefore be reemphasized that Haas and Carneiro treat the role of conflict in different, even though potentially complementary, senses.

Haas's archaeological treatment of internal class conflict and the use of centralized force is bolstered by ethnographic evidence from Hawaii and the Zulu, again indicating his willingness to search widely for useful comparative data. His caveats concerning the general weakness of the data for the comparative study of early states notwithstanding, it might be best at this juncture to recognize the general validity of the stratification-conflict model as tested here, while recognizing that an equally strong case could probably be made for the internal structural dependencies (integrative features) of any sociopolitical system as complex and as large as the early state.

In Part III, "Evironmental Factors in State Formation," Cohen (Chapter 4) and MacNeish (Chapter 5) review the role of the physical environment as an explanatory variable in the growth of state level polities. Those who are familiar with the earlier writings of these authors (in particular, M. Cohen 1977; MacNeish 1964, 1967, 1971b) will discover that they have brought earlier ideas to bear upon the present issues, although hardly in the sense of slavish repetition.

Cohen suggests that the phenomenon of state development should be viewed from two perspectives. The first, which is evolutionary in emphasis, seeks to discover general parallel adaptive strategies in the several areas of pristine state development. The second, whose emphasis is historical, addresses the question of why some populations achieved early pristine statehood while others did not. Although Cohen believes that a single explanation may be able to account for a *general,* essentially worldwide, evolutionary trend "in the direction of centralized hierarchical government," he considers it possible that the *particular* appearance of true states in certain areas of the world may have been "in fact random outcomes of historical processes . . ." That is, although he believes that an explanation of general evolutionary trends may be posited, only particularistic analysis may be able to account for specific local variations: multilinear evolution is nothing more than the historical epiphenomenon of more general evolutionary processes.

Cohen's general explanation of the worldwide trend toward increasing political centralization is a variation upon the thematic question addressed in his book, *The Food Crisis in Prehistory* (M. Cohen 1977). In the present case this question asks "why many independent human populations began to organize themselves hierarchically at about the same time after so many millennia of egalitarian structure." The answer to this problem has its origin in worldwide population pressures that Cohen believes led to the abandonment of a hunting-gathering way of life in favor of agricultural strategies. The net effect of this transformation was to increase caloric production per unit of space while narrowing the scope of the ecological niche. Increased ecological vulnerability resulting from the decline of traditional buffers among farming populations resulted in the development of various social and economic responses that functioned to reduce the stresses of increasingly risk-filled situations. Among the responses to such stress were the development of storage systems, the increase of interregional trade in both luxury goods and subsistence products, and the growth of centralized authorities who played a major role in providing economic security.

Cohen's contrast between general parallel adaptive responses that led to increasing centralization and, in particular, local adaptive responses that led to the appearance of true states—which are therefore the "epiphenomena" of general evolution—would appear to contribute to a solution of a problem implicit in Carneiro's discussion. That is, Cohen appears to be concerned, in Carneiro's terms, with differentiating between explanations that might account for "chiefdoms" and those that would account for "states," whereas Carneiro sees the latter as the logical result of the inexorable processes set in motion during the rise of the chiefdom. Carneiro's unitary theory cites the potential territorial extent of a polity as a key factor in state formation, whereas Cohen would argue that no such single key factor may be discovered.

MacNeish's chapter is an ambitious effort to identify significant parallels among four worldwide regions of pristine state formation (Mesoamerica, Peru, the Near East, and the Far East). These parallels include both a series of twelve developmental periods with associated sociocultural forms and a complex set of necessary (i.e., environmental) and sufficient (i.e., sociocultural) conditions that, according to MacNeish, account for the shift from one developmental period to the next. He sees, then, striking similarities in the process of evolution toward statehood throughout the world.

MacNeish's empirical odyssey begins with the summary results of his and his associates' remarkable Tehuacán Valley study. The Tehuacán materials, which form an unbroken sequence from early collectors through "pristine national states," serve as the basis for a highland Mesoamerican variation of the comparative sequence. Against this ideal typology he poses another ideal type: a lowland Mesoamerican variation with certain differences in the sociocultural features of periods IV through XI, differences that are ultimately traced to environmentally distinguishable conditions. Between the highland and lowland types there is a gradient of variations not included in this chapter. Perhaps the most striking distinguishing feature of the highland–lowland dichotomy is his contention that systems of centralized leadership in the highlands tended toward the secular, whereas those of the lowlands were more sacred or religious in nature. We feel certain that this will be one of the more controversial aspects of MacNeish's discussion. Was the Olmec priestdom civilized center (X–L) really more "sacred" than the Tehuacán Palo Blanco chiefdom administrative center (X–H); or was Tikal (an XI–L sacred city state) really more "sacred" than Teotihuacán (an XI–H secular city state)? Some might also argue that MacNeish's pristine national states (XII) are actually secondary phenomena and that the sacred and secular city states (XI) more accurately represent his search for the pristine state.

MacNeish's efforts to establish empirical parallels between developmental periods and environmental variations in Mesoamerica, Peru, and, to a lesser extent, the Near East and the Far East is a stimulating one, although regional specialists will surely discover room for argument. This, of course, is MacNeish's aim, as he argues that monocausal theories like those based upon population pressure and warfare are insufficient in light of the importance of "real sufficient conditions," such as highland–lowland interaction spheres, the capacity for large food surplus production, and well-organized exchange systems. Such sufficient conditions have their origins in a universal set of broadly similar environmental factors, so that MacNeish's argument is far more deterministic than that of Cohen – and more universal in its scope than the multilinear approach of Sanders and Webster (1978). It should be emphasized, however, that MacNeish stresses the tentative nature of his hypotheses and his hope that they will encourage more detailed comparative study.

The authors of Part IV, "Ideological Factors in State Formation," each notes that modern archaeology has tended to understress the

importance of ideology – religious ideology, in particular – in theories of prehistoric change. It is Coe's view (Chapter 6) that a highly
uniform, conservative cosmological orientation functioned throughout pre-Columbian Mesoamerica to legitimize the countinuity of
stratified, centralized societies. Keatinge's contribution (Chapter 7),
likewise, emphasizes the central role of religious ideology in the
centralization process and in the spread of civilization, but he argues
further that religion was an "enabler or catalyst," used by rising
political forces to gain control over the manipulation of populations
and their strategic resources. Finally, Freidel (Chapter 8) argues that
culture itself has been slighted as a causal factor in theories of state
origin and that the process must be understood, at least in part, in
terms of the special nature of the ideological underpinnings of early
civilization. Although these three authors are hardly in agreement
on all issues, their emphasis on the forms and functions of ideology
in state formation suggests a new trend in archaeological theory, one
for which there is ample reinforcement in contemporary ethnographic and ethnohistorical thinking.

Coe, like Freidel, contends that the materialist orientation of much
recent archaeology has blinded investigators to the manifested importance of ideology as a central feature of the early state and as a
central factor in state formation. Religious ideology, in particular, he
argues, is known to be a destroyer of the status quo as well as a
creator and maintainer of stability. Religious ideological differences
must therefore be central to any understanding of the differences
between "widely divergent forms of social, cultural, political, and
even economic life" throughout the several world areas of state formation. It is clear from Coe's statements, as well as from those of
Keatinge and Freidel, that a broader examination of ideology as a
factor in sociopolitical and economic change shifts our focus from
the state per se to more general questions about the nature of the
development of *civilization,* of which the state is but a feature, an
organizational epiphenomenon. The implications of these concerns
are discussed later in this chapter.

Readers familiar with Coe's writing will not be surprised by the
importance that he places on what he believes to be the conservative
continuity of the Mesoamerican world view or cosmology, at least
from Early Classic through Postclassic times. Such continuity, Coe
suggests, may have extended from Olmec times, although Formative
period evidence for Olmec religious content is far from satisfactory.
It is clear, however, that religious ideology played a major role in the
establishment both of the Olmec centers, such as San Lorenzo, and
the later highland Classic period city of Teotihuacán. His interpretation of the rapid formation of such centers, whose conceptualization
was apparently rooted in publicly expressed religious motifs, rests on

the plausible assumption that ideological innovation is more rapidly communicated among large numbers of people than are innovations in other spheres of life. Although he does not explore such innovation in terms of specific political stimuli and consequences, its implications for an understanding of the political activities that characterize increasing centralization of power are considerable. Somewhat surprisingly, Coe raises the possibility of the importance of religious revitalization movements in this process, only to pass over the idea for want of evidence prior to the lowland Maya Classic "collapse." As we suggest later, there is reason to believe that any religious innovation in an increasingly complex society may well be symptomatic of the presence of such movements.

Keatinge, focusing upon the Chavín data from Peru, suggests that the initially peaceful spread of a religious cult or movement, which appears to have had a set of common ideological themes, "provided both the means and sanctions for an increasing secularization in the goals of developing societies, goals whose emphasis became inexorably politico-economic." A Chavín-influenced religious movement penetrated a number of widely spaced local societies and was ultimately influential in the "initial fostering of interregional trade and communications" and "the development of economic and redistributive systems." Central to this process, he argues, was the establishment of pilgrimage centers under some degree of centralized authority, coupled with increasingly centralized controls over long-distance trade and other forms of communication between far-flung regions (cf. R. E. W. Adams 1977:94). What Keatinge adds to an interpretation of the importance of ideology in the establishment of centralized power is, then, the idea that universalizing religious beliefs serve as the "enabler or catalyst" in the formation of secular controls on a supralocal basis.

Keatinge argues further that the presence of large-scale and elaborate ceremonial structures in both pre-Chavín coastal and highland Peru indicates that politically controlled labor in the service of religion had long been available to these Peruvian polities. The later spread of a Chavín-influenced cult was thus built upon earlier ideological conceptions of the nature of power as supernaturally legitimized, and the effects of Chavín expansion were in the form of local syncretisms serving to legitimize further externally introduced secular controls. The oracle centers, which appear to have been part of the process of increasingly centralized controls, served as a means of defining new priesthoods intermediary between the gods and the common people. One is reminded of Helms's somewhat parallel argument that protohistoric and sixteenth-century Panamanian chiefs enhanced and increased their authority by their specialized knowledge of foreign, distant places, knowledge that was incorporated into definitions of their own sociopolitical and religious roles (Helms 1979:131–43). Priesthoods are the human sources for the external legitimation of emerging states, whereas chiefs seek to legitimize their own authority by increasing their personal charisma: In both cases the argument for the political role of religious ideology is compelling.

The use of "naked coercive force," Keatinge maintains, is not evident in the spread of the Chavín cult. The sanctions supporting increasing centralization were religious rather than military in nature. Ideology may then be the functional equivalent of the conflict that was believed by Carneiro, Haas, and others to be so essential in the growth of state institutions. Keatinge does not seem to be arguing that his views constitute an aspect of an "integrative" (as opposed to "conflict") model of state formation, yet the use of supernatural sanctions by a ruling elite may well imply something other than the threat of human military solutions to social breakdown. We can only conclude that there is something unsatisfactory about the conflict-integration dichotomy; for if Keatinge's reconstruction is reasonably correct, we are finding increasingly centralized power, presumably in the context of increasingly powerful supernatural sanctions but with no apparent evidence of open conflict. We would presume that the *threat* of conflict between groups in such increasingly stratified societies, generated from below, is as great as the threat of conflict from supernatural sources. All that we can hypothesize concerning this potential standoff of power is that its resolution (whether in the form of social reform, a religious cult movement from below, the appearance of a new and more powerful ruling elite-inspired supernatural threat) may not be readily evident in the archaeological record. Alternatively, the evidence may be there, but the investigator who, being intellectually committed to other questions, is unable to ascertain or interpret it. We will return to these problems.

Freidel's "Civilization as a State of Mind: The Cultural Evolution of the Lowland Maya" (Chapter 8) is an explicit plea for a recognition among archaeologists for the centrality of ideational (i.e., cultural) factors in the study of sociopolitical change.

To Freidel the principal issue at hand is not the evolution of the state itself but, rather, the "cultural evolution" of civilizations. He regards the state to be but one aspect of complex society, or society characterized by hierarchy; and in such complex societies state religions are a principal means by which both the social hierarchy and its attendant symbols are made manifest to the society at large. The evolutionary process leading up to this interdependency between state ideology and hierarchy cannot, Friedel argues, be reduced to materialist explanations in which ideology is regarded as epiphenomenal. Rather, he would suggest that, "cultural realities themselves are intrinsically dynamic, that social action is predicated upon cultural definition rather than the reverse, and that social organization will change as the cultural reality structuring it changes."

Following this line of reasoning, he proceeds to launch an ambitious reinterpretation of the differences between Late Preclassic highland and lowland Maya society. The issue that concerns Freidel is why the highland pioneers who settled the Maya lowlands in Preclassic times established a unified cultural tradition that during the Classic period became "one of the great and enduring civilizations of the ancient world," whereas the precocious highland centers stabilized into a set of locally differentiated, "balkanized" polities characterized by regional cultural variation. Finding various earlier ecological and economic explanations of these dichotomous cultural developments unconvincing, he seeks to discover differences in the highland and lowland cultural systems themselves that might shed light on the issue. Central to these differences was the development of hieroglyphic monuments in the lowlands, which he believes, "registered the advent of radical, elitist cult practices." Whether such cult innovations originated in the highlands or the lowlands is not yet clear, but their destruction in the highlands following the vulcanism that occurred toward the end of the Late Preclassic spelled the end of the hieroglyphic tradition as a major form of monumental scale communication in that region. In the lowlands, however, hieroglyphics in association with other forms of public art became a central, symbolic expression of the power of state level religion and, therefore, of state government itself.

Although hieroglyphic writing may have played such a role in the lowlands in early Classic times, this is not yet clear for the Late Preclassic. In a detailed analysis of monumental art styles in the Late Preclassic highlands and lowlands, Freidel attempts to demonstrate that even at that early date, monumental art, especially symbolic architectural decoration, was used in the lowlands as a universalizing form of ideological communication; in the highlands, however, monumental art reflected the localization of cultural tradition. Such use of architecture as an artistic medium appears to be strictly a lowland phenomenon and is interpreted by Freidel as indicative of the emphasis that the developing lowland pioneers in this "peripheral" region placed upon "central, communitywide public ritual as a means of social organization." The nature of this stylistic practice is explored in comparative terms, and the suggestion is made that the symbolism of public architectural art was widely shared throughout the Late Preclassic lowlands; such shared traditions were, it is argued, the groundwork for the cultural unity of Classic period lowland Maya civilization. In a stimulating final section Freidel explores the idea that the lowland Maya standardization of centralized religious institutions opened up avenues for an accelerated inter-chiefdom trade in sumptuary goods, resulting in increasing mo-nopolization of scarce and desirable goods by an increasingly power-ful hierarchy. The final outcome, in Friedel's view, was thus the "cultural invention" of the state, the locus of power for civilization.

Freidel's argument is complex and thought provoking. We suspect that it will generate significant controversy on several fronts, both empirical and theoretical. Although readers may find his underlying premises extreme and his dismissal of opposing points of view premature, the issues that he raises are substantial and intellectually stimulating.

The problem of definition

One of the most pervasive difficulties arising from the existing lit-erature on state origins seems to be that of formulating a generally acceptable definition of the typological category of pristine "state." What might appear to be a rather simple first step is seldom a straightforward empirical exercise, for most definitions have been derived from certain theoretical biases. When we follow a common circular pathway, the next step is to find ethnographic evidence for the existence and covariation of the pertinent variables. Then, of course, comes the task of confirmation, which ideally relies upon archaeological data recovery. The outcome of this kind of exercise is a proliferation of competing although, perhaps, equally valid defini-tions. This state of affairs may be quite useful for the stimulation of polemic debate. Nevertheless, it might also be argued that a central purpose of any definition should be to derive generalizations and understanding about what is being observed. This purpose is inher-ently impossible when definitions and their referents differ from author to author.

Like Fried, we disagree with Hoebel's view that "where there is a political organization there is a state. If political organization is uni-versal, so then is the state" (Hoebel 1949:376, cited in Fried 1967: 228). Also, like Fried (1967:229–30), we agree that the state cannot be defined by structural features alone, as, for instance, by the pres-ence or absence of a legislature, a bureaucracy, or any other such derived manifestations. Rather, following Fried (1967:229–42), the state might best be characterized at this stage of investigation as a type of institutionalized political action: all states wield centralized power in an order of socioeconomic stratification, regardless of whether this power is manifest or latent, raw or subtle. Whatever the form of power, the "paraphernalia of structured control" (Fried 1967:230) will guarantee the order of stratification and the alloca-tion of basic resources. Nevertheless, there are two basic difficulties (one theoretical and one practical) in accepting Fried's further arguments concerning the *origin* of the pristine state in terms of his political definition of that institution.

The theoretical difficulty stems from an uncertainty as to whether political repression actually forms or creates the state or whether, instead, it is primarily concerned with maintaining the positions of prestige and differential access to basic resources that would have arisen due to the prior origin of the state. The question is, Did the power of the state cause the transition to statehood? On the basis of its circularity, the proposition sounds inprobable.

The practical difficulty with Fried's definition raises more troublesome questions. Although we are in accord with this emphasis on the activity of the state in wielding power once it appears, such defined activity, even though easy to test within an historical framework, is exceedingly difficult to discover archaeologically. This practical difficulty is particularly troublesome, for in order to test propositions about the *transition* to pristine states, the investigator must work exclusively with archaeological data. Power is an elusive quality, and when used most effectively it may well be all but hidden. Merely finding a locus of power is insufficient evidence for the state; the discovery of what particular ends are realized by that power is also necessary. Sanders (cited in Hill 1977:307) is certainly very optimistic in claiming that "You can measure . . . the degree to which they are forced to pay taxes, or carry their disputes to a central authority, and so on. I think there are a whole series of such measures of power that we can get at archaeologically." Without belaboring the point, we feel that the archaeological technology of discovery is not yet sophisticated enough to distinguish Sanders's measurements from those provided by means of relatively straightforward data on trade, authority (as opposed to power), or unbalanced reciprocity. The more subtle information is not readily accessible in the archaeological record. What *is* accessible are the products of that political exercise of power. These products have been called "civilization" elsewhere (cf. Adams and Culbert 1977).

Ronald Cohen (1978a:2–5) provides a review of these problems of definition, characterizing the following patterns among commonly used definitions of the state.

Definitions based upon stratification
Identified with Marx and Engels and more recently Fried, these definitions reflect the view that the emergence of states was due to institutionalized inequity in which some ruling group has better access to life-sustaining resources. It is the category of definition that we have just considered.

*Definitions stressing the structure of government and/or
information-energy exchanges*
Used by Herbert Spencer, Henry Maine, and Service (1975), these
definitions stress the loss of local autonomy to a centralized and
hierarchical system. Wright and Johnson (1975) and R. N. Adams
(1975) examine the transactions involving the flow of decisions and
energy resulting from this pattern. This view seems more acceptable
as the criteria are archaeologically observable. However, because
managerial statuses and their resulting hierarchical arrangements
"always *derive* from and are made legitimate by a power source"
(Binford, in Hill 1977:308), our remark regarding power as a defini-
tive characteristic of states, yet notoriously difficult to pinpoint, is
also appropriate here.

Definitions based upon diagnostic traits
This category is certainly out of style. R. Cohen (1978a:3) states, "it
is next to impossible to obtain a set of traits that applies to more than
a few societies." However, as mentioned earlier, it is important to
attempt to outline some archaeological manifestations of the state
phenomenon, as this is necessary to understand the origin of pristine states. Whereas the material manifestations (or traits) of centralized power (such as hierarchical levels of consumption and distribution and complex exchanges of information, energy, and goods)
abound; archaeologists are not able to excavate power itself; nor can
they recover the social action underlying hierarchical units (cf. Flannery 1972).

In addition to the problems just cited, and in fact further com-
pounding them, there is a common confusion between what is meant
by the state versus the broader category of "civilization." Service approached this difficulty by maintaining that a state "is integrated by a
special mechanism involving legitimatized force. It constitutes itself
legally; it makes explicit the manner and circumstances of its use and
forbids other use of force by lawfully interfering in disputes between
individuals and between corporate parts of the society" (Service
1962:173–4). The concept of *civilization,* on the other hand, incorporates aspects of social complexity (castes, classes), more intensive systems of redistribution, marketing and trade, urbanism, technology,
and so on (Sanders and Price 1968:44–5). The formal distinction
among these classes of phenomena often breaks down, however, as
was the case when Service (1975) attempted to find archaeological
evidence for the state and, in fact, seemed to find only civilization. It
would seem that the distinction may be important from a practical
standpoint only under two conditions–if one were actually distinguishing the evolution of government independent of other institu-

tions or if one could provide an example of an "uncivilized" state or a civilization without state government. In practice, it would appear that neither condition is often, if ever, satisfied. We readily admit that the archaeological confirmation of the process of state formation may be accessible only because we are able to discern the consequences (i.e., civilization) of the process (i.e., the origin of the monopoly of power).

Beckner (1959) and later Sokal and Sneath (1963) have suggested that modern scientists might profitably reexamine a concept stated long ago (Jevons 1877:682–98). Their discussion of the concept – involving the procedures by which scientists attempt to categorize classes of phenomena – seems particularly germane to the conceptualization of the state and civilization. Most formal categories or classes are based upon Aristotelian logic. That is, a definition of the class attempts to capture the essence of that group: its "real nature" or "what makes the thing what it is" (Sokal and Sneath 1963:12). In formal logic this "real nature" gives rise to properties that are considered as inevitable consequences: "the essence of a triangle on a plane surface is expressed by its definition as a figure bounded by three straight sides, and an inevitable consequence is that any two sides are together longer than the third" (Sokal and Sneath 1963:12). Logical systems of this sort are considered systems of analyzed entities. This form of reasoning, however, is patently inappropriate for the consideration of a definition of a "state", because the relations among causes, processes, and consequences comprise a system of unanalyzed entities whose components resist being inferred from the various definitions of the state that have thus far been offered. This line of reasoning, which specifies that each property of the class be unique to that class, and therefore a necessary condition for inclusion, has been termed a "monothetic" grouping.

In contrast to this line of reasoning Beckner has offered the following "polythetic" arrangement:

> A class is ordinarily defined by reference to a set of properties which are both necessary and sufficient (by stipulation) for membership in the class. It is possible, however, to define a group K in terms of a set G of properties f_1, $f_2, \ldots, f_n$ in a different manner. Suppose we have an aggregation of individuals (we shall not yet call them a class) such that:
> 1. Each one possesses a large (but unspecified) number of the properties in G.
> 2. Each f in G is possessed by large numbers of these individuals and
> 3. No f in G is possessed by every individual in the aggregate.

> By the terms in (3), no f is necessary for membership in this aggregate; and nothing has been said to either warrant or rule out the possibility that some f in G is sufficient for membership in the aggregate (Beckner 1959:22).

For our purposes, it is not necessary to specify conditions that would provide an applicable hierarchy, as is required for a formal taxonomy. However, this form of reasoning may provide us with a way to provide a definition of the state without resorting to the circularity so common in such enterprise. For example, it is quite common to define a "state" as a natural category comprised of character complex "X." Thus every member of the category "state" (both known and unknown forms) is expected to possess X. Conversely, possession of the character complex X defines the state. Henceforth the state as defined by X assumes a degree of permanence and reality completely out of proportion with the tentative basis upon which it was initially proposed. Circular reasoning arises when new characteristics, instead of being evaluated on their own merits, are definitionally ruled out by the prior category of X. This form of prejudgment entirely ignores the fact that the state based upon character complex X has been *assumed* but not *demonstrated* (Sokal and Sneath 1963:6 – 20).

In a polythetic arrangement, on the other hand, we might (arbitrarily) suggest that some sixty unweighted, nonoverlapping characters might best represent the category "state." Those sixty characters could be derived from archaeological manifestations best referred to at present as "statelike." After some experimentation we might discover that any thirty characters associated together offer convincing evidence that we are, indeed, dealing with a state. With repeated manipulation of the characters (the numbers and kinds of which could be potentially infinite) and some actual temporal control, we might gain access to additional information regarding characteristic growth cycles in various kinds of polities. As new modes of archaeological discovery are suggested, such new information might easily be added to the existing system.

Following such a procedure might provide at least four benefits: (1) We would not be methodologically trapped (although we are admittedly affected) by our a priori definitions of the state. (2) We would have more fully comparable data. (3) We would be dealing with the systematic relationships among a number of institutions in addition to politics (i.e., the broader characteristics of what might be considered to be "civilization"). (4) We would possibly learn new information about state formation and the growth of civilization by noting repeated covariation between certain characters. Once there is a consensus regarding the acceptable numbers and kinds of variables, we might find that certain cases would be dropped from consideration as states, consequently enriching our understanding of chiefdoms; whereas others might be added on purely empirical grounds, challenging some of our preconceptions regarding the prehistoric distribution of states.

After factoring out those characters that are repeatedly associated with early states, we may then be in a position to offer a contextual definition of the state. Although we are aware that there will be strong objections to such an empiricist view of the definitional problem, experimentation along the lines suggested might well serve in the long run to challenge certain generally accepted prior assumptions, thus increasing the potential for more effective theory building.

The problem of method and theory

Stages and typologies

In another context Leach (1961) has characterized the practice of anthropological typology as something akin to butterfly collecting. We would agree with this assessment, even as it applies to those ideal types known as cultural evolutionary "stages," were it not for the fact that typology and classification provide a means of producing a basic shorthand of comparison and analysis. The understanding of the evolution of complex societies has benefited considerably by the traditional evolutionary stage models proposed by Fried (1967), Service (1962), Steward (1955), and White (1949). Employment of the comparative approach by these authors has stimulated the attempt to discover universal evolutionary processes and sequences. Attempts to introduce a multilineal evolutionary model, "in which different evolutionary trajectories relate to variations in the natural environment" (Sanders and Webster 1978:250) seem to have added flexibility to the primarily unilineal models of earlier writers. Nevertheless, structuralist arguments of this kind, in and of themselves, seem to add little to our understanding of the *transformational* process of cultural evolution (cf. Friedman and Rowlands 1978a:250). Sanders and Webster's position appears actually to be only a rather sophisticated form of possibilism, a model that "stresses several evolutionary trajectories, each conditioned by a distinctive permutation of environmental variables" (Sanders and Webster 1978:281).

The delineation of various evolutionary stages is useful in the sense that such ideal types provide starting points for the description of pertinent sociocultural and environmental variables interacting synchronically and morphostatically, omitting their morphogenic properties altogether. Like the palaeontologist's description of various stages in an organic evolutionary sequence, the sociocultural evolutionary stages proposed by these various anthropologists are simply conceptualized segments of nature (or culture) that help to make it understood. This is as it should be, for it appears that misplaced teleological arguments are the most common outcome of structural "explanations" of cultural evolution. Rather than regarding sociocultural stages themselves as the objects of transformation, it would be more useful to recognize that self-interested individuals (or, perhaps, small common interest groups) act rationally in situations of scarcity, stress, or incomplete information, whereas larger units of social or cultural analysis may not in fact represent the locus of such goal-oriented behavior. Therefore an analysis of the transformation of one state in an evolutionary sequence to another must consider an analysis of individuals or smaller units acting in concert in order to achieve perceived ends, whereas the state itself should not be regarded as "being forced" to acquire some emergent quality and thus to transform itself. Such an approach leads to the view of interlocking subsystems; and although complex, empirically grounded, and subject to considerations of stochastic variation, it provides a better understanding of change than the structuralist model does.

Political factors
Regardless of the particular evolutionary model that one accepts, it is clear that the process of state formation embodies increasing scales of inclusiveness in every sphere of human life. Various scholars have offered causal explanations of this differentiation of new functional units that exert ever increasing control over all human relations. One of the more commonly heard polemics concerning this trend is the dichotomization of "conflict theories" *versus* "integrative theories" (Fried 1978:38; Service 1978:21; Haas, this volume). It has occurred to us that both "conflict" and "integration" may be present at the same time within any sociopolitical context, because the origin of a specific political condition (exploitation on the one hand, or beneficence on the other) may have little or nothing to do with the perceptions of those being ruled. Whether the control exercised is benevolent or malevolent, it appears to be a universal feature of any hierarchical polity that the perceptions of how interests are best served are constantly manipulated by those who monopolize power. It is the success or failure of rulers in convincing those being ruled that may ultimately determine the success or failure of the history of individual polities, regardless of the nature of that rule or the motivations of the rulers. The exclusivity of these perspectives is thus questionable, even though it should be recognized that vested interest groups or individuals do in fact act in part to maintain their own interests. (Here it might be noted that Earle [1978] suggests that such interests are best met when there is a minimizing subsistence

production strategy to one in which production is maximized due to political intervention.)

Economic factors
Within the economic sphere more complex societies provide an increase in the scale and intensity of trade and external communication, a trend that appears to be largely a function of the maintenance at ever higher levels of consumption of ruling elites through their demand for luxury or sumptuary goods (Earle 1977; Freidel, this volume). Yet it must be stressed that his trend seems to be a gradual process of increasing control and diversification of exchange that predates the state itself. Ranked societies in the ethnographic record characteristically elaborate such systems of balanced and unbalanced reciprocity in the maintenance of leaders and their retainers and kin (Peebles and Kus 1977). Chiefdoms known from ethnohistorical sources (Helms 1979), as well as archaeologically documented stratified societies (Rathje 1971b) experienced rising demands for critical and sumptuary goods obtainable – which thus became all the more valuable in the legitimization of elite-controlled trade – only at great distances. In some cases centralized control over trade may well have functioned to average resources across complex microenvironments, especially in times of stress (Isbell 1978).

Rising demands, distribution requirements through time and space, and other elements of an expanding economy may all be indicators of the gradual loss of economic diversity (see Cohen, this volume). These trends lead in turn to the establishment of special function elites as manipulators of a territorially diversified economy. This positive feedback process comes about due to the increasing energy content of the total system as increasing numbers of consumers compete for increases in the output of the relatively declining number of producers. The process is complemented by and eventually dependent upon an increase in political scale to manage increasingly complex networks of redistribution. The reward in the process for the managers is, of course, power; and power may be easily converted to goods. Once set in motion, the process spirals.

Ideological factors
Finally, the appearance of the first states marks an increase in ideological scale, reflecting the inclusion of more territory and people under systems of commonly held ideational propositions and concepts of sanctity. As Rappaport has pointed out, larger scale societies become increasingly intolerant of ideological diversity. Common ideological elements function to mark off politically and socially relevant groups: "sanctity helps keep subsystems in their place" (Rappaport 1971:36). Thus the shift in ideological scale matches and comple-

ments the growth and integrated diversification of the polity and economy. As these processes represent interrelated systemic and sub-systemic changes, the prime mover question (which causes which?) appears to be untestable. Although ideology has recently been archaeologically unfashionable (Fritz 1978; Willey 1976), it is nevertheless clear to us and to several of the contributors to this volume that religious ideology in particular was consciously manipulated during periods of increasing social complexity. The effect of this manipulation was to overcome the tendency of the wider system to fragment as well as to legitimize internal differences of power and wealth.

In the closing section that follows we explore this interpretation of the role of ideology in more detail. In summary, we should emphasize that a thorough understanding of the origin of the state requires that we refine our understanding of several areas of investigation. The first is in the construction of an abstract model of evolutionary stages that provides us with the "hardware" of a black box analogy. That is, if we could thoroughly understand the fundamental character of both the chiefdom and the state, we would be in a much better position to postulate the factors that might best explain the conversion from one stage to the next. Although progress has been made in this direction, much remains to be explored.

A second area is in the proposal of plausible multiple causes that, acting on the structure as defined by the model of evolutionary stages, will upset and eliminate one or more homeostatic mechanisms, thus setting in motion what Maruyama (1963:166) has called "morphogenesis" or a deviation-amplifying mutual causal process (permanent systemic change). What concerns us is that because so many probable hypotheses have been advanced, we are faced with either of two possibilities: All of the proposals, save possibly one, may be wrong; or, alternatively, all may be correct, but for different times and places. Sanders and Webster (1978) take the latter position by proposing a multilineal evolutionary model in which different variables become operant because of variations in the external environment. Although it must be agreed that differences in environment will stimulate different cultural responses to systemic perturbations, we have already noted our view that Sanders and Webster's model is a form of possibilism with the same drawback that hinders any possibilistic model. That is, possibilism, can explain the presence of certain features at particular times and places but it cannot explain their absence.

We are therefore led to suggest a third, little understood area of investigation of a process that we conceive as being both stochastic and epiphenomenal (cf. Cohen, this volume). It is stochastic because the perturbations brought to the system by various "causes" are, under normal conditions, systematically "resisted," returning the system to its original form. The question therefore becomes, How much stress can a system undergo before it begins to transform into a different system? This process may be considered epiphenomenal, for it is a product of the relationship between the structure and the perturbations: It has the quality of emergence, taking as many forms as the various causes that precede it.

In sum, we consider an appropriate preliminary structure (a mature chiefdom, perhaps) to be a necessary condition for the transition to statehood. We also consider the various causes, such as stratification (Fried 1967, 1978), warfare under conditions of circumscription (Carneiro 1970), political control of an increasing economic sphere (Isbell 1978; Earle 1978), environmental limitations under conditions of population growth (Netting 1972; Sanders and Webster 1978), irrigation (Sanders 1968; Wittfogel 1957), class conflict (Diakanov 1968), and complexes of several of these (R. McC. Adams 1966) as comprising one or more necessary conditions for this transition. These conditions, together with the necessary condition (stochastic epiphenomenon) produced by an appropriate form and degree of stress, could be considered as constituting sufficient conditions for the emergence of the pristine state.

In the following concluding section we tentatively explore the idea that religious revitalization, through the mechanism of crisis cults, may well have been a common stochastic response to situations of stress, leading ultimately to the institutionalization of state religious systems. These, in turn, as Keatinge has argued, in this volume, ceased to be epiphenomenal as they began to serve as the pathway to the institutionalization of centralized power.

Crisis cults in the transition to statehood

Chapters 6 to 8 appear to point part of the way toward an improved understanding of the process of state formation. In the remarks that follow we explore somewhat further the implications of these interpretations of the role of religious ideology as a primary factor in the initial centralization of political systems. Such interpretations, we would argue, give pause to any systemic model that regards the role of ideology in the "infrastructure" of any early state as secondary. Godelier, a Marxist critic of such models as constructed by the "vulgar materialists," has emphasized the infrastructural status of religion among all peoples. Referring to the Inca state, he has written,

> This belief in the Inca's supernatural abilities, a belief shared by the dominated peasantry and dominant class alike, was not merely a legitimizing ideology, after the fact, for the relations of production; *it was a part of the internal armature of these relations of production* (Godelier 1978a:10; emphasis in original).

And elsewhere,

> Belief in the divinity of the Inca, the son of the Sun, and
> in the supernatural efficacy of his powers, a belief shared
> alike by the dominated peasantry and the dominating ar-
> istocracy, was not merely a surface or a phantasmic reflec-
> tion to the social relations. It was an internal part of the
> exploitative politico-economic relations endured by this
> peasantry. This belief could not have been a mere legiti-
> mation after the fact of an existing state which could have
> existed and developed without this belief. The belief itself
> was a source of the peasants' obligation to the Inca and
> therefore a source of their consent to his domination and
> to a form of subjection which did not necessarily require
> physical coercion by an army or police force to be ac-
> cepted (Godelier 1978b:13).

The Incas were, of course, the last in a series of state-supported New
World empires, and Godelier does not in this context address the
process by which the deification of the ruling class came about in
Andean prehistory. The point, however, is that the belief system is
regarded by some Marxists to be an integral factor in the social relations of production, functioning in the last analysis to conceal the "internal structure" of reality from "consciousness" (Godelier 1978a:4).
Religion, then, is not an institutional realm but, rather, a functional
aspect, in the case of a complex society, of the maintenance and reproduction of the social relations of production.

A similar perspective on the functions of religious ideology, although in this case from the perspective of the evolutionary adaptations of living systems, has been outlined by Roy A. Rappaport
(1971) in his brilliant article, "The Sacred in Human Evolution."
Rappaport, true to his ecological biases, regards religious rituals and
their sacred underpinnings (or sanctity) in terms of their "informa-
tional aspects" and "their place in the cybernetic processes of adaptation" (Rappaport 1971:25). That is, ritual and sanctity are universal
elements in human evolution, contributing to the living system's ability to maintain itself in a fluctuating environment and to transform
itself "in response to directional environmental changes" (Rappaport
1971:24; cf. Drennan 1976b). Without discussing the finer points of
this argument, we understand Rappaport to be making the following
generalizations about the special role of ritual and sanctity in human
evolution.

All ritual, Rappaport argues, serves to communicate information
about the status of human social relations; it reduces ambiguity to the
barest minimum in a world dominated by ambiguous and conflicting
external signals. Religious rituals are distinctive in that they allow the

utterance of propositions ("Hear, oh Israel, the Lord our God, the Lord is One"), which have no material referents and are therefore unverifiable. Their truth, however, is unquestioned by the faithful; they are sacred or inbued with sanctity (Rappaport 1971:29). Nevertheless, of course, sacred statements are often extended to sanctify real world affairs. Without such "ultimate sacred propositions" and the "sanctification of discourse," human society could not exist, for such propositions alone are guarantees of the truthfulness of symbolic discourse. Simply stated, the sanctification of discourse protects society from the insecurity and anarchy that would be generated by a band of liars. In this sense, sanctity reduces the effects of stress. Although sacred propositions must therefore be as old evolutionarily as language itself, the affect that humans associate with rituals probably long predates the idea of sanctity.

Rappaport also invokes the notion of control hierarchies – systems of subsystems of subsystems, and so on. In the case of social control hierarchies, the self-interests of higher levels of the hierarchy manipulate sacred propositions, which have no material referents, to suffuse with sacred content material statements concerning information that lower order levels of the hierarchy need in order to operate. In any hierarchical system, as for instance, in a system of agricultural production, lower order levels might tend to make decisions on the basis of their immediate interests. Regarding higher level regulation as arbitrary, criticism and recalcitrance would threaten the stability of the control hierarchy.

> However, to phrase regulation in moral or mythic terms – that is, to sanctify it – is to place it beyond criticism and to define recalcitrance as sacrilege. Sanctification transforms the arbitrary into the necessary, and regulating mechanisms which are arbitrary are likely to be sanctified (Rappaport 1971:35).

Sanctity therefore "helps to keep subsystems in their place" (Rappaport 1971:56), serving in many kinds of societies as the "functional equivalent of political power" (Rappaport 1971:37).

Noting that until relatively recently in human history religious ritual and sanctification managed to provide for the regulation of relatively large societies in the absence of discrete human authorities (Rappaport 1971:38), Rappaport concludes that the appearance of such authorities came hand in hand with the sanctification of their authority. The early states, which were at least initially theocratic, invested their rulers with sanctity. Such sanctity "provided a foundation for the regulatory prerogative of discrete authorities, perhaps even permitting their emergence" (Rappaport 1971:39).

Anthropologists, as opposed to some students of religious history, have been hesitant to tackle the question of the evolution of concepts of the sacred, even as they apply to the evolution of political forms. Wallace has proposed a four-stage typology of religions, suggesting that,

> religion began with (1) societies that possessed both individualistic and shamanic cults; proceeded to (2) societies with individualistic, shamanic, and communal cults; then went to (3) societies with individual, shamanic, and communal cults, plus ecclesiastical cults devoted to a pantheon of Olympian deities; and finally produced (4) societies with individualistic, shamanic, and communal cults, plus ecclesiastical cults devoted to a singular monotheistic conception of deity – that is, a high god who, while not usually the sole supernatural entity or manifestation, nevertheless has unquestioned sovereignty and ultimate power over both man and all other supernatural entities (Wallace 1966:256).

Richard Adams has equated stages (1) and (2) with band and tribal level organizations, whereas stage (3), representing beliefs in "some larger, more distant, more encompassing wellspring of 'power'," corresponds to chiefdoms and kingdoms (R. N. Adams 1975:237). This latter "stage" would seem to correspond with Wallace's in that increasing hierarchy in the social, political, and economic spheres fosters religious beliefs concerned with the morality of behavior "between peers and between persons in positions of relative super- and subordination" (Wallace 1966:257).

Wallace's insights, however, fail to cope with the critical relationship between what we may assume to be the identification of early political authorities with sacred power and the processes that led to the allocation of such power to these authorities. R. N. Adams (1975:238) has observed – in our view, correctly – that charisma, which must have been a feature of early political/religious leadership, is, so to speak, "in the eye of the beholder." That is, charismatic qualities are assigned to individuals in times of stress, when positive activity is regarded as impossible, or problems as unsolvable, in the absence of legitimate leadership held by means of allocated power. Adams's emphasis upon the consensus that must underlie the initial granting of power to charismatic authority is an important one, for it adds a limiting temporal dimension to the sanctification process seen by Rappaport as being essential to the maintenance of social control hierarchies (cf. Weber 1968). A shared sense of crisis *leads to* the allocation of power to a charismatic leadership. However, routinization will, we may assume, threaten the allocated power of the authority unless either (1) the sense of crisis is maintained (suggesting, perhaps, that charisma must be renewed by allocating more authority to one or another leader) or (2) the sense of crisis is effectively overcome by a political leader's increasingly effective use of force.

We suspect that Adams has oversimplified a complex situation by suggesting that "spiritual or theistic charisma" is primarily a phenomenon of chiefdoms, fragmented states, and millenarianism, whereas "political charisma" is characteristic of the trends toward political centralization in certain areas of the world during the last several centuries (R. N. Adams 1975:239). Although he may be correct in observing that the secularization of authority tends in many cases to be associated with the growth of polities of scale, where authorities are no longer "able to reciprocate with conduct that will work to the benefit of a very large number of people" (R. N. Adams 1975:239), some great empires, such as that of the Inca, did manage to retain a full measure of sacred authority for their leaders, despite (or perhaps because of) the secular demands that their control entailed. The implication of the stubborn survival of sanctity as a principle of hierarchy is that sanctified leaders, once fully established, reduce their vulnerability to popular disillusionment by means of effective crisis management in the sphere of what Rappaport would refer to as unverifiable sacred propositions. That is, if the top level of the control hierarchy can effectively maintain a monopoly over the flow of information pertaining to certain sacred events that filter downward through the system, any crisis in these events may be attributed to inadequate or inappropriate behavior at the lower levels of the system. Only the sanctified leader can observe and interpret these events, and only his bureaucracy of sacred and secular officials can communicate them downward. Only the common person, powerless in the face of the sanctified threat, can ultimately ward off the effects of divine crisis, whether this be by means of tribute, sacrifice, or service. The sanctified leader and the system that he monopolizes would thus seem to be an ideal example of Romer's Rule, which maintains that "the initial survival value of a favorable innovation is conservative, in that it renders possible the maintenance of a traditional way of life in the face of changed circumstances" (Hockett and Ascher 1964:137, quoted in Rappaport 1971:24). We will return to this problem later.

If sanctified, charismatic leadership is in fact a universal feature of the early state, we might well ask whether or not there is a universal process by which the sanctification of leadership comes into being. Although the conditions of comparative historical and ethnographic analysis are not conducive to the identification of pristine cases, we believe that some insight into this process may be gained by the study of what has variously been called millenarian movements, revitalization movements, or crisis cults. Although such cults that are known to us have appeared largely in acculturative situations or among subgroups of a state level society, they appear to be so ubiquitous in human history that we might well assume that they are as ancient as sanctified, charismatic leadership itself. As we follow this line of reasoning, it may therefore be useful to explore briefly the idea that the origins of political systems characterized by the sanctification of legitimate authority may be sought in the recognition of the universality of cult responses to various forms of crisis (cf. Netting 1972:234). Such a perspective is attractive in that it does not demand a universal set of particular necessary conditions for the appearance of the cult response but, rather, rests on the assumption that *crisis* as a generally necessary condition will under certain circumstances result in a series of events that may well lead to the establishment of a sanctified authority. The conditions that determine a particular state of crisis, or the conditions promoting stress, are highly variable; however, once in place, the responses to such conditions may well be remarkably uniform.

Although the comparative study of crisis cults (the term that, following LaBarre [1971], we have chosen to use) has been pursued intensively by social anthropologists and historians, archaeologists seem to have taken little note of such phenomena. This avoidance may be attributable to the hesitation of archaeologists to extrapolate ideological processes from their data, particularly in recent years when "materialist" explanations have been more fashionable in archaeological circles. It was, of course, during this period that the crisis cult literature was most fully developed. A second factor in this avoidance, however, may have been the assumption that such cults, which seem to occur during times of stress associated with rapid cultural and economic change, are primarily phenomena of the modern world. Research in the Americas, in particular, has tended to associate signs of early civilization and political centralization as a gradual process of stabilization rather than as a symptom of overwhelming, dislocating change. Ideological continuity has often been stressed as opposed to ideological revolution; early civilization has been viewed as the harbinger of panregional cosmological codification instead of as a moment of cultural distress in an ongoing series of transformations in which the political stakes in sanctified leadership were increasing at geometric rates.

Wallace (1956), whose formulation of "revitalization movements" was among the first systematic treatments of this subject, argued that the principal function of new religious movements was to offer a ritualized means of coping with crisis at the community level:

> When most, or even many, of a community's members are unable to maintain a satisfying image of self because their

culture or their fellow citizens, or both, are making it impossible to realize the values they have learned to take as
goals and models, then the customary individualized procedures for achieving personal salvation may no longer be
effective . . . Under circumstances of anomie . . . and pervasive factionalism . . . a new religious movement is very
likely to develop, led by a prophet who has undergone an
ecstatic revelation (comparable to becoming a shaman),
and aimed at the dual goal of providing new and more
effective rituals of salvation and of creating a new and
more satisfying culture (Wallace 1966:157–8).

Wallace's formulation recognizes that such movements arise out of
conditions of stress upon the sociocultural system by such factors as
"climatic and biotic change, epidemic disease, war and conquest,
social subordination, or acculturation" (Wallace 1966:159). Such
stresses create anomie and disillusionment, characterized by both
individual and social symptoms of disorganization and disorienta-
tion. The "revitalization process" that follows such conditions, he
argues, follows a universal paradigm of events, resulting, if "successful," in the routinization of the charismatic leadership that formu-
lated the sociocultural innovations inherent in the cult itself (Wallace
1966:162).

LaBarre, in a *tour de force* review of the literature, referred to such
responses as "crisis cults," by which he meant

any group reaction to crisis, chronic or acute, that is cultic.
"Crisis" is a deeply felt frustration or basic problem with
which routine methods, secular or sacred, cannot cope.
Any massive helplessness at a critical juncture may be a
crisis . . . The term crisis cult basically includes any new
"sacred" attitude toward a set of beliefs; it excludes the
pragmatic, revisionist, secular response that is tentative
and relativistic . . . [It] does not prejudge "primitive" or
"civilized," superior or inferior, innovative or traditional,
dispossessed or elite, colonial or interclass, majority or minority culture . . . And, finally, the term assumes that
there is no cult without crisis, and that much as the body
sometimes responds inappositely to stress . . . so also does
the mind (LaBarre 1971:11).

Perhaps LaBarre's major contribution is his insistence that there can
be no theory of crisis cults based upon a predictable set of variables
that create crisis. He considers in detail various theories of
causality – political, military, economic, messianic, "great man," acculturation, and psychological stress theories – and concludes that no

single cause or concatenation of causes can be invoked universally (LaBarre 1971:26–7). Crisis, he seems to argue, is the condition of humans; for any ideology is an artificial, symbolic, construct that may not suffice to cope with the nonhomeostatic nature of the real world.

This discussion leads us to the general conclusion that a salient feature of the process that characterized all the early transitions from small societies that were basically egalitarian or weakly stratified to their historical derivations, which were characterized by greatly increased scale and allocated power, was that of the cultic response to crisis. The very phenomenon of rapid centralization and increasing scale implies that crisis is an imminent feature of the process and that the omnipresence of the evidence of supracommunity level sacred symbols in the archaeological record leaves little doubt that the response to crisis embodied the routinization of cultic behavior in the increasing sanctification of political leadership. This process must find its origins, of course, in the factors that led societies to abandon the elaborate systems they had devised in order to maintain a standoff in power relations – a standoff that characterized power relations in the manipulation of material and linguistic symbols as well as in the means of subsistence for most of human history.

This standoff survived in some areas of the world until recently, as in Melanesia, where elaborate and highly symbolized systems of exchange served to balance out any long-term confrontations of power in either the material or spiritual spheres of life (see also Netting's discussion of the Kofyar priest-chief [Netting 1972:221–7]). As Weiner (1976) has emphasized in her study of exchange systems among the Trobriand Islanders, in such a Melanesian society, with only the weakest development of allocated power relationships, the norms of cross-cutting exchanges preclude the unbridled pursuit of self-interest. Perhaps even more important, however, is that Trobrianders do not tolerate open confrontation over the use of supernatural powers that can affect community life, although some individuals have access to such power. Confrontation over supernatural power, which unlike the symbolic powers of the material exchange system are not universally available, is perceived as dangerous to the balanced self-interests of the community at large:

> Confrontation lifts the mask of myth, and all individuals are made to face the reality of power with which they must cope. This revelation reaffirms the danger of social interaction while simultaneously confirming the need to contain competition within lines of exchange so that individual intent remains balanced by the constraints of exchange . . . From time to time, (this) treaty of peace must

momentarily be broken. But in these moments myth is reformulated once again out of fear of reality, a reality of power (Weiner 1976:225).

Thus to break the treaty of peace in an egalitarian society – or we might add, to break the treaty of peace in a stratified society based upon the allocated power of sanctified leadership – is to transform the myth that hides the reality of power. The new myth literally creates a new reality of power, a reality that is highly tolerant of absolute power and is couched in a language that sanctifies the use of that power. (That such "new realities" are essential to modern crisis cults explains, of course, the fear in which they are held by established authorities and the degree to which such authorities attempt to limit their influence.) The question that still eludes us, however, is the nature of the crisis that is likely to lead to the collectively innovated new myth, which we have asserted results from the routinization of the crisis cult. What were the crisis conditions with which initially stratifying societies had to cope? Undoubtedly they were many and varied, but the following three general situations must have been among them at varying times and places:

Agricultural intensification
Population pressure, it is often assumed, resulted in changing social relations of production in the agricultural sphere, gradual at first but increasing in rapidity with transformations in the division of labor and increasing the potential for conflict over lands subject to agricultural intensification. Increasingly differential control over land and labor, regarded by many to be the essence of the centralization process, may well have been brought on by a perceived crisis in human relations vis-à-vis the environment. The crisis would only momentarily be "solved" by the sanctification of those who monopolize differential control, however.

Increasing population and increasing intensification stimulate further conditions of crisis – recognition of the ecological hazards of agricultural specialization, recognition of the increasing limits of productivity and thus the increasing potential of surplus value, and recognition of the real uses of power in the form of agricultural tribute payments to sanctified leaders – conditions that ultimately generate crises that result in the sanctification of new centralized powers over the total agricultural system (see Netting 1972).

Social conflict
Intimately related to the effects of agricultural intensification is the growth of larger sedentary communities. Factional conflict, especially in situations of physical and social circumscription, may well

have been a central feature of such growth. The content of such conflict would have been varied and pervasive, prime material for the development of crisis cults. Here we may recognize the functions of the sort of externally directed expansionism that Carneiro (this volume) cites for the development of early chiefdoms. However, we are more inclined to see such expansionism as closely attuned to internally generated movements that granted sanctified power-holders the legitimate right to pursue external conquest. Such processes of sanctification, we may assume, however, predated the pressures for external conflict.

Cultural conflict

If expansionism was in fact a characteristic of early stratified societies, a central problem of these societies must have been that of incorporating their neighbors into a cosmological order that transcended local cultural differences. In such situations there would have been a parallel to modern crisis cults in acculturative situations, wherein colonized societies react with the formulation of alternative cosmic orders and, in some cases, with the routinization of new political systems that are "better suited" to the new political and economic reality. Simultaneously, we would hazard to guess, there may have been crisis cult efforts devised by the sanctified leadership of the conquering polity designed to co-opt the colonized society in a higher order syncretistic cosmology that incorporated elements of belief common to both systems. Such processes would suggest that the problems of empire building, which in some cases (as among the Inca) involved the absolute abstraction of a cosmological order, encompassed varying cultural traditions in the total expansionary chiefdoms and protostates (cf. Drennan 1976b:358–9).

On a slightly different level, Helms, in her study of contact period Panamanian chiefdoms, has emphasized that sanctity was often achieved by adopting foreign cults that added an aura of mystery and power to the ritual behavior of the sanctified chief (Helms 1979). In other words, the Panamanian chief obtained new power from afar in the form of knowledge unavailable to the common person. As in the case of expansionism, cultural differences were mediated by sanctified powerholders. In both cases, sanctified power overcomes the threat of crisis generated by cultural difference, as the routinized cult surpasses the individual knowledge of society's members.

Lewis (1978) has proposed that small-scale political maneuvering and the use of military charisma may act in a similar manner in the development of centralized authority. Cultural conflict may be inherent during periods of positive feedback, due to the nature of relations between those whose control resources are related to *security* as opposed to those whose control resources are related to *efficiency*. Such conditions would be particularly crucial during periods of population pressure (cf. Netting 1972). Another stochastic process has been documented by Saxe (1977), who describes the systemic changes that occurred in the Hawaiian Islands as a consequence of contact with Europeans; in this case the changes entailed the rapid transformation of a complex chiefdom to a state. Secondary state formation, as in the Hawaiian Islands case, inevitably has this stochastic element; yet no other kind of polity, we maintain, would experience this transformation unless the other structural preadaptations were present.

In search of the state
Our remarks have suggested the qualitative nature and the relative rapidity of the processes of pristine state formation. Such transformational rapidity is, of course, known from historic cases of secondary state formation. It must also be emphasized that although it is useful to reflect upon the general evolutionary process of social stratification, this broad, widely distributed process should be distinguished from the narrower conditions that resulted in state formation (see Cohen, this volume).

If we agree that a form of society resembling the chiefdom as defined by Carneiro (this volume) was the logical and probable empirical *threshold* toward a system in which the power of sanctified authority was allowed to approach its pragmatic limits, we are forced to ask what *special conditions* and *general processes* might have characterized the several first steps taken across that threshhold. The general process toward statehood, we have suggested, may well have been characterized universally by the cultic response to crisis, resulting in a rapidly increased sacred and secular authority of power-holders and the extension of that authority to include previously independent political units. The conditions of crisis that brought this general process into play, however, were stochastic in nature. In each particular case, then, we are potentially faced with the documentation and analysis of unique historical circumstances, as well as with the discovery of more general processes.

The methodological implications of this perspective have yet to be fully examined, much less resolved and empirically explored. Notwithstanding, it is clear that if in fact state formation processes were in certain aspects qualitative in nature and characterized by religious and political transformations under conditions of rapid change, then the archaeological identification of such processes should be feasible. The regional approaches offered by Keatinge and Freidel in this volume present evidence that appears to confirm our assumption that increasing political stratification was associated with the relatively rapid widespread distribution of unified, publicly symbolized religious conceptions. Because the early state must have been, we have maintained, a regional phenomenon, methodological control over regional analysis must be emphasized in the study of the transition phenomenon. Because the process must have been rapid, considerable temporal control will have to be maintained. Because the process must also have been discontinuous, representing sudden replacement of earlier sacred symbolic systems or their integration into newly introduced religious conceptions (see Keatinge, this volume), interpretation of such ideographic evidence must be treated with the same care as that of the evidence for the particular form of the *material* expansion of the political economy.

The chapters of this volume indicate that although significant progress has been made toward the archaeological identification of both the general process and the individual historic sequence of state formation in the New World, there is considerable work yet to be done. This work must continue to address theoretical as well as methodological and empirical issues, and interpretations at each level must be well informed by the comparative products of historical and ethnographic study. The issue at hand – the transition to statehood – is far more than a passing fancy of a small intellectual community. The issue, in fact, thrusts the archaeologist into the realm of modern society, for "the rulers" have not abandoned us since the initial advent of the state:

> We do not really know whose rules we obey. We can identify some of our most immediate rulers . . . We can recognize those philosophers, thinkers, religious leaders of whose contributions we are aware. We do not know all the others, countless, who deriving one from the other, stretch far back in history (Sereno 1968:166).

PART II

Sociopolitical factors in state formation

2

The chiefdom: precursor of
the state

ROBERT L. CARNEIRO*

Perhaps the main conclusion to emerge from the conference that precipitated this volume is that we still know very little about chiefdoms.[1] And the corollary to this conclusion is, naturally enough, that we need to know more. After all, the state has become a major object of study for anthropologists, and chiefdoms are the antecedents of the state.

Yet the great interest that has existed in states is only now beginning to be matched by a similar interest in chiefdoms. In fact, until relatively recently, the existence of the chiefdom as an evolutionary stage was hardly recognized. "Despite the fact that chiefdoms are numerous and are found widely separated on the globe," wrote Service in 1962, "they have not been set off as a distinct form of society, significant in their own right" (Service 1962:173).

Since Service wrote those lines, though, the picture has changed. Chiefdoms have begun to attract the eye of anthropologists. Thus Colin Renfrew (1973:542) has even called chiefdoms "a fashionable concept." In this paper I would like to take a closer look at chiefdoms, examining their attributes, the process that gave rise to them, and their position in the course of political evolution.

The most significant factor about chiefdoms, in my opinion, is that they represent the first transcending of local autonomy in human history. With chiefdoms, multicommunity political units emerged for the first time. It could not have been an easy step to take because it took some three million years to achieve. During more than 99 percent of human history, local autonomy prevailed in human society, and no permanent aggregation of communities into larger political units seems to have occurred prior to the Neolithic. It was only during the last 7,500 years that the first steps were taken in supravillage aggregation.

But although it took a long time in coming, when it finally took

*I would like to express my gratitude to Laila Williamson, my research assistant, for her help in assembling and digesting the materials on which this chapter is based.

place this step proved to be no isolated or tentative one. Within a few millennia of the rise of the first chiefdom a veritable explosion of chiefdoms occurred in many parts of the world. And in most of these areas, within a millennium or two of the first chiefdoms, states arose.

The transcending of local sovereignty and the aggregation of previously autonomous villages into chiefdoms was a critical step in political development – probably the most important one ever taken. It crossed a threshold, and once crossed, unlimited further advance in the same direction became possible. The emergence of chiefdoms was a *qualitative* step. Everything that followed, including the rise of states and empires, was, in a sense, merely *quantitative*.

Chiefdoms thus constitute a major stage in political development. At the lower end of this development, they mark the end of the era of autonomous villages; at the upper end, they usher in the state.[2] These contributions make chiefdoms well worth examining, and therefore I would first like to trace briefly the history of the concept of chiefdoms.

The history of the concept of chiefdoms

Surprisingly, the term "chiefdom" is relatively new in anthropology. In its current sense it was first offered by Kalervo Oberg in 1955. However, it was given its greatest impetus by Elman Service in 1962 when, in his very influential book, *Primitive Social Organization*, he proposed the chiefdom as a general evolutionary stage. But the concept of chiefdom, if not the term, precedes both Service and Oberg, stemming from the work of Julian Steward.

Chiefdoms are particularly well represented in the Circum-Caribbean area, and much of volume 4 of the *Handbook of South American Indians* (Steward, ed., 1948) is devoted to a description of the chiefdoms of this region. Because it was Julian Steward who first spotlighted these chiefdoms, let us see how this occurred and examine Steward's comments about them.

When Steward began working on the *Handbook*, the chiefdoms of the Circum-Caribbean had long since ceased to exist. They had either been exterminated or else deculturated down to the level of autonomous villages, the "Tropical Forest" level. Thus Steward (1948a:xv) wrote that it had "been supposed that the culture of the Antilles and nothern Venezuela should be classed with those of the Tropical Forest." However, evidence to the contrary was beginning to accumulate.

First, according to Steward (1948a:xv), came the work of Samuel Lothrop (1937), whose "summary of the ethnography found in early documents of the Conquest period of Panamá and his ar-

chaeological work at the late pre-Conquest site of Coclé furnished
cultural evidence of peoples who can scarcely be recognized as the
precursors of the modern *Cuna*." Shortly thereafter, wrote Steward
(1948a:xv), Paul Kirchhoff undertook "a thorough perusal of all
the available early chronicles bearing on the peoples around the
Caribbean Sea, and he points out that, far from having a primitive
culture such as that observed among their descendants of the past
century, these tribes were highly developed." While editing the
Handbook of South American Indians, Steward examined Kirchhoff's
evidence and was impressed by it. "It was mainly at his suggestion,"
Steward (1948a:xv) wrote, "that the editor [Steward himself] segre-
gated the articles on the tribes of this area from those of volume 3
of the *Handbook* ["The Tropical Forest Tribes"] and grouped them
in the present volume."

In his summary article to volume 4 of the *Handbook, The Circum-
Caribbean Tribes,* Steward (1948b:2–3) characterized Circum-
Caribbean culture as follows:

> The tribes carried on intensive farming, which outranked
> hunting, gathering, and fishing in its productiveness and
> which supported a dense population and large villages.
> The typical community was a large, compact, planned
> village of several hundred to several thousand persons. It
> consisted of pole-and-thatch houses arranged in streets
> and around plazas, and it was surrounded by a palisade.
> In the village were temples, special residences for chiefs,
> and storehouses.
>
> Society was characteristically stratified into three or
> four classes. The village chief stood at the social pinnacle,
> and in some areas he ruled over federations of villages or
> tribes. Characteristically he lived in a large house, re-
> ceived tribute, had many wives and retainers . . . , wore
> special insignia and ornaments, was carried by his subjects
> in a litter, and at death his body was either mummified or
> desiccated and placed in a special house or temple, or it
> was buried, accompanied by wives and servants . . . There
> was rarely an organized priesthood, for in most of these
> tribes the shaman, and in some the chief, functioned as
> intermediary between the people and their gods. Simi-
> larly, the noble class tended to merge with that of the
> chiefs, except where extreme stratification occurred . . .
>
> Wealth was a major factor in the status of chiefs and
> nobles, and it was produced by . . . [their] large house-
> holds, together with some tribute from commoners and
> even from other tribes.

In describing the advanced cultures of the Circum-Caribbean, Steward focused on the attributes of the chief. He tended to depict the chiefdom in terms of the status, privileges, and perquisites of its head. Thus in the preceding quotation he spoke of the chief's special house, the large number of wives and servants he had, his special insignia of office, the fact that he was carried in a litter, the mummification of his body, and the burial of his retainers with him at this death. However, except to say that "in some areas he ruled over federations of villages or tribes," Steward did not portray Circum-Caribbean chiefdoms in terms of their political and territorial structure.

Steward saw the Circum-Caribbean type of culture as an evolutionary stage. In South American cultural development, the Circum-Caribbean level had grown out of the Tropical Forest level, and in turn had given rise to the Andean level. In discussing the emergence of the Andean level of culture, Steward said it had developed out of a "Formative" level, using the correlative archaeological term. But he proceeded to describe the Formative in exactly the same terms he had used to depict Circum-Caribbean culture at contact times. Indeed, he did so explicitly (Steward 1948b:8). However, Steward saw no hard and fast distinction between Circum-Caribbean and Andean culture and said that the latter differed from the former "more in elaboration than in essential form or content" (Steward 1948b:7).

Despite the fact that he dealt extensively with chiefdom-level societies in the *Handbook,* nowhere in this work did Steward use the word "chiefdom." Nor did he employ *señorío* or *cacicazgo,* the terms generally used by early Spanish chroniclers in referring to chiefdoms. Thus, although he described an important type of society in considerable detail, Steward left it unnamed.

In 1955 this type of society was given the name "chiefdom" by Kalervo Oberg in his article, "Types of Social Structure among the Lowland Tribes of South and Central America." Oberg proposed a typology of sociopolitical units that, although he applied it only to lowland South and Central America, consisted of general developmental stages, which, as Daniel Gross (1973:187) later put it, was "untainted by a historical particularist approach." That is, it could be applied anywhere in the world where substantial political evolution had occurred. Oberg's typology was:

1. Homogeneous tribes
2. Segmented tribes
3. Politically organized chiefdoms
4. Feudal type states
5. City states
6. Theocratic empires

In his article Oberg used the term "chiefdom" quite unselfcon-

·sciously. He did not claim to have coined it, nor did he say he had derived it from anyone else. As far as I know, this was the first time this type of political unit was given a distinct name. In characterizing chiefdoms, Oberg (1955:484) wrote:

> Tribal units belonging to this type are multivillage chiefdoms governed by a paramount chief under whose control are districts and villages governed by a hierarchy of subordinate chiefs. The distinguishing feature of this type of political organization is that the chiefs have judicial powers to settle disputes and to punish offenders even by death and, under the leadership of the paramount chief, to requisition men and supplies for war purposes.

Oberg proceeded to cite some of the same features of chiefdoms that Steward had, such as the fact that paramount chiefs had many wives, were carried in litters, and lived in large houses. But it is clear that, unlike Steward, Oberg defined chiefdoms in terms of political hierarchy and territorial control rather than the high status of the chief.

In 1959 Steward once again turned his attention to the subject of South American chiefdoms in his book, *Native Peoples of South America,* coauthored with Louis Faron. By then Steward had read Oberg's article and had evidently been influenced by it. His definition of a chiefdom (a term he now used) involved the incorporation of many villages into a larger political unit. Thus he spoke of "a number of small multicommunity societies, which have been designated . . . 'chiefdoms' . . . " (Steward and Faron 1959:174). And on the next page he wrote: "While 'chief' usually denotes the leader of a band or village, we extend its meaning to designate leadership of several communities which we call 'chiefdoms' " (Steward and Faron 1959:175).

Steward further divided chiefdoms into two subtypes, militaristic and theocratic (Steward and Faron 1959:177). However, at the upper end of its range, he expanded the concept of chiefdom to include societies more complex than those to which Oberg had applied the term. Thus Steward spoke of "strong chiefdoms like that of the Chibcha, or Muisca" (Steward and Faron 1959:175), which Oberg (1955:485) had classed as a feudal type state.[3] Already, then, we see the beginnings of a problem that still troubles us today: Where do we draw the line between a chiefdom and a state?

Although written just prior to the appearance of Oberg's article, and thus not employing the term "chiefdom," Marshall Sahlins's *Social Stratification in Polynesia* (1958) was a milestone in the discussion of this type of society. In this work Sahlins dealt with fourteen Polynesian islands, most of which were at the level of chiefdoms.

Indeed, largely through Sahlins's book, Polynesia has come to be regarded as the area of chiefdoms par excellence.

Yet in characterizing complex Polynesian societies in terms of evolutionary level, Sahlins did not use strictly political criteria. For example, he did not emphasize the power and functions of the chief as such or the number of villages that he controlled. Instead, he used the degree of social stratification to rank the Polynesian societies in his sample. His plan, he said, was "to order Polynesian societies on a stratification gradient" (Sahlins 1958:1).

Sahlins distinguished four levels of social stratification for Polynesia and assigned each of the fourteen societies in his study to one of these levels on the basis of its degree of social stratification. Arranged in order of descending amount of stratification, these four levels were: Group I (Hawaii, Tonga, Samoa, Tahiti); Group IIa (Mangareva, Mangaia, Easter Island, Uvea); Group IIb (Marquesas, Tikopia, Futuna); and Group III (Pukapuka, Ontong Java, Tokelau).

In a general way, it can be said that these four levels of social stratification are correlated with different levels of political organization. Reading the attributes cited by Sahlins for each of the four levels, one can roughly equate a type of political organization with each of them. I would say that chiefdoms are best represented by Groups IIa and IIb. Below this level, the societies in Group III seem to be little more than autonomous villages, whereas those in Group I seem well on their way to becoming states, if they are not so already.

Although Sahlins emphasized those characteristics of Polynesian chiefs having to do with social status and prestige, he also listed some of their more directly political attributes. These included the "ability of chiefs to confiscate goods of others by force in some cases," and the "ability to inflict secular punishment on wrongdoers including [the] ability to kill or banish those who infringe chiefly rights" (Sahlins 1958:11). However, he seems to have regarded these attributes not so much as touchstones of chiefdoms as political entities but, rather, as indicators of a high degree of social stratification.

Sahlins made it quite clear early in his work that he thought the basis of power and prestige for the Polynesian chief was *redistribution*. Indeed, it was through his *Social Stratification in Polynesia* that the concept of redistribution was reintroduced into anthropology and began to gain the wide usage it enjoys today.[4] In his introduction Sahlins wrote that "Everywhere in Polynesia, the chief is the agent of general, tribal-wide distribution," and "derives prestige from his generosity," and that in turn, "his prestige permits him to exercise control over social processes . . ." (Sahlins 1958:xi). It is clear from this and other passages that for Sahlins, chiefdoms had an economic basis rather than a political one.[5]

The first full-blown exposition of the nature and basis of chiefdoms came in Elman Service's *Primitive Social Organization* (1962). Service appears to have been strongly influenced by Sahlins's work on Polynesia[6] and, like him, saw chiefdoms as having an economic rather than a political basis. Thus he wrote that "the rise of chiefdoms seems to have been related to a total environmental situation which was selective for specialization in production and redistribution of produce from a controlling center" (Service 1962:143–4). Redistribution was, for Service (1962:144), "basic . . . in the origin of this type of society . . ." Indeed, he asserted (Service 1962:144) that "Chiefdoms are *redistributive societies* with a permanent central agency of coordination" (emphasis in the original).

Service also noted that social stratification was an important element of chiefdoms. "The most distinctive characteristic of chiefdoms as compared to tribes and bands," he wrote, "is . . . the pervasive inequality of persons and groups in the society. It begins with the status of chief as he functions in the system of redistribution. Persons are then ranked above others according to their genealogical nearness to him" (Service 1962:154–5).

But although the chief enjoyed high status, his power was limited: "Chiefdoms have centralized direction . . . but no true government to back up decisions by legalized force" (Service 1962:159).

In concluding his chapter on chiefdoms, Service summarized some of their attributes, repeating his assertion that they are based upon redistribution of goods rather than upon the reciprocal exchange characteristic of tribal society. The central collection of food involved in redistribution permitted the chief to subsidize craftsmen, so that superior arts and technology could be produced. The ability to mobilize and feed a sizable labor force also enabled a chiefdom to produce large public works, such as irrigation canals, terraces, temples, temple mounds, and even pyramids (Service 1962:170).

Like Sahlins, Service saw chiefdoms as essentially *economic* in origin and function. He failed to perceive their basically political nature. Thus he took practically no notice of the fact that chiefdoms are *multicommunity* political units. Likewise, he failed to give due attention to the growth of chiefdoms by the forceful incorporation of separate villages or other chiefdoms.

In his well-known book, *The Evolution of Political Society* (1967), Morton Fried does not deal with chiefdoms as such. He cites Sahlins's and Service's discussions of them, though, and agrees that the concept of chiefdom "genuinely bridges a previous level of organization, the acephalous society, with the state" (Fried 1967:169). What Fried does discuss at great length is what he calls "rank society," which some anthropologists since Fried, thinking they are following him, tend to equate with chiefdoms. For Fried, rank society, although no longer fully egalitarian, like the band or the simple village, is not yet stratified, like the state.

But Fried's "rank society" seems to span a greater evolutionary distance than Service's "chiefdom." At its lower end, rank society is found in autonomous villages scarcely removed from an egalitarian social structure (Fried 1967:174, 175, 183). In fact, Fried (1960:721) says that even the higher statuses in rank society "are devoid of privileged economic or political power . . ."

Fried is much more interested in the social status of the members of rank society than in its political organization. And presumably because of this preoccupation, he virtually ignores the chiefdom, which is essentially a political form.[7]

Service's book *Primitive Social Organization* was widely read and became enormously influential. It affected the thinking not only of ethnologists but also of archaeologists. Perhaps the most whole-hearted acceptance and thoroughgoing application of the concept occurs in the work of the British prehistorian Colin Renfrew. Renfrew (1976:260) found in Service's discussion of the chiefdom the type of political entity he thought must have characterized Britain and Western Europe during the late Neolithic and early Bronze Age. In his book *Before Civilization* (1976), Renfrew makes extensive use of the notion of chiefdom to interpret European prehistory.[8]

For example, Renfrew (1976:170) argues that the stone temples of Malta "are too big to have been the product of single small and independent farming villages," but must have been built by chiefdoms (Renfrew 1976:168). "The essential feature of chiefdom society," he says (1976:170), "is the marked social hierarchy, in which status is governed to a large extent by birth . . ." But he also says that "a whole series of villages, each with its petty chieftain, can be linked together in a social unit, all owing allegiance to one chief" (Renfrew 1976:171).

Following Sahlins and Service, Renfrew (1976:172) considers redistribution a fundamental element of chiefdoms. He speaks of "the great capacity of chiefdom society for mobilization, for organizing considerable bodies of men who can devote much labor to the fulfillment of some task essential to the well-being of the community" (Renfrew 1976:172–3). The three features of a chiefdom that make this possible, he says, are (1) a large population, (2) solidarity within the labor force, and (3) redistribution as a means for supporting the labor force undertaking public works.

It was a society having these attributes, says Renfrew (1976:173, 253), that built the great stone temples of prehistoric Malta and the henges of late Neolithic Britain. And he suggests that, to further our understanding of these accomplishments, we look at historically known chiefdoms in other parts of the world, like the Southeast of the United States, Africa, and especially Polynesia, where similarly imposing stone structures were built (Renfrew 1976:256–9, 174–81). These ethnographic parallels, he thinks, reveal to us the same general political structure reflected archaeologically in Neolithic Britain and Malta (Renfrew 1976:173–4).

The characterization of chiefdoms
Having examined others' conceptions of the chiefdom, I would now like to offer my own. *A chiefdom is an autonomous political unit comprising a number of villages or communities under the permanent control of a paramount chief.*

This is a minimal definition. It focuses on what I consider essential to the concept of chiefdom. It excludes what is incidental or subsidiary. To be sure, chiefdoms are usually characterized by many more traits than this, and we need to determine what these additional traits are in order to flesh out the concept. But trying to include them in the definition, I think, merely encumbers it. And no guarantee is afforded that the characterization of a chiefdom will get at its essence. Thus Renfrew (1973:543; 1974:73) lists twenty separate features of a chiefdom, not one of which, in my opinion, is central to the concept.

The definition offered here needs little comment. I included the word "permanent" in order to exclude cases such as Plains Indian tribes from being considered chiefdoms. During the summer buffalo hunt twenty or so bands of a Plains tribe might come together and elect one of their number as chief, assigning considerable authority to him. But this authority was strictly temporary, lapsing in the fall when the tribal gathering split up and the constituent bands went their separate ways.[9]

The definition of a chiefdom I have offered is structural. It focuses on territorial and political forms. It specifies that in a chiefdom a number of villages, forming a lower level of organization, have been united into a higher level, governed by a superior chief. In defining chiefdom in this way I am following Oberg. But I have also been influenced by the typology of political organization proposed as far back as 1876 by Herbert Spencer (1967:48–52). In that scheme, Spencer classified the societies of the preindustrial world into four types:

1. Simple
2. Compound
3. Doubly compound
4. Trebly compound

Simple societies are ones in which each village (or band) is autonomous. In *compound* societies previously autonomous villages have been aggregated into a larger territorial grouping under a paramount political leader. Although Spencer did not give this type of society a label other than "compound," we can readily equate it with a chiefdom. In *doubly compound* societies several compound societies have in turn been reaggregated into a still larger political unit. This unit we may equate with a state. Finally, *trebly compound* societies are ones in which doubly compound societies have once again been reaggregated into a still larger political unit. This unit might perhaps be called an "empire."

In summary, Spencer's typology classifies societies according to the number of levels of political organization they possess: *one* (=autonomous village), *two* (=chiefdom), *three* (=state), and *four* (=empire).

This typology has the advantage that it is easy to apply. Not only is the number of levels of political organization in a society readily ascertainable ethnologically, it is, as we shall see, inferable archaeologically. It is thus no accident that some archaeologists have looked with favor on a two-level definition of a chiefdom and a three-level definition of a state.

Thus Gregory Johnson (1973:10), although couching his remarks in the language of decision-making theory, writes that "states minimally have a three-level decision hierarchy above the general population, and chiefdoms a two-level hierarchy . . ." And the European archaeologist Sarunas Milisauskas (1978:249) concurs: "I maintain that state societies in Europe should have at least three hierarchical levels of administration. For example, a king, ruler, or oligarchy at the top, then regional governors or administrators, and then village heads at the bottom. (As noted previously, societies with two levels of administration were classified as chiefdoms and with one level as tribes.)"

I am quite ready to accept a two-level definition of a chiefdom. I am not so sure about a three-level definition of a state. I think one might want to specify functional as well as structural criteria in defining a state. But I prefer to postpone discussing this problem until we deal with the transition from chiefdom to state later in this chapter.

Types of chiefdoms

A great deal of political evolution is encompassed between autonomous vilages (or tribes) and the state.[10] It is thus not enough to say that this evolutionary span was filled by "chiefdoms," and let it go at that. Chiefdoms varied greatly among themselves in size, strength, wealth, complexity, and other characteristics. Therefore we need a typology of chiefdoms.

Some anthropologists have distinguished kinds of chiefdoms, using attributes other than their relative degrees of development. Julian Steward (Steward and Faron 1959:177), as we have seen, contrasted militaristic and theocratic chiefdoms. And Colin Renfrew (1974:74) says that the archaeological evidence from Neolithic Britain suggests the existence of two types of chiefdoms, "group oriented" and "individualizing." "Group-oriented" chiefdoms were "societies where personal wealth in terms of valuable possessions is not impressively documented [in the archaeological record], but where the solidarity of the social unit was expressed most effectively in communal or group activities," such as the building of long barrows or henges. In "individualizing" chiefdoms, "a marked disparity in personal possessions and in other material indications of prestige appears to document a salient personal ranking, yet often without evidence of large communal meetings or activities."

A more widely applicable typology focuses on the levels of development of chiefdoms. Several anthropologists (e.g., Milisauskas [1978:165] and Steponaitis [1978:420]) have proposed dividing chiefdoms into two types, *simple* and *complex*.[11] This is a step in the right direction. But two levels do not do justice to the range of evolution found among chiefdoms. I would propose a three-level typology of chiefdoms: *minimal, typical,* and *maximal.* A *minimal* chiefdom is one that meets the minimal requirements of a chiefdom (as I previously defined them) but does not go far beyond them. A *typical* chiefdom is one that is clearly a chiefdom, with elaborations in many aspects of its political and social structure, but still well below the level of a state. A *maximal* chiefdom is one that has become large and complex enough to approach the threshold of the state.

Looking first at minimal chiefdoms, the question arises, How small can a chiefdom be? Theoretically, it can be as small as two villages, as long as both of them are under the control of a paramount chief. But chiefdoms of this absolutely minimal size, although they must have existed at some time, were no doubt fugitive and transitory. I am not familiar with any instance of one. It seems to me, however, that a chiefdom comprising a dozen or so villages has a fair claim to being considered minimal. One such chiefdom is Kiriwina in the Trobriand Islands. Malinowski (1922), in his *Argonauts of the Western Pacific,* gave a fine brief description of this chiefdom, and I have quoted it at some length in Appendix A.

The island of Futuna was also divided into minimal chiefdoms. Villages had one hundred to two hundred persons, and there were five to ten villages in a chiefdom. Each village had a chief, an *aliki fenua,* who along with one or two other village functionaries, formed a "district" council, the *fono,* which was presided over by a paramount chief, the *aliki sau* (Sahlins 1958:85–7, 188–90). "The chiefs, acting as individuals, exercised some claim on the resources of their villages for use in feasts . . . and for entertaining visitors. Chiefs probably could not force contributions for such occasions" (Sahlins 1958:87).

Typical chiefdoms were well represented in the southeastern United States by groups such as the Natchez, Creek, and Cherokee. The latter, for instance, when visited by William Bartram in 1773, had a well-organized chiefdom consisting of some sixty villages with a total population of around 11,000 (Renfrew 1976:256). The chiefdoms that filled the Cauca Valley of Colombia also appear to have been at the middle level of political organization (Trimborn 1949:207–74).

The best known examples of maximal chiefdoms are probably Hawaii and Tahiti. Because they were approaching the level of states, we shall consider them in more detail later when we deal with the transition from chiefdoms to states.

The distribution of chiefdoms
How prevalent were chiefdoms in the non-Western world at the time of first European contact? There were several areas where chiefdoms predominated. Polynesia is probably the best publicized of these, largely because of Sahlins's pioneer work on the chiefdoms of that region.

The Circum-Caribbean area no doubt had the largest number of chiefdoms of any region in the world. They must, in fact, have numbered in the hundreds. The Cauca Valley of Colombia alone contained no fewer than eighty chiefdoms (Trimborn 1949:245).

Chiefdoms also flourished in sub-Saharan Africa. That Africa is not always thought of as an area of chiefdoms is probably because the social anthropologists who have worked there have generally spoken of the more evolved African soceties as "kingdoms" or "states." But I am convinced that a careful examination of African political ethnography would reveal many examples of chiefdoms.[12] Indeed, Donna Taylor's (n.d.) recent study has done just this.

The southeastern United States, as already mentioned, is another region where chiefdoms were common, the Creek, Cherokee, and Natchez being only the best known.

Did the Northwest Coast have chiefdoms? Many anthropologists believe they did (e.g., Service [1962:150, 153, 169–70]; Sanders and Price [1968:49, 81]; Flannery [1972:403]; Farb [1978:143]). It is, of course, a matter of definition, but by my definition it did not, because the tribes of that area had not gone beyond the level of autonomous villages. Let me quote two specialists on this area who support this view. Kalervo Oberg (1955:476), speaking of the Northwest Coast generally, stated that "no political organization appeared, the chiefs remaining ceremonial, economic, or war leaders of kinship groups, their ties to the members of their respective groups being composed of kinship rights and obligations." And more recently and emphatically, Leland Donald (1979:4) has written, "Nowhere on the Northwest Coast was there regular political unification above the local community level and even the Nootka federation was no exception to this."

This raises the question of whether it is possible for chiefdoms to arise at all among societies subsisting entirely, or largely, on a wild food basis. The answer appears to be *yes*. A bona fide ethnohistorical example is provided by the 16th century Calusa of southern Florida, who subsisted largely by fishing, supplemented by gathering and hunting (Goggin and Sturtevant 1964).

Archaeologically, the region where culture evolved furthest on a seemingly wild food basis was the coast of Peru, with its great wealth of marine resources. Here, as early as the Preceramic VI period, there were, according to Lanning (1967:59), "some hints of the existence of stratified societies and of sociopolitical organization which transcended the level of the village . . ." And Moseley (1975:104) asserts that "the Peruvian data . . . demonstrate that the foundation of civilization [on the coast] . . . arose out of a subsistence pattern that was not dependent upon cultivated foods." (But see Wilson [1981].)

It seems, then, that agriculture per se is not essential to the rise of chiefdoms. Where wild food sources are unusually abundant, reliable, and essentially sedentary, chiefdoms may occasionally arise.

The antiquity of chiefdoms

When did chiefdoms first arise? The answer to this question naturally varies from region to region. It also depends, in part, on the definition of a chiefdom, and upon this score archaeologists are by no means in agreement. However, allowing for uncertainties based upon the lack of a standard definition and upon the problems of inferring the existence of a chiefdom, however defined, from archaeological remains, here are a few dates that archaeologists have offered.

In the Near East, where the world's first chiefdoms arose, their initial appearance has been put around 5500 B.C. (Flannery 1972:403). In Britain, chiefdoms are said to have been in existence by 4000 B.C. (Renfrew 1973:540), whereas in central Europe they occurred by 3000 B.C. (Milisauskas 1978:167).[13]

Turning to the New World, chiefdoms may have arisen in Peru by 2000 to 1800 B.C. (Lanning 1967:57, 59, 78, 90), in the Olmec area of Mexico between 1500 and 1200 B.C. (Sanders and Price 1968:15; Sanders and Webster 1978:290), in the Valley of Mexico about 900 B.C. (Sanders and Price 1968:15), in the Valley of Oaxaca by 850 B.C. (Blanton et al., 1979:374), in Highland Guatemala from 800 to 500 B.C. (Sanders 1974:97, 111), in the Lowland Maya area by 350 B.C. (Ball 1977:111), and in the southeastern United States by A.D. 1200 (Flannery 1972:401).

It is worth noting that the various parts of the world where chiefdoms made their initial appearance were *not* the areas where they were most common around A.D. 1500 The areas where chiefdoms first arose were, of course, the areas where they had longest to develop, and as a result, a number of them evolved into states. Thus by A.D. 1500, many areas where chiefdoms had flourished millennia before no longer showed any trace of them. This was true of much of Mesoamerica and Peru, where chiefdoms no doubt abounded in Formative times.[14] It was also true of the Valley of the Nile, where the forty or so administrative units called *nomes*, into which Dynastic Egypt was divided, were the only vestiges of a time when the valley was occupied by chiefdoms. Service (1962:153) is surely right when he says that chiefdoms preceded the West African states of Dahomey, Benin, and Ashanti. Indeed, scratch any preindustrial state deep enough and you will find chiefdoms underlying it.

The role of chiefdoms in prehistory

Much of the recent flurry of interest in chiefdoms has been generated by the "new archaeologists," who are concerned with the sociopolitical structure of the societies whose remains they unearth. Many of these archaeologists have dug in regions of relatively high culture, where political evolution reached the level of chiefdoms or beyond. Thus they often have to make a determination about the presence or absence of chiefdoms at sites they have excavated. But there is still much difference of opinion among them about the nature of chiefdoms and their role in the course of political development. Accordingly, let us look more closely at this problem.

Service (1962:143) speaks of chiefdoms as "a *stage* in general cultural evolution," and I think he is quite right. However, not everyone agrees. Herbert Lewis (1978:8), for one, thinks that "the chiefdom, redistributive or otherwise, as a stage in political evolution is a misleading sort of myth." And Sanders and Webster (1978:281) likewise do not consider the chiefdom as being a necessary stage between egalitarian society and the state. They argue, in fact, that most pristine states arose from egalitarian societies without ever having been chiefdoms.

What do they put in place of chiefdoms? To them, the "main evolutionary trajectory" leading from egalitarian society to the state passed instead through Fried's "stratified society." However, they do not make it at all clear how their version of Fried's stratified society differs in its political structure from Service's chiefdom. As they describe the two, they seem pretty much the same. Thus I think Sanders and Webster's "stratified society" and "chiefdom" can be collapsed into one category. And accordingly, their multilinear model of political development reduces essentially to a unilinear one.

But if my analysis is wrong, and the two categories will not collapse into one, then there is a certain irony in Sanders's use of Fried's "stratified society" in reconstructing political development. For Fried (1967:185), "stratified societies" had reached true social stratification but were nevertheless "lacking political institutions of state level." He considers social stratification to be a necessary precondition for the state, at least for pristine states: "each pristine state certainly had to traverse this stage or level" (Fried 1967:185n.). "Once stratification exists, the cause of stateship is implicit and the actual formation of the state is begun, its formal appearance occurring within a relatively brief time" (Fried 1967:185).

This "relatively brief time" must be brief indeed, because actual cases of stratified societies that have not yet evolved into states "are almost impossible to find . . ." (Fried 1967:185). In fact, Fried readily admits: "Societies that are stratified but lack state institutions are not known to the ethnographer. Indeed, as argued elsewhere, pristine examples of such societies have probably not existed on our planet for 2,000 years or more" (Fried 1967:224).

It is truly a fugitive stage that has not been seen on the face of the earth for the last two millennia. And this is especially true because during that time scores if not hundreds of states have emerged. Is it possible that true social stratification is really an *accompaniment* of the state and not a precondition for it? If so, then the supposed prestate occurrence of stratification would be a phantom concept. And it is puzzling that Sanders, who once stood four-square behind chiefdoms as a necessary stage in the rise of the state (Sanders 1974:108–11), should have turned away from that solid substance to embrace a phantom.

Another theorist who is disinclined to see the chiefdom as a stage between egalitarian villages and the state is Malcolm Webb (1973). Webb believes that the state is based upon the acquisition of large amounts of wealth from outside its own borders, either by conquest or through trade. This much wealth, he believes, chiefdoms simply do not have. Nor can they acquire it, because the political leader of a chiefdom is "dependent upon [the] free obedience" of his people and thus he cannot compel them to pay taxes or draft them to labor on his behalf (Webb 1973:378). For such a society, then, says Webb (1973:378), "progress beyond the chiefdom level would be impossible."

Webb (1973:378) admits that the power of the head of a chiefdom "may grow by slow accumulation until the point is reached at which . . . [his] commands will be unfailingly obeyed." But somehow, he thinks, a chiefdom can never cross the Rubicon and become a state.

Chiefdoms, then, are evolutionary dead ends for Webb. They either remain chiefdoms, or, more likely, break down into their component units. Thus Webb (1973:379) speaks of "the tendency of large chiefdoms to break apart . . . , then to reunite only to fall apart again . . ." He believes that "any expansion of the system to the point of linking disparate groups, of undertaking novel tasks . . . or of requiring innovative policy-making causes the system to snap" (Webb 1973:379).

If Webb does not see the chiefdom as intermediate between autonomous villages and the state, it is not clear what he would interpose between them. But how can whatever stage he interposes not have multivillage aggregations, a paramount chief, and some degree of centralized control over food and labor – in short, the basic attributes of a chiefdom? I fail to see, then, how Webb can really dispense with the chiefdom as a stage in the rise of the state.

Let me restate my opinion that the only route to the state is through chiefdoms – at least through chiefdoms as I have envisioned and described them. Anyone who doubts this must show how a group of autonomous villages could aggregate and organize themselves into a state without going through an intermediate stage with the essential features of a chiefdom. The gap is just too large to be spanned in one leap. I have never heard of such a leap being made, and I invite anyone to show me an instance of one in the historical record. And if they cannot present an historical example, let them at least try to offer a plausible explanation of how such a jump might have occurred. I for one concur with Timothy Earle (1978:2) when he says, "Since archaeological evidence now suggests that chiefdoms temporally precede states in many areas, a good argument may be made for the evolutionary development from chiefdom to state."

The archaeological identification of chiefdoms
Theory aside, the fact remains that the archaeological period that in American archaeology is termed the "Formative" was, in many parts of the world, a period of explosive development of chiefdoms. In some areas this development went on to produce states, whereas in others it stopped at chiefdoms. But whether the chiefdom was early or late in an area, an archaeologist working in a region where they occurred must sometime ask, "How can I tell if I am digging up a chiefdom?"

In order to answer this question one must first have some definition of a chiefdom. It helps immeasurably if the definition is one with archaeological correlates. Thus the European prehistorian Sarunas Milisauskas (1978:248) has said that "Archaeologists should define state societies [and he would also include chiefdoms] in such a manner that they can demonstrate the existence of state societies [or chiefdoms] with archaeological data . . ." A number of archaeologists have in fact already suggested what kinds of archaeological remains can reveal the presence of a chiefdom.

One diagnostic feature that has been proposed is the presence of monumental architecture. This would consist of architectural remains large or elaborate enough to have required the organized labor of more people than would have lived in just a single village. Thus Colin Renfrew (1973) has used the occurrence of long barrows, henges, and causewayed camps in the late Neolithic of Wessex to infer that the people who built them were organized into chiefdoms. Similarly, he noted that the stone temples of Malta "are so large, and involved so much labour, that they cannot have been the work of small local groups . . ." but must have been wrought by chiefdoms (Renfrew 1976:166).

This criterion is probably applied most readily in distinguishing the archaeological remains of chiefdoms from those of autonomous villages.[15] But a problem is likely to arise toward the other end of the scale. When is an earthwork or a fort or a tomb imposing enough to be beyond the capacity of a chiefdom to construct? That is, when would it reflect the organized effort of a state? The line is not an easy one to draw.[16]

A second way in which the existence of a chiefdom may be inferred archaeologically is through the identification of ceremonial centers. The fact that these centers were fewer in number than the villages they ostensibly served would suggest that these villages were politically unified. Thus Lanning (1967:78) cites the building of large ceremonial centers at Río Seco and Chuquitana (El Paraíso) on the central coast of Peru around 2000 to 1800 B.C. as providing evidence of a form of society clearly above the autonomous village level. Lanning does not identify this form of society, but to judge from his comments, we can surmise that it was a chiefdom.

A third way of inferring the existence of chiefdoms archaeologically is by finding differentiated burials in which the differences in the quantity and quality of the grave goods points to a categorical distinction in status among a few individuals, presumably chiefs, and the general populace. This criterion has been used, for example, by the European archaeologist Milisauskas (1978:166, 167, 245, 289) to decide whether excavated sites in central Europe represent autonomous villages or chiefdoms.

Although generally useful, this criterion encounters difficulties at both ends of its application. Even in autonomous villages, chiefs may sometimes be sufficiently honored or wealthy to be buried with significantly more and finer grave goods than anyone else. And at the upper end of the scale, how much finery does it take to indicate that the burial was that of the ruler of a state rather than the head of a chiefdom?

A less direct but more ingenious method of inferring the existence of chiefdoms involves the plotting of settlement sizes for all contemporary archaeological sites in an area against the frequency of these sizes. If all the settlements were autonomous villages, we would expect their sizes to be distributed more or less evenly around a single mean. In an area of chiefdoms, though, a different result would be expected. Because chiefdoms have capital villages or towns that tend to be significantly larger than any other settlement in the political unit, plotting settlement sizes against frequencies for them would produce a bimodal curve. The higher peak in the frequency curve might be at, say, 100, if that were the average size of villages in the chiefdom. On the other hand, the smaller peak might be at, say, 500, if that were the average size of capital villages in the chiefdoms of the region.[17]

This same technique can, of course, be used to determine, archaeologically, the presence of states. If we define states as having three levels of administrative centers – villages, district centers, and a state capital – then plotting settlement sizes against their frequencies would yield a trimodal curve. This conclusion is based upon the reasonable assumption that each successive type of settlement was distinctly larger than the one immediately below it. And if the state had advanced to the point that it had four levels of settlements (districts having been grouped into provinces with provincial capitals), then the curve for settlement size would be expected to have four modes.

Archaeologists are not content, however, merely to identify chiefdoms. They are eager to try to account for them, too. "If anthropologists are to understand the evolution of chiefdoms," says Earle (1978:6), "it must be through archaeological and ethnohistorical research and not another ethnographic project." He is confident of the results. "Archaeological evidence for chiefdom organization," he writes, "is both varied and extensive, and future archaeological work should offer opportunities to study the evolutionary process involved in the formation of hierarchical societies" (Earle 1978:7).

The origin of chiefdoms

Accordingly, let us now turn to the question of how chiefdoms arose. But first, let us consider the general problem of causation with regard to political forms.

With "systems theory" so much in vogue in archaeology today there is a tendency for theorists to view causation as a ramifying network of factors ("parameters"). Thus the more one tries to trace causal responsibility, the more diffuse and attenuated it becomes. This tendency is rather like the view of the older functionalists, who spurned the notion of causation altogether and argued that because everything in a social system is interrelated to everything else, one could not assign causal primacy to one or even a few factors. Everything had coequal influence. If there was to be causation at all, it had to be a sort of democracy of causes.[18]

It is certainly true that most theorists nowadays have only harsh words to say about "monocausal" theories. I do not share this prejudice. There is nothing wrong with a monocausal theory if it works. Ideally, as scientists, we want to make our explanations as simple and economical as possible. We want to reduce the causal elements to the fewest number that will do the job. If a single cause can explain a phenomenon, so much the better. Of course, if one factor is not enough, then we increase the number of causal factors in our theory until our explanation becomes satisfactory. We may well end with multiple causation, but a multiplicity of causes, if it comes to that, should be thought of as a necessity, not a virtue.

In discussions of monocausal theories of the origin of chiefdoms (or of the state, for that matter) two things are sometimes confused. First, there is the nature of the explanation proposed to account for a given chiefdom. This explanation can be simple or complex. It can encompass one cause or many. Next, we have the question of whether a single theory, simple or complex, will account for the origin of chiefdoms generally, or whether several theories will have to be invoked. These two issues are quite separate. Thus it is entirely possible that a rather complex theory might be required to account for chiefdoms but that the same theory might then be universally applicable; that is, it might explain the rise of chiefdoms everywhere. In that case, chiefdoms would have arisen by what Mark Cohen calls "parallel adaptive responses." This explanation would be monocausal in the sense that only one theory was required to account for all chiefdoms. But it would be "multicausal" in that it combined several causal factors.

Whether the best theory of the origin of chiefdoms will be monocausal or multicausal (in either sense) cannot, of course, be decided beforehand. It will emerge only after successive attempts have been made to account for the rise of chiefdoms in many parts of the world.

However, in pursuing this endeavor, we should be on our guard against allowing a superficially bewildering diversity among chiefdoms to be taken, ipso facto, as proof that only a multiplicity of theories will account for them all. We must be ready to tease out of the evident variety of conditions, those few factors, however subtle or hidden, that may be the common causes of chiefdoms everywhere. My bias, then, which I openly proclaim, is to favor a *unitary* theory of the origin of chiefdoms. Accordingly, I will entertain alternative or subsidiary theories, not as a desideratum, but only as I am forced to by the facts.

The question of how chiefdoms arose is not an easy one. As Service (1962:145) noted, "No one has observed the actual origin of a chiefdom." Or if someone did, and recorded the process in detail, neither Service nor I have yet discovered it. But let us proceed to discuss some of the factors and theories that have been proposed to account for chiefdoms.

Chiefdoms and technology

Was it technological advance that gave rise to chiefdoms? Evidently not.[19] There are many examples of chiefdoms that had the same technology as their neighbors, who remained at the autonomous village level. The Taíno chiefdoms of the West Indies, for example, had a subsistence technology essentially the same as their Arawak-speaking cousins on the Guiana mainland, who lived in autonomous villages. Both used simple digging sticks in planting, and neither added fertilizer to the soil.[20]

Indeed, Barry Isaac (1975:139) is ready to argue that chiefdoms could have arisen even on a wild food basis. Thus he writes: "In areas where wild resources were already tightly clustered, sociocultural evolution easily could have proceeded to the chiefdom level in the absence of agriculture. We will probably discover more instances of this as . . . archaeology . . . becomes more sophisticated."

The difficulty of accepting the possibility that people with a simple, Neolithic technology could have built the impressive archaeological remains represented by long barrows, causewayed camps, and henges made British prehistorians favor the theory that the makers of these remains must have been more advanced technologically than the Neolithic folk of Britain, and had, in fact, come from the Mediterranean. The Carbon 14 recalibration, which showed these British remains to be contemporaneous with, or even to predate, European manifestations of a similar architecture, led Colin Renfrew (1976) to argue that they were not the products of diffusion, but indigenous developments in Britain. They were products, Renfrew argued, of a society organized into chiefdoms with the power to mobilize and direct large amounts of human labor, rather than the result of any sophisticated technology.[21]

The fact is that chiefdoms everywhere are basically manifestations of a certain form of organization instead of representing a particular level of technology.[22] Indeed, the elaborate technology sometimes found among chiefdoms is often the *effect* of their political organization rather than its *cause* (see Carneiro 1974). It may well have been the power of late Neolithic chiefs, which permitted them to command the labor of artisans and to spur them to experiment with new materials and techniques, that really fostered the onset of the technological era we call the Bronze Age.[23]

However, a distinct technological advantage, such as the possession of superior weapons, could accelerate, and in some cases even precipitate, the formation of chiefdoms. There is evidence from Japan (Sansom 1958:14–19) that the first major steps toward state formation on that island were taken by chiefdoms that had been in contact with China. From there, they had obtained iron weapons that permitted them to conquer their enemies, who were armed with only bronze ones. It seems quite possible that the first chiefdoms of Japan were formed by peoples armed with bronze weapons (also obtained from China), which permitted them to subjugate their neighbors, who had only stone or wooden ones.

If the rise of a chiefdom on the large island of Hawaii was achieved with a native military technology, the extension of Hawaiian hegemony to the rest of the island chain was certainly facilitated by the adoption of guns from the Europeans (Service 1975:155; Webb 1965:33).

Theocratic origins

Service (1962:171) writes of chiefdoms: "sometimes the priest and chief are the same person. For this reason many chiefdoms have been called theocracies with considerable appropriateness." Sanders and Webster (1978:270) say that in a chiefdom "the person of the chief is almost sacrosanct, and he frequently plays a vital sacerdotal role." Malcolm Webb (1973:379) states that "chiefdoms, especially those whose size and complexity approach the maximum for the type, inevitably are theocracies."[24]

Some have gone so far as to suggest that it was because of the chief's religious authority that he was able to create a chiefdom in the first place. I frankly doubt this. In my opinion, religion played a *consolidating* role in the development of chiefdoms, not a creative one. As we pursue our study of chiefdoms we must be careful to distinguish those factors that merely strengthened the chiefdom from those that gave rise to it.

Social stratification

Few would quarrel with Service's (1971:140) statement that "chiefdoms are profoundly inegalitarian." Some theorists are so impressed by the social inequalities found in chiefdoms that they see the chiefdom as largely a political reflection of these inequalities. How do these social differences arise? This is not easy to answer. Kent Flannery (1972:402), for one, says that "One of the thorniest problems in cultural evolution is the origins of hereditary inequality . . ."

Morton Fried, who has had much to say on the subject, sees status differences arising out of differential access to strategic resources.[25] How does this differential access itself arise? Fried is quite clear about what factor did *not* produce it. He writes: "Whatever emerges

when we attempt to show how ... [the evolution of ranking and
stratification out of an undifferentiated egalitarian base] occurred, it
seems evident that it will not be related to any prior evolution of
military organization or command" (Fried 1967:105–6). But he is
nowhere near as clear about what *did* give rise to ranking and stratification. In fact, he leaves the question essentially unresolved.

Whatever their origin (which I will return to later), differences in
social status are neither the touchstone of chiefdoms not their cause.
Such differences may invariably accompany chiefdoms, but they are
epiphenomena – the products of political power rather than the
source of it.

Redistribution

By far the most popular explanation of the rise of chiefdoms is based
upon the notion of "redistribution." We have seen that Sahlins and
Service both made redistribution the sine qua non of chiefdoms, and
many have followed them in this belief. This is true not only of
ethnologists[26] but also of archaeologists. Indeed, "redistribution" has
become as fashionable in archaeology as "area cotradition" and "interaction sphere" once were. For example, Colin Renfrew (1976:171–3,
214–16) in *Before Civilization,* makes redistribution the key to the rise
of chiefdoms in the late Neolithic of Britain and Western Europe.
Indeed, it is probably safe to say that most anthropologists today
regard redistribution as the most important single factor in the rise of
chiefdoms.

In my opinion, though, this view is mistaken. Redistribution is not
the main road to political evolution but only a blind alley. What a
chief gains from redistribution proper is esteem, not power. Power
accrues to him only when he ceases to redistribute food and goods
wholesale and begins to appropriate and concentrate them. But before pursuing the argument against redistribution theory, I would
like to make a brief survey of its history.

It was the German ethnologist Richard Thurnwald (1932) in his
Economics in Primitive Communities who first put forward the concept
of redistribution. Thurnwald noted that in the economic systems of
primitive peoples there were two important processes, *reciprocity* and
redistribution. Reciprocity, he thought, was universal among the simplest societies, but redistribution had evolved later:

> By the formation of an upper layer, the economic area
> outgrows self-governing communities and the process of
> uniting a number of them into a compact body begins ...
> There is thus created an organization based, on the one
> hand, on the contributions and services of the dependent
> class, and, on the other, on the power of distribution pos-

sessed by the heads of families in the leading stratum (Thurnwald 1932:85–6).

The economist Karl Polanyi read Thurnwald and accepted a number of his concepts, including reciprocity and redistribution. Polanyi contended that primitive societies were characterized by

> the absence of the motive of gain; the absence of the principle of least effort; and, especially, the absence of any separate and distinct institution based on economic motives.[27] But how, then, is order in production and distribution ensured? The answer is provided in the main by two principles of behaviour not primarily associated with economics: *reciprocity* and *redistribution* (Polanyi 1945:54).

The operation of these two principles, Polanyi thought, were sufficient to keep primitive economies running smoothly. We need not discuss reciprocity here but we should consider how Polanyi viewed redistribution. He saw this mechanism operating through the principle of "centricity."

> The institutional pattern of centricity, which is present to some extent in all human groups, provide[s] a track for the collection, storage, and redistribution of goods and services. The members of a hunting tribe usually deliver the game to the headman for redistribution. It is in the nature of hunting that the output of game is irregular, besides being the result of a collective input. Under conditions such as these no other method of sharing is practicable if the group is not to break up after every hunt . . . Among some tribes . . . there is an intermediary in the person of the headman or other prominent member of the group; it is he who receives and distributes the supplies, especially if they need to be stored. This is redistribution proper (Polanyi 1945:56, 58).

Believing that centricity was "natural" to human societies, Polanyi did not find it necessary to account for it. He also made no effort to distinguish sharply between "redistribution" as carried out by a village chief and by an absolute monarch. Following Thurnwald, he included in the concept of redistribution everything from the "voluntary sharing of game by hunters" to "the dread punishment which urges the *fellaheen* to deliver their taxes in kind" (Polanyi 1945:59). Indeed, he maintained that "redistribution was present on a gigantic scale in the civilization of the Pyramids" (Polanyi 1945:57).

There is a world of difference between these two forms of redistribution, however. At one end of the scale we have the complete and equitable reassignment of a village's harvest back to its producers by a chief who is merely a temporary and benign custodian of it. At the other end there is enforced appropriation of part of a society's food supply by a powerful ruler for his own benefit and that of a small ruling elite. Not to emphasize the vast difference between the two, strikes me as a major oversight.[28]

Again following Thurnwald, Polanyi (1945:58) believed that chiefs achieved their power by "the manner in which they redistribute the goods." He thus seemed to favor an economic rather than a political explanation of the rise of what we now call chiefdoms. But he failed to inquire into this problem very deeply. In discussing Trobriand economics, for example, Polanyi did not ask himself why the paramount chief of the little chiefdom of Kiriwina had the power to acquire food from the various villages under him. He considered this power to be merely an exemplification of the principle of centricity and thus not to require explanation.

Marshall Sahlins (1958) was much influenced by Polanyi, and when he wrote *Social Stratification in Polynesia,* borrowed his concept of redistribution and used it to account for the varying degrees of power among Polynesian chiefs. Thus he wrote:

> Everywhere in Polynesia, the chief is the agent of general, tribal-wide distribution. The chief derives prestige from his generosity. In turn, his prestige permits him to exercise control over social processes, such as production, upon which his functions of distribution rest. Consequently the greater the productivity, the greater the distributive activities of the chief, and the greater his powers (Sahlins 1958:xi).

If the roots of chiefly power lie in redistribution and the roots of redistribution lie in productivity, where did the roots of productivity lie? Sahlins (1958:249) saw productivity as a function of environment and technology. Surplus production would occur if environmental and technological factors permitted it. Thus he sometimes used phrases like "to cope with the problem of surplus production," as if, under the appropriate conditions of environment and technology, a surplus of food would automatically arise (Sahlins 1958:250).

However, as I have argued elsewhere (Carneiro 1961:53–4; 1970:733–4), although the *potential* to produce a food surplus is inherent in any agricultural system, its *actualization* will depend upon economic incentives or political coercion. In Polynesia, there were no economic incentives such as markets, where surplus food could be exchanged for other commodities. But there *was* political coercion. And the stronger the chief, the more food he could exact from his subjects. Surplus production in Polynesia, as elsewhere, was thus largely a function of strong political power rather than the other way around.

Let us look more closely at the relationship between chiefly power and redistribution. As long as a chief merely returns everything he has been handed, he gains nothing in wealth or power. Only when he begins to keep a large part of it, sharing with his retainers and supporters but not beyond that, does his power begin to augment.

But the power of a chief to appropriate and retain food does not flow automatically from his right to collect and redistribute it. Villagers freely allow a chief to equalize each family's share of meat or fish or crops through redistribution because they benefit from it. But they will not willingly suffer the same chief to keep the lion's share of food for himself. Before doing this, he must acquire additional power, and that power must come from some other source.

The word "redistribution" is often used very loosely. Whenever the word is applied in describing the activity of a chief we should ask two questions: (1) "What percentage of the food or goods taken in by the chief is actually redistributed?" (2) "To what percentage of the population are they redistributed?" For chiefly disbursement to be genuine redistribution, both percentages should be high. If the percentages are small, what we have is not real redistribution at all, but something more akin to *taxation*. And it is in taxation that the sinews of government really lie. When a chief can compel the populace to turn food and goods over to him, which he can then apply at will, he is at last manifesting power.[29]

By the selective distribution of food, goods, booty, women, and the like the chief rewards those who have rendered him service. Thus he builds up a core of officials, warriors, henchmen, retainers, and the like who will be personally loyal to him and through whom he can issue orders and have them obeyed. In short, it is through the shrewd and self-interested disbursement of taxes that the administrative machinery of the chiefdom (and the state) is built up. However, the chief who does this is no longer a redistributor. He is an appropriator and a concentrator.

To these theoretical arguments let me add some empirical evidence. Recent reexaminations of the movement of goods that actually occurs in chiefdoms indicates that this movement is more like taxation than redistribution. Thus, for the Natchez, Steponaitis (1978:422) says:

> Collection of tribute within this system took a number of different forms. At one extreme was sporadic tribute, which stemmed from a chief's right to demand goods or labor from the people under his jurisdiction at any time. It is clear from the accounts that such sporadic demands

were not uncommon. More regularly scheduled tribute collections also took place, however, the people usually bringing their goods to a place in or near the political center of the district in which they lived.

Summarizing his findings for chiefdoms generally, Steponaitis (1978:420) noted: "What formally appears to be redistribution in complex chiefdoms is functionally more akin to the collection of tribute than the institutionalized sharing of surplus."

In her comparative study of political organization among thirteen chiefdoms of eastern and central Africa, Donna Taylor (n.d.:16) found that "the chieftaincies of the sample were not typically 'redistributive' societies, as these have been described by Sahlins and Service . . . In fact, the organized collection and redistribution of regional production specialties was described for only one of the most centrally organized societies examined (Lozi)."

Even in Polynesia, the archetypal area of redistributive chiefdoms, the workings of redistribution turn out to be rather different from the way Sahlins and Service depicted them. Thus Steponaitis (1978: 425), after a brief survey of Tahitian chiefdoms, concluded:

> Chiefs could . . . demand goods or labor from their sub-chiefs and commoners at any time. Large-scale levies would be imposed at the commencement of public-work projects, at the arrival of visiting dignitaries, and for the equipping of war parties. More regular contributions from commoners were received as first fruits offerings and at various other ceremonial and ritual occasions.

A similar picture emerges from the other major chiefdom of Polynesia, Hawaii. In their close scrutiny of redistribution in Hawaii, Peebles and Kus (1977:425) observe:

> During the Makihiki [the major agricultural festival of Hawaii] the paramount chief and his entourage passed twice through each district under his control. The acknowledged function of his peregrinations was to perform the necessary agricultural rites and to collect taxes. These taxes, in the form of offerings to [the god] Lono, were amassed by the *konohiki*, the local landlords and agents of the chief, and were placed on altars within each *ahupua'a* [dispersed settlement]. If the offerings were adjudged sufficient and acceptable then the *kapu* (tabu) which had been placed on the lands and products of the district prior to the Makihiki was removed.

Peebles and Kus (1977:425) then quote David Malo that, on the twentieth day of the Makihiki, "the levying of taxes was completed and the property that had been collected was displayed before the god . . . : and on the following day . . . the king distributed it among the chiefs and the companies of soldiers throughout the land . . . *No share of this property, however, was given to the people*" (emphasis mine, RLC).[30]

Peebles and Kus (1977:425, 426) conclude their reexamination of Hawaii by saying:

> There is no hard evidence for a redistributive network in which subsistence items flowed to and through the office of the paramount chief . . . contrary to the traditional view of the chief as the focal point in a redistributive network through which subsistence goods moved and diverse, ecologically specialized villages were united, we are faced with a diametrically opposed organization and behavior. In Hawaii the chief is *imposed* on local production . . . (emphasis in the original).

Summarizing their conclusions for chiefdoms generally, Peebles and Kus (1977:421) state: "we find that the central concept of redistribution is neither a univariate phenomena, [*sic*] a causal factor, nor a constant correlate of chiefdoms."

Thus it may not only have been an accident but an error by which the concept of redistribution became attached to that of chiefdom.[31] The result has been a muddying of the waters, which continues to obscure our understanding. If we are to explain the origin of chiefdoms, we must set aside the notion of redistribution and look elsewhere. We must seek the source of power that permitted a chief actually to tax his subjects and not just give back to them the goods they had previously brought him.

Warfare and the chiefdom
The mechanism that brought about chiefdoms is, in my opinion, the same one that brought about states, namely, war (see Carneiro 1970: 734, 736).[32] This has not been more generally recognized because many anthropologists are still disinclined to see warfare as instrumental in political evolution.[33] Thus Fried (1976:596), although conceding the importance of war at the state level,[34] asks, "Where is the evidence that there has been an intertribal struggle for existence in cultural evolution?" Barry Isaac (1975:138) asserts that "a chiefdom level of development could be reached rather gradually, without anyone's being killed or forcedly subjugated as a direct consequence." In fact, Isaac (1975:138) sees conquest warfare as "merely the final step in the formation of large states."

However, anyone who has delved into the archaeological, historical, and ethnographic literature on chiefdoms and their immediate precursors, whether in Europe, Africa, the Pacific, the Circum-Caribbean, or the Southeast, cannot help being impressed by the overwhelming evidence for intensive warfare among these societies.[35] It is my contention that this warfare led, under certain specifiable conditions, to the rise of chiefdoms.

Warfare alone is insufficient to account for chiefdoms. It is extremely widespread in primitive society, and yet chiefdoms did not arise wherever it occurred. Additional factors had to be present for warfare to fuse autonomous villages into chiefdoms. Of prime importance among these factors was environmental circumscription. Briefly, the circumscription theory runs as follows. As population density increases,[36] and arable land comes into short supply, fighting over land ensues. Villages vanquished in war, having nowhere to flee, are forced to remain in place and to be subjugated by the victors.

Chiefdoms arose most readily in environmentally circumscribed areas, such as islands and narrow valleys. But they could and did arise elsewhere. They arose, for example, in lowland Guatemala, where the circumscribing factor was not the natural environment but population.[37] Following Chagnon, I have called this phenomenon "social circumscription" (Carneiro 1970:737–8). But social circumscription is never as tight as environmental circumscription. Defeated groups can, to some degree, escape through the interstices of their surrounding neighbors. Thus it takes longer to amalgamate defeated villages into a chiefdom where only social circumscription is operative (Carneiro 1972:74–6). Doubtless, for this reason chiefdoms arose among the lowland Maya five hundred years later than they did in the environmentally circumscribed valleys of Mexico and Oaxaca.

As already stated, with sufficient population density, chiefdoms can occur almost anywhere through the operation of social circumscription. Besides the lowland Maya area, chiefdoms arose in this way over much of Europe north of the Alps during the late Neolithic and early Bronze Age. This also appears to be the way in which chiefdoms arose in West Africa.

I should add one qualification, though. Chiefdoms may arise without the necessity of actual warfare and conquest. For one thing, villages may be coerced into yielding their sovereignty by the threat of force rather than by its exercise. Also, a chiefdom may be formed by the confederation of a number of previously autonomous villages. This may appear to be a "voluntary" act, but the fact is that almost invariably confederacies are formed under duress.[38] Villages decide to amalgamate for greater protection against their enemies. Thus confederation fits better among "coercive" explanations of the origin of chiefdoms than among "voluntaristic" ones (see Carneiro 1970:733–4).

As Service noted, the chiefdom was a *stage* in political development. It was the necessary precursor of the state. No state is known to have arisen directly from the fusion of autonomous villages. All seem to have been formed through the coalescing of groups already aggregated into supravillage units. Such units were, by my definition, chiefdoms. Moreover, because the aggregation of villages occurs only through war, or the threat of it, any theory of the origin of chiefdoms that foregoes this mechanism is severely handicapped.[39]

Warfare and social stratification

Warfare, moreover, provides a means of explaining the origin of ranking and social stratification. Thus it does what Fried's "differential access to strategic resources" was unable to do. As waged at the chiefdom level, warfare generally leads to the taking of captives. At first, these captives were sacrificed, but later they began to be spared and turned into productive members of the society. However, their productivity was unwilling: labor was forced from them by enslaving them. When a large and distinct enough body of war captives had developed in the society, social classes could be said to have begun.[40]

I have long been struck by the fact that no society seems to have just two social classes. Societies appear to go from one class (or no classes) to three. Why? An explanation in terms of warfare provides the answer. The two social classes that are added to a society as it develops are a lower class and an upper class, and the rise of these two classes is closely interrelated. The lower class, as previously stated, consists initially of war prisoners who are turned into slaves and servants. At the same time, however, an upper class also emerges, because those who capture and keep slaves, or have slaves bestowed on them, gain wealth, prestige, leisure, and power through being able to command the labor of those slaves. Thus warfare, while enhancing the status of the chief, also purveys the same benefit, even though to a lesser degree, to his most loyal followers and successful warriors.

The difference between "rank" societies and "stratified" societies need not detain us here. During the early stages of a politically evolving society, differences in wealth, status, and prestige are not sharply demarcated among its members. Status differences between them tend to grade into one another in a continuous series. But after the process has continued long enough, fixed and formal social classes crystallize out of this gradient of unequal social statuses.

The growth of chiefdoms

Having made an effort to account for the origin of chiefdoms, I would now like to discuss their growth. The growth of chiefdoms has two aspects: (1) the increase in the area of land held by chiefdoms, as opposed to that still in the hands of autonomous villages, and (2) the increase in size of individual chiefdoms. Let us deal with each in turn.

Once chiefdoms begin to form in a region, the process proceeds rapidly. The military advantage that size alone confers on a society means that even a minimal chiefdom will have a significant edge over its neighbors if they are still independent villages.[41] As a result, it will not be long before autonomous villages as such will cease to exist. Either they will be defeated by and incorporated into one of the existing chiefdoms or they will join forces with other such villages in a defensive alliance, which will itself tend to become a chiefdom.

Not only does this process take place rapidly, it proceeds at an ever quickening pace. This theoretical expectation is supported by a bit of "experimental" evidence. A series of simulations carried out by my research assistant, Laila Williamson, strongly suggest that chiefdom formation is an accelerating process. Thus if in a small valley it took a certain amount of time for, say, forty autonomous political units to be reduced to twenty, it would take much less time for these twenty to be reduced to one.[42]

Chiefdoms grow largely by accretion. But just how does this accretion take place? When chiefdom A defeats and engulfs chiefdom B, does chiefdom A incorporate chiefdom B as a single subordinate political unit, or does A dissolve away B's existing superstructure and assimilate it in the form of separate villages? I am not sure yet that we can answer this question with any degree of assurance.

However, the answer has important implications. If a victorious chiefdom generally incorporates a defeated enemy as individual villages rather than as a single unit, then the successful chiefdom will simply grow in size without elaborating in structure. It will remain at the two-level stage of political organization. How many villages, though, can be held together by a paramount chief in this way without the need for further development of structure? At what point will it become necessary to aggregate the encompassed villages into districts under subchiefs, thus creating an intermediate level between villages and the paramount chief?

Again, this question remains largely unexplored. We know from the Cherokee, for example, that as many as sixty villages can be included in a chiefdom without a middle level of political leaders having to arise between village chiefs and the paramount chief (Gearing 1962). But how many more than sixty villages can be successfully accommodated into such a two-level chiefdom? And if three levels of organization develop, do we then (following Spencer's structural criteria) consider that the chiefdom no longer exists, but has given way to a state? Once again, it is easier to raise some of these questions than to answer them.

When we inquire into the level of political complexity that a chiefdom can attain, another variable we must consider is the size of the territory within which the chiefdom develops. The rule seems to be: The smaller the area in which a chiefdom arises, the easier it will be to unify. At the same time, the smaller this area, the lower the level of complexity the unifying chiefdom can attain (see Carneiro 1972: 74–6).

This can best be illustrated with island chiefdoms, such as those of Polynesia. Given two islands, the smaller one can be expected to be politically unified first, but the larger island, when finally unified, will have a more complex chiefdom.

The scale of a chiefdom depends largely upon the number of people whose labor the paramount chief can control. The more individuals in a chiefdom, the greater the amount of food they can be made to produce. And the more food produced, the greater the surplus the chief can siphon off. Because it is by means of this surplus that a chief feeds himself and rewards his warriors, officials, retainers, artisans, and all the other subordinates who contribute to the elaboration of the chiefdom, it is clear that the larger a chiefdom's territory, the more complex it can become.

Compare, for example, Pukapuka and Hawaii. Each island was politically unified into a chiefdom, but they were chiefdoms of a vastly different order. Pukapuka, being a tiny island, could support only a small chiefdom with little political elaboration (Beaglehole 1938:234–7). But Hawaii, being a large island, supported a chiefdom that, in magnitude and complexity, dwarfed that of Pukapuka.

From chiefdom to state
Finally, the question we need to consider is, When does a chiefdom become a state? Isaac (1975:140) calls this "a thorny problem." And Sanders and Marino (1970:9), after surveying the archaeological evidence for the New World, say that "The most difficult problem of identification lies in the attempt to separate chiefdoms from states."

To a certain extent this is a matter of definition, but that does not necessarily make the problem any easier to solve. In Fried's (1968: 145) opinion, "it is impossible to offer a unified definition of the state that would be satisfactory even to a majority of those seriously concerned with the problem." If that is true of defining a state, it is at least as true of drawing the line between a chiefdom and state.

There is no question, however, that a continuous process of political development leads from autonomous villages, through chiefdoms and states, to empires. Our task is to draw lines at certain points through this continuum to set off significantly different parts of it. Although this is partly arbitrary, it is not entirely so. Only if the lines between stages are drawn at appropriate points will the most salient features between contrasting forms stand out.

Much difference of opinion exists as to whether certain societies were chiefdoms or states. For example, was Hawaii a chiefdom or a state? Earle (1973:9–10) calls Hawaii "an excellent example of an advanced chiefdom organized only slightly below the state level." And Sanders and Price (1968:82) note that "the unusually large Hawaiian chiefdoms had structural features approximating those of states . . ." But they are nevertheless reluctant to call it a state. Where *do* we draw the line?

It has become common to characterize the state as having a monopoly on the use of force. Elman Service, for one, sees this attribute as distinguishing states from chiefdoms. The state, he says, has a "monopoly of force, as opposed to the power of a chief . . . who might if necessary hold an *advantage* of force . . ." (Service 1962: 171). Barry Issac adopts the same distinction. "The major difference between a chiefdom and a state," he writes, "is that only in the latter does some person, body, or office have a monopoly on the legitimate use of force within the polity" (Isaac 1975:143).

But this criterion is flawed. Many societies that, I dare say, Service and Isaac would both want to call states, lacked a monopoly on the use of force. This was true, for instance, of the Anglo-Saxon kingdoms. Thus in the laws promulgated by the tenth-century Anglo-Saxon monarch Aethelstan, we read (Attenborough 1963:163), "And he who is before others in killing a thief, shall be the better off for his action and initiative by [the value of] twelve pence [taken] from our common property." Thus not only could any subject of Aethelstan take it upon himself to kill a thief, he was actually rewarded for doing so by the king.

A recent comparative study of African political organization by Donna Taylor (n.d.) has shown the same thing. In a number of African societies that have other earmarks of states, private parties could take personal action in the case of certain crimes.[43] And I am sure that as soon as anthropologists drop the shibboleth that states have a monopoly on the use of force, we will hear of considerably more such cases.

Of course, states do eventually monopolize police power, but this takes place at an advanced level of state organization, not at its threshold. As Sanders and Webster (1978:274) observe, "monopoly of coercive force was weakly developed in early states . . ." Thus this criterion, despite its current popularity, fails as a marker for the existence of the state.

Criteria of state organization
I have already discussed Spencer's doubly compound form of society as providing a possible structural criterion for the state. Were we to follow this usage, we would say that a society had become a state as

soon as it had developed three levels of territorial and political organization: (1) the local level, consisting of individual villages, (2) the district level, comprising a number of villages organized into larger political units, and (3) the state level, encompassing a number of districts, fused into a single, overarching polity.

Using this criterion, we would have to conclude, for example, that the largest political units of Tahiti, called *fenua*, were really states rather than chiefdoms because they had three tiers of political and territorial organization:

> Each *fenua* was internally composed of smaller administrative districts called *patu*, which were further subdivided into even smaller units called *rahui*. Corresponding to this territorial structure was a three-tiered hierarchy of political offices. The *fenua* as a whole was ruled by a chief. Directly below him were a number of subchiefs, each of whom had jurisdiction over a *patu*. Officials of lowest rank were stewards (*ra'atira*) who each had charge or a *rahui* (Steponaitis 1978:423–4).

Now, merely because this three-level structural criterion is easy to apply does not mean that it is entirely satisfactory. Certainly before committing myself to it I would like to examine a good number of three-level societies to see if they also exhibited certain functional criteria that I consider hallmarks of a state.

What are these functional criteria? In "A Theory of the Origin of the State" (Carneiro 1970:733) I offered a definition of the state, which, with only a minor change, I offer here again, "*A state is an autonomous political unit, encompassing many communities within its territory and having a centralized government with the power to draft men for war or work, levy and collect taxes, and decree and enforce laws.*"

More elaborate definitions of the state have been offered (e.g., Flannery 1972:403–4; Sanders and Webster 1978:274).[44] Such definitions, however, are sometimes so extensive and involved that it is hard to say whether they are intended as strict definitions or merely as characterizations. If they are characterizations, they raise the question of whether all the traits enumerated in them, or only a preponderance of them, must be present for a society to be counted as a state.[45]

I believe the three functions previously cited – the power to draft, the power to tax, and the power to enforce law – are the most crucial and therefore the most diagnostic ones of a state. They are the functions that permit a society, eventually if not immediately, to manifest all the other attributes commonly associated with states. Thus they are the ones that should be used in a minimal or essential definition of the state.

Let us return now to the question raised earlier, namely, "Do three-level societies ("states" by a structural definition) invariably, or at least generally, exercise these three state powers?" I have made no special study of this question, so I cannot answer it conclusively. However, an example is at hand of a three-level society that did *not* manifest all three of the basic state functions – Tahiti.

We have seen that the several *fenua* of Tahiti qualify as states under a three-tier structural definition. However, they fail to qualify as states on the functional requirement of law enforcement. R. W. Williamson (1924:III, 16–17) has described the Tahitian legal system as follows:

> the official system of administration of justice was put into motion in connection with offences against the chiefs rather than as between the people themselves. It is stated that justice was not enforced by any law or regularly administered, though a chief did sometimes punish his immediate dependents for faults committed against each other, or even the dependents of other chiefs, if the offence was committed in his district; that there was no regular code of laws, and, except in cases of offences against the king or chiefs, rulers were seldom appealed to; that criminal punishment was unknown, except in the selection of obnoxious characters for occasional sacrifice; that the people obtained satisfaction with their own hands, whether justly or unjustly, for every injury received.

It appears, then, that three-level societies do not always meet our functional requirements for a state. Thus if we adopt these functional criteria, we cannot assume that every three-level society known archaeologically, historically, or ethnographically will automatically qualify as a state. What proportion of them will do so remains to be determined.

Now, the converse question can be raised. Do all societies that meet the *functional* criteria of statehood previously specified have three (or more) levels of political organization? Again, I have made no special study of this question, but I think it is likely that they do. But if such a society lacked three levels, would we consider it a state? My inclination is to wait until we find such an exception before being forced to take a stand.

When I first proposed a functional definition of a state, my concern was to present the hallmarks of a full-fledged state. My concern then was not with the delicate matter of distinguishing chiefdoms from states. In trying to make this distinction now, I want to emphasize that it is not a question of all or none but, rather, that it involves crossing a threshold in a continuum. Undoubtedly, most societies that we would want to call chiefdoms rather than states show at least the rudiments of conscription, of taxation, and of law enforcement.[46] After all, were these elements not present to some degree in a chiefdom, it could not hang together. It would tend to split apart and revert back to autonomous villages, or else succumb to a neighboring chiefdom that was better organized.

But the presence of a continuous gradation does not mean that there are no sharp and important contrasts within it. A draft is more than a call to arms. Taxation is a greater obligation than voluntary contributions. And promulgated laws are more strictly sanctioned than mere custom. Somewhere along the line, as we examine the evolution of these functions, a significant threshold is crossed; a categorically stronger and more complex society arises, which we want to call a state rather than a chiefdom. Our job, then, is to specify as precisely as possible where this threshold lies and when it has been crossed.

Our most pressing need right now is for a detailed comparative study of chiefdoms from all parts of the world and at all levels of development. Only when such a study has been made will the essential features distinguishing chiefdoms from states clearly stand out. When they do, we will be able to formulate them into useful categories. The data for such a study are scattered but exist in abundance. Now that the interest in chiefdoms has quickened, we can expect that more and more scholars will turn to this task. As they do, the chiefdom will begin to emerge from the penumbra, where it still lies, into the full light of understanding.

Notes

1 As recently as 1978 Timothy Earle (1978:6) wrote, "Although chiefdoms are critical for understanding evolutionary processes, . . . [they] are presently poorly defined and poorly understood."

2 I do not consider the "tribe" to represent a universal stage in political development. The tribe, in Service's sense, is a loose agglomeration of communities of peoples of similar culture given a certain amount of coherence by such things as "pantribal sodalities," but lacking any permanent and effective means of political integration. Although in some cases chiefdoms no doubt arose from tribes, in many cases they did not, arising instead from autonomous villages.

3 Sanders and Price (1968:81) classify the five Chibcha polities as chiefdoms rather than as states because of "The lack of architectural remains comparable to those of Mesoamerica and the Central Andes . . ."

4 We shall trace the history of the idea of chiefly redistribution later in this chapter.

5 In his later work, *Tribesmen* (1968:24–5), Sahlins again pays more attention to the supposed economic basis and function of the chiefdom than to a characterization of its political structure.

6 By Oberg's work as well: "The concept of *chiefdom* first came to my attention when Kalervo Oberg (1955) used it to designate a type of lowland South American society that lay between segmented tribes and true states. I borrowed it as the name for a full evolutionary stage in *Primitive Social Organization* (1962). I have found the conception of this intermediate stage enormously useful in several problems, and use it throughout this work" (Service 1975:15n.–16n.).

7 It is perhaps worth noting that Fried rejects the notion (which he says Sahlins and Service accept) that the "tribe" is an intermediate stage between autonomous villages and the state. "I do not believe that there is theoretical need for a tribal stage in the evolution of political organization," he says (Fried 1967:173). Instead, he believes that "tribalism . . . is a reaction to more recent events and conditions" (Fried 1967:173). That is, he sees the formation of tribes as a response to colonial expansion by state societies.

8 The major thesis of this book is that the recent revision of the radiocarbon time scale has forced on European archaeologists the conclusion that chiefdom-type societies, capable of impressive architectural feats, were as old or older in Western Europe as in Eastern Europe. Therefore, "whereas many of the changes seen in the material record were formerly viewed as the consequence of a 'diffusion' of culture from 'higher' centers, it is now clear that many developments, such as the development of monumental architecture and probably of metallurgy, were the consequences of processes operating locally" (Renfrew 1974:71).

9 Plains Indian tribes are also debarred from the status of chiefdoms because the definition requires a society to live in multiple communities, whereas a Plains tribe, although under the political control of a tribal chief, was aggregated into a single large camp.

10 Or, as Renfrew (1974:71) put it, "the . . . 'Neolithic Revolution' masks millennia of cultural development . . ."

11 Thus Milisauskas (1978:165) says, "While any chiefdom probably is located at a slightly different point along a range of increasing political complexity, the two different terms help us to discuss the relatively simple chiefdoms of the Middle Neolithic [of central Europe], and to differentiate them from the more complex polities of the Bronze and Iron Ages."

12 Service (1975:330) says, "*Africa* had a tremendous number of chiefdoms in early colonial times, but the great increase in the slave trade and warfare caused the collapse of many, while others became full-fledged states."

13 And were still in existence three thousand years later when Tacitus (1970:110–13), in his famous work, *Germania*, gave us a brief glimpse of what they were like.

14 "At Kaminaljuyu, it seems almost certain that, prior to the evolution of a fully developed state-like political system, some kind of transitional phase must have occurred which is comparable to what Service is calling the chiefdom" (Sanders 1974:109).

15 It is, of course, not inevitable that a chiefdom will leave monumental architecture behind to give testimony to its existence. The chiefdoms that extended along the Amazon River, from Machiparo to Marajoara, did not. The only archaeological evidence of their high status is their elaborate ceramics.

16 Thus Sanders (1974:109) writes: "The problem with using [these] criteria [monumental architecture] is that it works well for small, simply organized chiefdoms and large, highly organized states but it is precisely [at] the intermediate level where chiefdoms are evolving into states that we are faced with a dilemma of how to make the distinction between them."

17 For example, Milisauskas (1978:157) writes: "Usually the large sites [of Middle Neolithic cultures in southeastern Poland] occur at least several kilometers from one another, and interspersed between them are smaller sites. The large Funnel Beaker sites may represent the seats of sociopolitical authority of small polities. The ranking lineage or family may have resided in the large sites and dominated

the groups residing in dependent settlements." The ratio of small settlements to large ones in this region was 6 to 1.

18 In their attempt to trace political evolution from egalitarian society to the state, William Sanders and David Webster (1978:280) strike a middle ground: "To some degree . . . our model is systemic rather than lineal. The fact that we ranked the factors gives the model a lineal quality, so that a purist might deny it systemic pretensions. In rejoinder, we would argue that any systemic model – if it is ever to have rigorous value – will have to include quantification of the variables; and if necessary, the result will be inequalities in the strength of the various factors."

19 "The increased productivity and greater population density of chiefdoms are not necessarily due to any particular technological development . . ." (Service 1962: 143).

20 Only in one small corner of Hispaniola, the Xaragua district, was irrigation practiced (Sturtevant 1961:72).

21 According to Cieza de León (1959:176), Inca civilization was built in essentially the same way: "The most amazing thing is how few tools and instruments they have for their work, and how easily they produce things of finest quality . . . They also make statues and other large things, and in many places it is clear that they have carved them with no other tools than stones and their great wit."

22 "chiefdoms are not always demarked by a particular technological innovation which would set them off from tribes and states, but are characterized by their form of social organization . . ." (Service 1962:144).

23 "Technology does not always develop of itself; the many millennia between the first hammering and annealing of copper in the Old World and its smelting and casting to produce useful objects documents this" (Renfrew 1974:85).

24 To cite one example: "The Natchez chiefdom was a theocracy, with both secular and sacerdotal authority embodied in the Great Sun" (Farb 1978:166–7).

25 For example, Fried writes (1967:186): "A stratified society is one in which members of the same sex and equivalent age status do not have equal access to the basic resources that sustain life."

26 Thus, for example, Mark La Gory (1975:73) asserts that "the greater the distributive activities of the chief, the greater his status and authority . . ."

27 In primitive society, Polanyi (1945:56) wrote, "the economic system is, in effect, a mere function of social organization." He summarized this view by saying that in simple societies the economy is *embedded* in the social relations (Polanyi 1945:63). The term "embeddedness" has since been picked up by anthropologists who now use it widely.

28 As an economist, Polanyi was perhaps overly impressed by the distinction between economic systems based upon the market and those that are not. But the importance of this distinction need not be allowed to obscure the enormous differences that exist in the ways that goods move in nonmarket-based societies.

29 In a recent work Marvin Harris (1979:92) has a fine summary of this process: "Other things being equal, all such systems tend to move from symmetric forms of redistribution (in which the primary producers get back everything they produce) to asymmetric forms (in which the redistributors retain more of what is produced for longer and longer periods). Eventually the retained portion of the harvest surplus provides the chief with the material means for coercing his followers into further intensifications [of production]. (For example, as in Hawaii, where the chief acquired a permanent military retinue.) Contributions to the redistributive portion of the economy gradually cease to be voluntary; soon they verge on taxation, and at that point, chiefdoms stand poised at the threshold of becoming states."

30 Timothy Earle (1977:226) has observed: "The redistributive hierarchy of the Hawaiian chiefdom functioned to mobilize goods to support the operation of the political superstructure; in short, redistributional mobilization *was a form of taxation*" (emphasis mine, RLC).

31 Or by allowing allegiance to a concept to blind one to what the data have to say. Thus Sahlins was well aware of the naked force with which Tahitian chiefs appro-

priated goods from their subjects: "The paramount chief's servant could enter a person's house, seize cloth, kill pigs, take the last breadfruit, and pull up the houseposts for firewood, while the owner, even if he were a subchief, would look on without saying a word. Ellis notes that farmers, on pain of banishment or of being used as sacrificial victims, had to supply produce for chiefs if they stopped nearby while traveling" (Sahlins 1958:39–40). Yet practically in the same breath he says "the redistributive ethic prevailed in Tahiti as it did elsewhere" (Sahlins 1958:40). (For a similar failure to see the facts for what they are because of an unquestioning adherence to redistribution theory see Farb 1978:166.)

32 The first social scientist to see that war held the key to explaining political evolution was Herbert Spencer, who wrote: "We must recognize the truth that the struggles for existence between societies have been instrumental to their evolution. Neither the consolidation and re-consolidation of small groups into large ones; nor the organization of such compound and doubly-compound groups; nor the concomitant developments of those aids to a higher life which civilization has brought; would have been possible without inter-tribal and inter-national conflicts" (Spencer 1882:241). Spencer devoted many pages of his *Principles of Sociology* to illustrating how the process had operated (Spencer 1967:33, 35, 37, 73, 74, 76, 100, 113–14, 117, 125, 215, etc.).

33 But the climate of opinion is changing. For example, David Webster (1975:465) has recently written: "As a result of my own work on the defensive system at Becan, an early Lowland Maya center . . . , I have become increasingly convinced that a predominant form of conflict – warfare – has played a significant role in cultural evolution."

34 "there is a deep and abiding association between the state as a form of social organization and warfare as a political and economic policy" (Fried 1968:149). Also, "it can be convincingly argued that the development of the state has been paralleled by growth in the scale of war" (Fried 1968:149).

35 Let me quote one example: "Warfare was endemic to the Southeast in both the Mississippian and the historic period. In the early sixteenth century the chroniclers of the DeSoto expedition . . . thought it important to record the day they passed into the lands of fortified towns. Even allowing for the overstatement to which these observers were prone, it would seem that in the interior of the Southeast warfare and alliance for war was a way of life. Almost every society encountered by DeSoto's army was either allied to or engaged in active hostilities with its neighbor. In many instances the chief of the territory where DeSoto was bivouacked sought an alliance with him to make war on an adjoining territory. In other instances the DeSoto party was attacked; in one battle they were routed, in several other engagements they were forced to flee. Such losses should be taken as accurate, even understated, and therefore the details of these battles speak highly for the military prowess of the Southeast societies" (Peebles and Kus 1977:444). (For an account of the intense warfare waged among the Cauca Valley chiefdoms of Colombia see Trimborn 1949:275–381.)

36 The cause of the population increase that began with the Neolithic and which led to the population pressure that helped give rise to chiefdoms is a separate problem. Nevertheless, it is a most interesting and important one, which I deal with in Appendix B.

37 Joseph Ball (1977:125–6) has explained the rise of chiefdoms in this region as follows: "Given the archaeologically and geographically inferred preconditions of growing population, a swidden agricultural subsistence system, and a circumscribed environment, I propose that supravillage-level sociopolitical organization first appeared in the Northern Maya Lowlands in response to territorial competition and expansionist warfare among its inhabitants. A combination of offensive – defensive alliances, absorptions of defeated groups, and tighter internal sociopolitical organization could have given rise to a number of larger, more powerful village communities. In the face of persisting need to extend their territories farther, maintain their holdings, and effectively organize composite populations of allied and absorbed villages, these gradually would have stabilized as true ranked societies or chiefdoms."

38 This is exemplified by the Cherokee, about whom Gearing (1962:118) writes: "I have referred to the Cherokee state [=chiefdom] as voluntary, meaning by that that none of the units which joined exercised force on others of the units. This sense of voluntarism does not intend to preclude duress on all the units from some external source." Indeed, just prior to this passage, Gearing (1962:109) says: "Cherokee villages began their career toward statehood under conditions of external duress . . ."

39 Against the argument sometimes raised that there is no archaeological evidence of warfare in a region known to have produced chiefdoms, one can answer that even intense warfare does not always leave imperishable traces. What evidence would an archaeologist digging in Yanomamö territory five hundred years from now find of the acute and recurring warfare among them today?

40 At a later stage the slave class is augmented by adding to it native-born members of the society itself – usually people who have defaulted on their debts or who have been sold into slavery. For example, Mendelsohn (1949:1) writes: "The earliest Sumerian . . . slaves . . . were captive foreigners . . . to be followed later by imported foreigners, and finally by natives who were reduced to the status of slavery because of debt." Thus the origin of slavery is *extra*societal, but it later becomes *intra*societal as well.

41 Thus Service (1962:151) remarks, "once a chiefdom (even slightly developed) is pitted against mere tribes it will prevail, other things being equal." Sanders and Price (1968:132) observe, "Chiefdoms, with their tighter structure [than tribes], offer obvious military advantages over tribes, so that chiefdoms evolving among tribal groups, stimulate the development of other chiefdoms." (See also Webster 1975:467.)

42 In actuality, though, the process may not be quite so "exponential" as I have painted it here. Chiefdoms do not only grow, they also split. The larger they are, the stronger the divisive forces within them. (As White [1959:103] says, "Other factors being constant, the degree of solidarity varies inversely with the size: the larger the group the less the solidarity . . .") Thus the reduction in the number of chiefdoms in a valley may slow down after a while and perhaps even reach an equilibrium of sorts, until something permits the process to resume its course and a single political unit is ultimately formed.

43 "the most centrally organized political – jurisdictional organizations in the sample were not characterized by certain features which various writers have considered diagnostic attributes of state society. Thus, central organization here did not have a monopoly of force, and the rights of individuals, and of local kin groups, to secure redress for wrongs, were not eliminated" (Taylor, n.d.:18).

44 However, Sanders (1974:98) also has offered a very succinct definition: "We will simply define the state here as a political system involving adjudicative powers and explicit manifestation of force."

45 Of the two dozen or so traits that Flannery (1972:403–4) cites for the state, how many can fail to be present before we must consider the society not to have been a state? It is interesting to note, though, that on a chart in this same article, in which Flannery (1972:401) must, in very brief compass, contrast the major stages of political development, he lists only five traits as distinguishing states from chiefdoms, and three of these traits are "military draft," "taxation," and "codified laws."

46 "All the qualitative components of the state were already present to some degree among advanced chiefdoms. The asymmetric redistribution of harvest surpluses already amounted to an incipient form of taxation" (Harris 1979:100).

APPENDIX A

On the island of Boyowa in the Trobriands, where Bronislaw Malinowski did much of his fieldwork, there were several small chiefdoms, the best known of which was Kiriwina. On a map of the Trobriands, Malinowski (1922:50) shows eighteen villages within the boundaries of Kiriwina chiefdom, although he says elsewhere that in wars between Kiriwina and the neighboring chiefdom of Tilataula, each could muster only some twelve villages for the hostilities (Malinowski 1922:66).

In *Argonauts of the Western Pacific*, Malinowski (1922:63–5) described clearly and succinctly the nature of the Kiriwina chiefdom, especially the powers and functions of its paramount chief. Because this is such a fine description of a minimal chiefdom, it seems useful to quote the following extracts:

> the main chief of Kiriwina . . . resides in the village of Omarakana. He is in the first place the headman of his own village, and in contrast to the headmen of low rank [that is, headmen of other villages], he has quite a considerable amount of power. His high rank inspires everyone about him with the greatest and most genuine respect and awe . . .
>
> Not only does the chief – by which word I shall designate a headman of rank – possess a high degree of authority within his own village, but his sphere of influence extends far beyond it. A number of villages are tributary to him, and in several respects subject to his authority. In case of war, they are his allies, and have to foregather in his village. When he needs men to perform some task, he can send to his subject villages, and they will supply him with workers. In all big festivities the villages of his district will join, and the chief will act as a master of ceremonies. Nevertheless, for all these services rendered to him he has to pay. He even has to pay for any tributes received out of

his stores of wealth ... But how does he acquire his wealth? And here we come to the main duty of the vassal villages to the chief.

From each subject village, he takes a wife, whose family, according to the Trobriand law, has to supply him with large amounts of crops. This wife is always the sister or some relation of the headman of the subject village, and thus practically the whole community has to work for him. In older days, the chief of Omarakana had up to as many as forty consorts, and received perhaps as much as thirty to fifty per cent of all the garden produce of Kiriwina. Even now, when his wives number only sixteen, he has enormous storehouses, and they are full to the roof with yams every harvest time.

With this supply, he is able to pay for the many services he requires, to furnish with food the participants in big feasts, in tribal gatherings or distant expeditions. Part of the food he uses to acquire objects of native wealth, or to pay for the making of them. In brief, through his privilege of practising polygamy, the chief is kept supplied with an abundance of wealth in food stuffs and in valuables, which he uses to maintain his high position; to organise tribal festivities and enterprises, and to pay, according to custom, for the many personal services to which he is entitled ...

Power implies not only the possibility of rewarding, but also the means of punishing. This in the Trobriands is as a rule done indirectly, by means of sorcery. The chief has the best sorcerers of the district always at his beck and call ... If anyone offends him, or trespasses upon his authority, the chief summons the sorcerer, and orders that the culprit shall die by black magic ... Only in extreme cases, does a chief inflict direct punishment on a culprit. He has one or two henchmen, whose duty it is to kill the man who has so deeply offended him, that actual death is the only sufficient punishment.

The great increase in population that occurred during the Neolithic has long attracted attention. The conventional explanation for this increase is that it was caused by the greater reliability in the food supply made possible by the adoption of agriculture. The starvation that periodically cut into the hunting populations of the Paleolithic, the theory runs, was virtually eliminated by agriculture. Villages were then free to grow.

However, recent studies of contemporary hunters and gatherers have shown that their mode of subsistence is much more rewarding and reliable than had been assumed, even in desert habitats. If we can project this condition back into the Paleolithic, it would appear that starvation was not the limiting factor in keeping Paleolithic populations low that it was thought to be. Thus the population increase that marked the Neolithic could not be attributed to the supposed increase in the reliability of the food supply under agriculture. The food supply was already reliable. But if the bounteousness of agriculture was not what produced the jump in human numbers, what did?

In an important but little known article, Robert W. Sussman (1972) has argued that the growth in population that accompanied the Neolithic was due to the effects of sedentism. As long as societies lived in nomadic bands, a woman faced the burden of having to carry her young children wherever the band went. Under these conditions, raising two infants at the same time placed an intolerable burden on her. She thus spaced her children relatively far apart (four years or so, according to Sussman [1972:258]). In this way, by the time she was ready to raise another child, her older one could walk and did not have to be carried when the band moved. And the most common and effective method of child spacing was infanticide.

Once societies settled down, though, raising infants became easier. Women no longer had to carry their youngsters long distances every few days. A woman could now raise children at somewhat shorter intervals.

It is obvious that with only a slight decrease in infanticide, a village whose population had been stable would now begin to grow. If in a Neolithic village of one hundred persons one woman in a decade allowed one infant to live, which she previously would have killed, the village would grow by 1 person every ten years. And an increase of 1 person every ten years in a village of one hundred is equivalent to an average annual rate of growth of 0.1 of 1 percent.

In an earlier work (Carneiro and Hilse 1966), we showed that an average yearly increase of just this magnitude was all that was needed to account for the big spurt in population that took place in the Near East between 8000 and 4000 B.C. Thus the decline in infanticide fostered by sedentism was all that would have been required to produce the enormous increment in human numbers that occurred in the Near East during this time, which in turn had such dramatic consequences for the evolution of culture generally and the rise of the state in particular.

3

Class conflict and the state in the New World

JONATHAN HAAS

Introduction: conflict and integration theories

Within the discipline of anthropology and the other social sciences there is a longstanding debate concerning the initial role of the state in the evolution of society. The origins of this debate may be traced at least as far as the time of Aristotle and Plato. On the one side there are what may be called *conflict* theorists (also "coercive," "class," or "radical" theorists – Service 1978; Lenski 1966), and on the other there are *integration* theorists (also "contract," "benefit," "consensus," or "conservative" theorists – Service 1978; Lenski 1966; Yoffee 1979). As first outlined by Marx and Engels and later developed in anthropology by Childe, White, Fried, and others, the basic conflict argument is that the state developed primarily as a coercive mechanism to resolve internal conflict that arises between economically stratified classes within a society. To quote Engels:

> As the state arose from the need to keep class antagonisms in check, but also arose in the thick of the fight between the classes, it is normally the state of the most powerful, economically dominant class which by its means becomes also the politically dominant class and so acquires new means of holding down and exploiting the oppressed class (Engels 1972:231).

On the other side of the argument, theorists, such as Spencer, Durkheim, Moret, and Davy, and more recently Service, have argued that the state developed not as a coercive mechanism to resolve internal conflict but as an integrative mechanism to coordinate and regulate the different parts of complex societies. Basically, they see the state as a nonpartisan institution of government that provides organizational benefits to the society as a whole, by playing a central role in activities such as warfare, trade, or irrigation. Although most of the arguments on both sides of the debate are based upon logical reconstructions and observations of historically known states, Service (1975) has made the first serious attempt to address the issue using archaeological evidence from the first prehistoric states. In his analysis of the origins of civilizations and the state Service (1975:282–6) specifically brings the conflict model to task. He maintains that the basic elements of this model, namely, economic stratification, class conflict, and the centralized application of force, are not readily apparent in the archaeological record of early state societies. He also argues, quite reasonably, that their absence stands as a confirmation of his integrative model. However, a close examination of his argument reveals that the debate is by no means resolved. Without going into a detailed critique of Service's entire presentation (Haas 1979:85–103), I would like to focus on his rejection of the conflict model.

Service's negative conclusions about the conflict model are based upon a more extensive than intensive review of the available literature on early states, and he does not attempt to test rigorously these conclusions in a specific body of data. Two steps are necessary in order to conduct such a test. First, each of the basic elements of the conflict model must be operationalized such that they are recognizable in the archaelogical record. In other words, how do we identify stratification, conflict, and the application of force in terms of the sites, houses, artifacts, bones, and the like that we find in the ground? Second, after figuring out how to recognize the different elements, one must examine the material record of individual state societies for appropriate positive or negative evidence of each. Unfortunately, it is much easier to formulate the testing procedure than to carry out the test itself. Archaeologists have usually not asked questions related to the internal organization of prehistoric polities and as a result have seldom gathered the kinds of data needed to determine clearly the presence or absence of the conflict elements in individual prehistoric states. However, it is possible to abstract some relevant data from different world areas of early state development, and this abstracted data can be used for at least a preliminary test of Service's negative conclusions.

Methodological problems

Before attempting such a test, however, we must address, if not resolve, two problems that are contained within the testing model. The first is related to the definition of the state, and the second is related to the virtual absence of relevant data from the very first states that may have arisen in any particular area.

In regard to the first problem there are a number of questions concerning what a "state" is and how one might be recognized archaeologically. Cultural anthropologists and archaeologists show little agreement on either of these issues, as can be seen by the variety of definitions and recognitional schemes that currently abound (e.g., Wright and Johnson 1975; Flannery 1972; Carneiro 1970, 1978; Webb 1975; Service 1975; Trigger 1978; R. Cohen 1978a). Although I have attempted to address both issues elsewhere (Haas 1979:165–222), they are too complex to tackle in the present context. Instead, I will avoid either taking sides or offering my own definition but will simply look at those prehistoric societies that scholars working in an area have referred to as "states." In all cases these societies have large populations and exhibit highly complex and centralized forms of organization. Such organization is manifested in large-scale construction projects, trade networks, and religious systems.

The credulous policy of accepting what others have called "states" inevitably introduces certain weaknesses into the test. In particular, there is the problem that societies called "states" by some scholars are called "chiefdoms" or "ranked societies" by others. By simply accepting the "state" designation, I cannot be sure if I am using data from an actual state or from a society at a lower level of cultural evolution. Although this problem presents difficulties for a more comprehensive analysis of prehistoric political organization, it does not seriously affect the critical points of debate between the conflict and integration positions. The basic issue is whether or not the first governments were based upon stratification, conflict, and force. The conflict position says they were, whereas the integration position says they were not. Therefore archaeological evidence of these three elements in early, large, complex, and centralized polities, regardless of what they are called, would provide confirmation of the conflict position at the expense of the integration position. Furthermore, all the societies that I consider here to be potential states were also reviewed by Service, who concluded that they specifically *lacked* any evidence of the three conflict elements. By reexamining the evidence from the same societies, which Service used to refute the conflict position and confirm the integration position, one can critically evaluate his argument and compare the two positions objectively.

Whereas Service used six major areas of early state development in both the Old and New Worlds, I will focus here only on the New World states of Mesoamerica and Peru as testing grounds for the conflict model (see Haas 1979:104–64 for an extension of the test in both the Old and New Worlds). The sample will be further restricted to the earliest stages of state development in both areas. Specifically, the Formative and Early Classic periods in Mesoamerica (ca. 1000 B.C. to A.D. 300 – Weaver 1972; Price 1976), and the Early Horizon and Early Intermediate periods in South America (ca. 800 B.C. to A.D. 700 – Lumbreras 1974b; Rowe and Menzel 1967) will be examined. The reasons for making this temporal restriction are primarily methodological. In both areas the later stages of political development are characterized by clear evidence of military expansion and the formation of "empires." Because the appearance of military empires will introduce an external element of conflict into the internal organization of conquered societies, it obscures the question of whether such conflict is inherent to the organization of a state. Even the most ardent of integration theorists is not going to argue that conflict and coercion are absent in an empire based upon conquest (see Service 1975:286). Consequently, the appearance of widespread military expansion is a rational cut-off point for studying the internal organization of developing state societies.

Although looking at the earliest societies that have been referred to as states alleviates the problems of definition and recognition, there is still a major problem with the overall testing model. Both the conflict and integration models of state formation are concerned primarily with the "pristine" (Fried 1960) emergence of states, that is, states that evolve without major economic, military, or religious influence from existing outside states. In both Mesoamerica and Peru it could be argued that, at best, only one or two localized societies evolved into states under pristine conditions. Furthermore, because the emergence of one state in an area can be expected to induce the emergence of other states, the pristine lifespan of *any* state can also be expected to be relatively short. Although the exact identification and lifespan of pristine states in Mesoamerica and Peru cannot be presently determined (and may never be determined, given the exigencies of the archaeological record), it can be safely assumed that in the 1,300 to 1,500 years of evolution being examined here, there will be a distinct minority of polities that might even have been truly "pristine" states. In other words, the vast majority of data related to prehistoric political organization in Mesoamerica and Peru must be drawn from secondary, rather than from pristine, states. Consequently, it might be argued that finding evidence of stratification, conflict, or force in early New World states does not constitute confirmation of the conflict model; rather, the evidence might reflect secondary elements in secondary states. At the same time, it can be argued that if we are going to make any empirical evaluation of the conflict-integration debate, we must make use of available data and compensate as best we can for its inadequacies.

In terms of the test at hand, it can be argued that with a conflict model, a *pattern* of stratification/conflict/force is established at the inception of state societies and can be expected to occur in later states as well as in the earlier ones. In contrast, with the integration model there is no inherent argument to the effect that the stratification/conflict/force pattern will emerge at some point after the state has emerged. The presence of such a pattern in nonconquest-based states would thus require an additional explanation that goes beyond the basic premises of the integration model. Consequently, if archaeological evidence of the stratification/conflict/force pattern is *consistently* found in a variety of early states in an area, Occam's Razor dictates that the conflict model be accepted as offering the simpler and more concise explanation of the data.

Thus recognizing that there are unresolved definitional and methodological problems inherent in an empirical evaluation of the conflict and integration positions, we now turn to see whether there is New World evidence of each of the basic elements of the conflict model.

Testing the model

Differential access to resources

The first element in the model is economic stratification. According to Fried (1967:186), stratification exists when some members of a society have greater access to basic resources than other members. Accompanying stratification is the division of the society into classes. Those persons with unrestricted or increased access to basic resources constitute one class, whereas those with restricted or reduced access to those same resources constitute another class. In reality, there may be a range of persons with greater or lesser access to resources, but it is to be expected that there will be a qualitative distinction between those persons with the greatest access and those with the least. In order to operationalize this concept of class stratification so it can be recognized archaeologically, we must address two issues: (1) defining and distinguishing the resources that are basic in a society and (2) determining how to recognize differential access to those resources in a material record.

"Basic resources" are essentially all the goods and products that are either absolutely necessary for, or significantly contribute to the probability of, survival and reproduction in a society. It quickly becomes apparent that it is impossible to devise a list of basic resources that applies to all societies. A car may be considered a basic resource in Los Angeles but a luxury resource in New York and a nonexistent resource in the pre-Hispanic New World. In other words, specific basic resources will vary tremendously from one society to another, depending upon environmental, technological, and historical circumstances. However, it is possible to distinguish *types* of resources that can be considered basic in all societies. Among the types of basic goods and products would be food, tools used for the production and preparation of food, and protective devices for coping with the physical environment and an antagonistic social environment. Everyone needs to eat something; everyone needs to have some means of obtaining food and making it edible; and everyone needs protection from the elements and potential enemies. This is not intended as an exhaustive list of all types of necessary or adaptively advantageous goods and products but, rather, as a tentative list to be used in an initial test of the presence or absence of stratification.

The identification of these general types of basic resources provides us with a means of addressing the second issue in operationalizing class stratification: that is, the archaeological recognition of differential access. Because there are direct material manifestations of all these types of resources, differential access in a stratified society should be reflected archaeologically in differential use, consumption, and/or proximity to those resources. Thus we look for unequal distribution of food, certain kinds of tools used for the production and preparation of food, and protective devices in the material record. Theoretically, stratification can be inferred if *any* of these things are found to be distributed differentially in a society. However, it is probable that stratification based upon unequal access to one type of resource will be accompanied by unequal access to other types as well. In other words, there should be a pattern of differential access, not just an isolated instance. An additional aid in determining stratification is to be found in luxury or sumptuary goods. Although such goods are not a useful indicator of stratification per se, they can be used to help interpret observed patterns of resource distribution. Generally, status and rank markers should parallel the patterns of economic stratification.

The three types of basic resources – food, tools, and protective devices – will be treated separately in order to specify how each can serve as a means of identifying a pattern of stratification in the archaeological record.

Food. This type of basic consumer resource will include all those comestibles that contribute to essential subsistence and nutritional balance. To detect unequal access to such comestibles, we must look for direct evidence of unequal consumption in either trash deposits or in skeletal remains. It is not enough, for example, simply to find large food storage areas in conjunction with high status residences. The central figures in a redistributive system may have quantities of food brought in and stored at their place of residence, but they may not eat better than others (Fried 1967:116–18). For more direct evidence of differential consumption of food, the upper levels of a stratified hierarchy should have trash containing food remains that reflect a better overall diet than that of the lower levels. Skeletal remains should also reflect differential access to a better diet in terms of the general health of individuals from different levels of the stratified hierarchy. If some members of a society have greater access to food, particularly higher quality and nutritious food, then it can be expected that these individuals would be healthier than those without such access. Thus the skeletal population from a stratified society should exhibit qualitative physical differences between groups of individuals with unequal access to food resources.

When turning to the archaeological record to test for stratification based upon access to food, I can find only two cases where the relevant nutritional analyses have been conducted. Both relate to skeletal analyses in Mesoamerica. I can find no similar analysis of any skeletal population in Peru and no nutritional analysis of trash deposits in either area. However, the available Mesoamerican data are enlightening. From the Mayan lowland site of Tikal, there is an in-depth study of burial materials, which are indicative of differential access to food resources. Haviland (1967) found that in the first century B.C. the men inhumed in elaborate burial tombs were approximately 7 cm taller than the men not buried in tombs. Furthermore, the difference between the tomb occupants and the nontomb occupants was a qualitative one. Although there was some gradation in height within each of the groups, there was a distinct gap between the shortest members of the former group and the tallest members of the latter. If it were simply the case that superior status was being bestowed on tall individuals, there should be a quantitative height scale with no such qualitative gaps. Although other explanations may account for this pattern, stratification based upon unequal access to foodstuffs, as argued by Haviland, is the most parsimonious (Haviland 1967:321).

More direct evidence of differential nutrition and access to foodstuffs comes from the Formative site of Chalcatzingo. In a superb recent study Schoeninger (1979) analyzed the chemical composition of bone minerals from skeletons uncovered at Chalcatzingo. She specifically examined the bone strontium levels, which in turn reflect the relative meat intake of individuals. The results were striking. Basically, she found that individuals in the highest status graves, accompanied by jade artifacts, had the lowest bone strontium levels and thus the highest meat intake. Middle status graves, with some grave goods but no jade, had significantly higher bone strontium levels and lower meat intake. Individuals in the lowest status graves with no grave goods had the highest bone strontium levels and lowest meat intake. Clearly there was differential access to basic food resources at Chalcatzingo.

It is fairly obvious that these two positive, but limited, cases do not definitively prove that stratification based upon unequal access to food was a widespread element in the development of early states in the New World. The problem in proving such a conclusion, however, cannot be attributed to an overwhelming amount of adverse evidence; rather, there is an abysmal absence of necessary evidence.

At the same time, what Schoeninger's study so nicely shows, when the difficult but critical kinds of analyses are conducted, is that concrete evidence of stratification based upon access to food *can* be found. Until such analyses are carried out on other sites in Mesoamerica and Peru, we will have no way of knowing if some members of the early New World states were consistently eating better than others. At present, we have no solid basis for making positive or negative inferences concerning the ubiquity of stratification based upon access to food resources. Information on the distribution of other types of basic resources, however, is more plentiful for the early New World states and does tend to be indicative of a general pattern of stratification.

Tools. This type of basic resource would include primarily agricultural implements and those items necessary for cooking, processing, eating and storing foodstuffs. The relative distribution of such tools may be indicative of stratification in two kinds of circumstances. In one case, certain kinds of tools may be technologically superior to other kinds (e.g., metal versus stone) and bestow an advantage on their owners in the production and preparation of food. Finding the superior type of tools concentrated in the hands (or rather the remains) of only a portion of a population, and the inferior tools associated with the remainder, would constitute evidence of a form of stratification. In the second case, large-scale labor specialization may lead to the concentration of all productive and preparative tools in the hands of only a portion of the population. However, finding such a pattern of concentration in the archaelogical record may be indicative of two very different kinds of stratification. One possibility is that the persons lacking the tools constitute a disenfranchised lower class that has only indirect access to the means of producing and preparing food. The other is that the persons without tools constitute an upper class that is exploiting the labor of those persons directly engaged in productive and preparative activities. Thus when radical differences are found in the distribution of tools, independent evidence, such as luxury goods and status markers, must be used to distinguish the relative position of the different strata.

Although there is more evidence on the distribution of tools than on the consumption of food, it is still less than satisfactory for a conclusive statement. In Mesoamerica there is evidence that obsidian, a common medium of preparative tools, was distributed equally in residences in the Valley of Oaxaca during the Early and Middle Formative periods (Winter and Pires Ferreira 1976). However, there are no data on obsidian distribution from the later periods, when archaeologists believe the state first emerged in the area (Flannery and Marcus 1976; Blanton 1976). Consequently, the earlier data have no bearing on the possible role of stratification in state formation. At the Formative site of Tlatilco, where several hundred burials have been excavated, some of the graves have few or no offerings of any kind, whereas others had abundant sumptuary goods as well as different kinds of stone tools and ceramic vessels (Porter 1953). Similarly, in Classic period Maya sites there is evidence of distinctly unequal distribution of specially crafted preparative tools in different burial assemblages. Higher status burials had more tools and tools of a higher quality than did lower status burials (Rathje 1970).

At the city of Teotihuacán in the Early Classic period, the presence of hundreds of craft workshops, where obsidian tools and other items were produced, is evidence of a large-scale division of labor (Spence 1967, 1973; Millon 1973). This division of labor is probably indicative of a highly complex system of stratification. The persons engaged in producing obsidian tools and other craft items would have increased access to those resources but restricted access to the food resources produced by other members of the population. In the case of the noncraft food producers the relative access would be reversed. At the same time, there are indications of an upper class elite at the site, to be addressed later, who may have had greater access to both craft items and subsistence products. Unfortunately, there has been insufficient work done at Teotihuacán (or at least published) to indicate the actual distribution, use, and consumption of either tools or food resources in the residences or trash deposits.

Turning to South America, there is direct evidence of unequal distribution of productive and preparative tools in general at the site of Pampa Grande, a Moche V city on the north coast of Peru. In one distinctly high status residential complex the associated artifactual assemblage contained no agricultural implements and no preparative tools. In fact, it contained no tools of *any* kind (Haas 1976, n.d.). In contrast, in the identifiably lower status residential areas, all types of tools occur regularly within the houses and in association with the domestic refuse (Shimada 1976). It can be inferred from this distribution that the persons in the higher status residence did not produce or prepare their own food resources but obtained them through the labor of others. Lower status persons, on the other hand, obtained their food through the utilization of the tools found in association with them. Thus the distribution of tools at Pampa Grande is indicative of differential access to food resources between low status groups that had to produce and prepare their own food and a high status group that did not.

For other early sites in Peru this type of distribution information on tools is not available. Again, the evidence for New World stratification in terms of the second type of basic resources is suggestive but not conclusive.

Protective devices. The third general type of basic resource includes the protective devices used for coping with the physical environment and an antagonistic social environment. Although artifacts such as clothing and weaponry fall into this general type, there is more abundant relevant data to be obtained in an analysis of architectural and housing patterns. With housing, stratification should be marked by differences in quality and location of residences. Differential access to the materials or labor necessary for house construction would be most directly reflected in qualitatively more spacious and technically superior houses for the upper strata than for the lower. Differential access to defensive mechanisms would be manifested in the location of high status residences within walled compounds or fortifications, whereas lower status residences would be located outside or at some distance from such defensive architecture.

In Mesoamerica there is evidence of stratification based upon access to housing and defensive architecture at Teotihuacán, at different sites in the Valley of Oaxaca, and at the Maya site of Tikal. At Teotihuacán there are large, spacious, and elaborate palatial residences in potentially defensible compounds in the center of the city and a range of smaller, more crowded, and simpler dwelling complexes in a wide belt around the center (Millon 1973). Although many of these lower status residential complexes are also surrounded by large compound walls, others are not (Millon 1973; Millon, Drewitt, and Cowgill 1973). In Oaxaca, where housing has been subjected to a more intensive statistical analysis than at other sites in Mesoamerica, Winter (1974, 1976) has found that there are qualitative intrasite differences among houses in the Classic period. There are three general types of houses in the valley, with a clear difference in size, arrangement, and number of rooms between the largest and most formal type and the other two. High status burials (measured in terms of luxury goods) are found in association with the larger houses, further supplementing the inference that differential access to housing, labor, and materials is at least one element in some form of class stratification in Oaxaca. At Tikal there is evidence of high status stone masonry residences in the area of the ceremonial center of the site; these are contemporaneous with lower status masonry and thatch residences in the surrounding area (Haviland 1970; W. Coe 1965b). The ceremonial center and both high and low status residences near it were also surrounded by a large defensive earth wall (Puleston and Callender 1967). Other low status residences located further from the center were not provided with this type of protection.

In South America evidence of unequal access to superior residences and protective architecture can be illustrated in a number of sites in the Moche area. At both Pampa Grande and the site of

Galindo in the Moche Valley (Bawden 1977) there are high status, formally laid out adobe residences, located in large adobe-walled compounds. These are contemporaneous with numerous irregular houses with trash-filled cobble walls located outside any form of defensible compound. At the earlier site of Moche there are also high status adobe residences in the ceremonial center of the site with lower status masonry residences clustered around the periphery (Topic 1977). Topic also believes there may have been a compound wall in the area of the central adobe residences, but the evidence for this is weak. As a whole, housing patterns in the Moche area indicate that some society members definitely had increased access to labor and superior building materials for the construction of residences and defensive architectural devices.

It is possible to cite some additional evidence of stratification in the New World states, but what I have given is the best evidence I can find. From the available body of archaeological data collected in Mesoamerica and Peru there is only a hint of the relative distribution of different types of basic resources. Although things like subsistence, tools, and housing receive considerable attention in the archaeology of pre-state societies, archaeologists working on developed states tend to concentrate their limited resources on larger scale issues, such as ceremonialism, long-distance trade, and the agricultural modes of production. This work is extremely important and necessary, but it fails to tell us whether or not the first states were based upon economic stratification. The small amount of relevant data that can be abstracted from work aimed toward other ends suggest that some members of New World states did have greater access to certain basic resources, and it certainly does not allow us to conclude that stratification was absent, as concluded by Service.

Internal conflict and the application of force
With the first step in the conflict model unconfirmed but at least suggested, we can still proceed to test the other parts of the model, namely, internal conflict and centralized application of force.˙ Because the different parts of the model are interrelated, finding evidence of internal conflict within the early states and of the application of forceful sanctions, would allow us to confirm the model, even in the absence of direct evidence for stratification.

Internal conflict. In regard to internal conflict, the basic argument is that under conditions of stratification the relationship between the unequal social strata is predicted to be one of conflict, expressed by some degree of sustained hostility and antagonism within the society. Persons with restricted access to resources would contest, rather than simply accept, the unequal distribution of those resources (Fried 1978). On the other hand, those persons with unrestricted or greater

access would attempt to protect or defend their privileged position
in the face of such contestation. This ongoing antagonistic relationship between social strata can be expected to be manifested in several ways:

1. The different strata to resolve or reduce daily tensions,
would not be expected to reside in immediate proximity
to one another. This would be seen archaeologically in the
separation and relative isolation of the higher and lower
status groups in a stratified society.

2. The group with greater access and a favored position
would be expected to institute defensive mechanisms to
protect physically their position in the face of prolonged
internal aggression or hostility. This would be indicated
by the presence of defensive mechanisms serving to protect *only* the higher status residences within a site.

3. Possible rebellion or revolution by the lower status groups
might also be expected. This would be manifested in the
form of violent internal measures taken to depose the
upper status group from their privileged position. To distinguish such internal rebellion from conquest, one should
characterize it by the lack of an influx of foreign elements,
and possibly by the selective destruction and abandonment, without replacement, of the high status residences at
a site.

In looking at the archaeological record for these three possible
manifestations of antagonism between social classes, we see that
there is much more conclusive evidence for this central element in
the conflict model than for the other two. Turning first to the
evidence from Peru, we note once again that the most conclusive
data come from the Early Intermediate period on the north coast.
The expected separation and isolation of high status residences
from other residences are manifested in a number of sites and
valleys. In the Virú Valley, Willey (1953:347–8) found that in the
cluster of sites known as the Gallinazo Group (ca. 300 B.C.) there
were very large stone-floored houses separated by several hundred
meters from contemporaneous village aggregations of twenty to
one hundred small rooms or houses (see also Bennett 1950). At the
later site of Galindo in the Moche Valley, lower status stone masonry houses are clustered on the hillslopes to the rear of the site,
whereas the higher status adobe houses are down below on a flat
plain area (Bowden 1977). In addition to this relative isolation, the
high and low status residential areas are separated by a massive
stone wall. Furthermore, the higher status residences at the site are
also surrounded by large, defensible compound walls. At the site of
Moche the high status houses are clustered together between two

huge pyramid structures in relative isolation from the lower status residences at the edges of the site. As already mentioned, there may also be a compound wall around portions of the central area of the site (Topic 1977).

At Pampa Grande separation and isolation of high and low status groups is extreme. The site is not located in a particularly advantageous military position, and there are no indications of protective mechanisms or fortifications erected to defend the immediate avenues of approach. Consequently, it can be inferred that defense was not a primary variable in the determination of the location and layout of the site. However, within the four square kilometers of the total site area there is one enormous walled compound and several comparatively smaller compounds. The wall around the main compound was 600 meters long, 400 meters wide, at least 4 meters high and 2 meters thick. Within the compound, architecture is generally sparse and most of it is arranged in a formal pattern. The dominant architectural feature inside is the massive platform mound or truncated pyramid, Huaca Grande (Haas 1976, n.d.). This structure is composed of a series of stepped terraces and platforms. The height above ground level of the various floors on this structure ranges from 10 to 55 meters. The only means of access up onto any of the upper levels is by way of a walled corridor/ramp. Access is further restricted by a number of cross walls or checkpoints along this ramp. To gain access onto the uppermost level of the structure required that a person pass through an additional baffling or zigzagging entry and another walled ramp. On the summit of the structure an elaborate, multiroomed, residential complex is located (Haas n.d.). This high status residence is thus not only separated and isolated from other residences at the site but is also a highly defensible stronghold against any possible internal acts of aggression or hostility. The indications that the site itself is not fortified or defensively located support the inference that the elaborate defensive measures surrounding the single high status residence are addressed to internally rather than to externally originating aggression.

Below Huaca Grande there is another large and formally arranged complex of rooms inside the compound walls. On the basis of surface indications this complex also appears to be composed of high status residences, but confirmatory excavations have not been conducted. There is another complex of rooms at the rear of the compound, which appears to be residential but is definitely not high status. These rooms are small, have rock and rubble walls, and are randomly arranged. However, although these rooms are within the compound and afforded the protection of the surrounding wall, equally massive walls separate and isolate this lower status complex from the probable residential complex at the front of the compound and from the access ramp leading up to the Huaca Grande room complex. In other words, the compound walls serve to isolate the interior residences from the majority of the site, and subdividing walls further isolate the higher status residences from the few lower status residences within the compound.

Work on the other smaller compounds at the site has not been focused on residential architecture; thus the extent of isolation and separation of residences cannot be determined at present. The investigations that have been carried out in these smaller enclosures have revealed structures associated with warehousing and storing certain agricultural resources, such as maize and cotton (Day 1976). The walls around storage and warehousing areas may be tentatively interpreted as preventative mechanisms against possible usurpation or theft of the resources.

Overall, there is clear evidence of isolation, separation, and internal defense of high status residences on the Peruvian north coast, and I would argue that this pattern can be adequately interpreted only as a manifestation of conflict between social classes. What about more direct evidence of actual conflict, however? Indications of rebellion or revolution in the Moche area are more limited and less convincing, but still present. Returning to Pampa Grande, almost all the platform mounds and high status adobe structures, including Huaca Grande and the residence on it, were burned and never reoccupied or utilized. In contrast, none of the excavated stone masonry structures in other parts of the site were burned. This selective pattern of burning, and the total lack of evidence of an intrusive occupation after the fire, point more to internal revolt than to external conquest.

Another interesting, though admittedly shaky piece of evidence of rebellion in the Moche area, has been uncovered at one of the platform mounds at the site of Moche. On Huaca de la Luna there is a graphic mural depicting an assortment of ceramic vessels and other artifacts rising up and actively rebelling against their users (Lumbreras 1974b:102). Whether this mural is a symbolic representation of human rebellion cannot, of course, be verified. Nevertheless, I believe it does illustrate that at least the concept of a rebellion was not unknown during the Moche occupation of the north coast.

Going back to Mesoamerica, there are two cases where different kinds of data point to intrasocietal conflict. One of these comes from the latest state in the period being considered and the other, from the earliest. At Teotihuacán separation and isolation of residential groups of different statuses are carried out on a grand scale. The vast majority of all the residences at the site are artificially isolated from one another by large stone compound walls (Millon 1973, 1976). The entire city, in other words, is composed of a series of separate walled compounds of both high and low status residences. However, the highest status compounds are all aggregated at the center of the city, and these appear to have been the first walled compounds built. In discussing the compartmentalization of Teotihuacán Millon (1976: 224) maintains that the division of the city into walled compounds was associated with "major conflicts, antagonisms, and tensions" among the city's residents. Thus internal conflict between social groups at Teotihuacán seems to have been a dominant element during the initial stages of occupation.

More direct evidence of conflict is found in the Olmec area of the Mexican Gulf Coast during the Formative period. At the central Olmec sites of La Venta and San Lorenzo between forty and sixty large stone monuments have been uncovered in the course of excavations (M. Coe 1968a, personal communication 1979; Drucker et al. 1959). These monuments, predominantly religious or political in nature, included large slabs or stelae carved with different scenes or figures, life-size representations of priests carrying babies, and the colossal stone portrait heads for which the Olmec are so famous. At each of these sites the majority of monuments had been deliberately and violently mutilated or destroyed (Drucker et al. 1959:229–30; M. Coe 1968a:86). Furthermore, the destruction of the monuments took place close to the time of abandonment of La Venta and just shortly before the abandonment of San Lorenzo. At both sites the deliberately destructive actions have been interpreted as resulting from internal revolt (Heizer 1960:220; M. Coe 1968a). Although it is possible that foreign invaders may have carried out or directed this work, revolution should be given preference, because there is no indication of a foreign intrusion in the area. In fact, Coe found that local pottery and figurine manufacture continued uninterrupted at San Lorenzo for a period of time after the destruction of the monuments (M. Coe 1968a:86).

An additional factor that points to internal revolt at La Venta in particular concerns an increase in labor output during the final occupation period. Throughout the occupation of La Venta the population contributed labor in transporting and carving stone monuments, in burying massive quantities of imported stone as religious offerings, and in building large ceremonial structures. During the final period of occupation they had the additional burden of quarrying and transporting over two hundred basalt columns, each weighing 2 tons and originating at a source over 50 linear miles away (Drucker et al. 1959:126). These columns were used in building two large stone tombs and in starting the construction of a large walled compound within the ceremonial center of the site. Although many columns were stockpiled at the site, the enclosure wall was never completed. Drucker et al. (1959:126–7) hypothesize that the additional burden of bringing in and erecting the columns was too much for the La Venta population, leading them to rebel. It is also significant to note that the apparent straw that broke the camel's back was the construction of a walled compound, which in other areas is used as a mechanism of isolating and protecting elite residences.

Overall, the evidence for internal conflict in the New World is considerably stronger than for stratification, but this too is still in need of further confirmation.

Application of centralized force. The application of forceful coercive sanctions in support of a system of stratification is the final basic element in the model. This element brings up a critical problem with Service's integrative analysis and evaluation of the conflict position. His essential argument is that the early governmental leaders in the archaic civilizations did not regularly appeal to violence as a means of gaining the compliance of their respective populations. Rather, they used positive means, including "engineering the consent" of the governed by the adroit use of supernatural powers; maintaining social control through an adjudicative or legal system; providing the offensive and defensive advantages of a centralized military; and providing the economic benefits of a redistribution system and/or trade network (Service 1975:291–6). What Service fails to see, or at least acknowledge, is that coercive force is inevitably covariable with a strong centralized government that supplies essential goods and services to a dependent population. Although it cannot be denied that in governing a population the early governmental rulers could have applied tremendous positive sanctions in providing beneficial ideological, judicial, military, and economic goods and services, neither can it be denied that those rulers could also have applied equally tremendous negative sanctions by *withholding* the same goods and services. Furthermore, if these goods and services are essential for social control, protection, and subsistence (as argued by Service), then withholding them is a negative sanction equally as forceful as the brute strength of a police force or militia.

Service does recognize that societal leaders have the power to withhold as well as to provide. For example, he states that in early civilizations the religious rulers utilized their control over the supernatural to apply both positive and negative sanctions in "engineering the consent" of the governed (Service 1975:294). Because negative supernatural sanctions have no direct physical impact, Service's claim that force was not used by early governmental rulers is unaffected. However, when control over economic or military resources is considered, Service fails to recognize the potential physical impact of using that control to apply negative sanctions.

In his discussion of the evolution of leadership Service states that the redistributive leaders in simple "bigman systems" have the power to reward and punish by giving out or withholding the goods they control (Service 1975:293). At the same time, he asserts that the leadership position of the bigman is dependent upon his successful and judicious management of the redistributive system. In this sense, a leader is "created by his followers, not by their fear of him but by their appreciation of his exemplary qualities"(Service 1975: 293). However, as Service points out, such a leadership system is inherently unstable due to its dependence upon the success of the leader. When such a society increased in size and social complexity, the necessary stability was provided by transforming the leadership system into a permanent, institutionalized government. Such a transformation would indeed provide stability to a developing hierarchy as Service contends. However, it concomitantly frees the leaders from their critical dependence upon the successful and judicious management of resources for the maintenance of their position. Freed of the dependency imposed on their evolutionary antecedents, permanent governmental rulers have qualitatively greater power to govern by reward and punishment through providing and withholding the economic goods and services they control. Viewed from this perspective, it is apparent that in "engineering the consent" of the governed the early governmental rulers could have applied materially forceful economic sanctions along with the materially forceless supernatural sanctions inferred by Service.

The failure to recognize that coercive force is an inevitable covariable of an essential benefit is exacerbated by Service's discussion of the effects of circumscription. He maintains that in all examples of early governmental development the societies were circumscribed either geographically or socially by the presence of external enemies (Service 1975:298; following Carneiro 1970). In cases of geographical circumscription, the governments provided integrative benefits in the form of efficient production and distribution of subsistence resources. In cases of social circumscription the government provided the benefits of protection from the enemy. By observing the ubiquity of circumscription, Service (1975:299) draws the conclusion that due to circumscription "the *benefits* of being part of the society obviously outweighed the alternatives." Furthermore, "the benefits of membership in the society must have been very obvious" (Service 1975:299). He then maintains that these obvious benefits helped enable the governmental rulers to govern without applying force. What Service does not point out in his conclusions is that under conditions of circumscription, there are *no* viable alternatives to belonging to the society. The only "choices" available to the members of such a society would have been death at the hands of an enemy, starvation in a sterile desert, or submission to the demands of the societal rulers. As stated eloquently by the philosopher David Hume:

> Can we seriously say that a poor peasant or artisan has a
> free choice to leave his country when he knows no foreign
> language or manners and lives from day to day by the
> small wages which he acquires? We may as well assert that
> a man, by remaining in a vessel, freely consents to the
> dominion of the master, though he was carried on board
> while asleep and must leap into the ocean and perish the
> moment he leaves her (Hume 1953:51).

Certainly the benefits of membership in the society would have been
obvious to the populace; equally obvious would have been the physically deleterious or lethal alternatives to membership. Thus the lack
of reasonable alternatives provided the rulers with an indirect but
nevertheless coercive and forceful means of ensuring the obedience
of the population.

Aside from seeing that rulers who provide essential benefits can
also apply force, one must also recognize that in the circumstance of
forceful repression actual coercive sanctions may be applied with
relative infrequency. If a ruler is able to demonstrate physically the
ability to apply such sanctions, then the threat of applying them may
be used as an effective mechanism for maintaining the subordinate
position of the lower status portion of the population (cf. Bierstedt
1950:73; Dahl 1969:86; Haas 1979:199–221). In other words, if
there is forceful resolution of conflict between unequal social groups
in the first states, it is not to be expected that the application of force
by the government will be omnipresent, nor will it be the only means
used to govern the population. Considerable insight into the way in
which the rulers of the early New World states could have utilized
coercive sanctions to maintain the system of stratification may be
gained from ethnohistoric examples of complex societies at or approaching statehood.

Two societies in particular, the Hawaiians of Polynesia and the
Zulu of South Africa, provide examples of highly complex political
forms that developed without overriding influence from outside
state societies. Service treats both societies as primitive states and
asserts that force or coercive sanctions were not used in either of
them as a successful means of governing or maintaining a system of
stratification (Service 1975:116, 285). However, upon examining
both of these cases, one sees that coercive sanctions were actively and
regularly applied against the lower status portions of the population
as a successful means of maintaining social control.

In Hawaii at the time of contact the paramount chiefs had managerial control over the distribution of land and water rights. They
also served as the foci for the collection and redistribution of economic resources. They used this economic control and central posi-

tion in a number of ways. They personally subsidized specialized craftsmen, enjoyed qualitatively greater consumption of numerous luxury goods, employed personal litter bearers, and lived in superior housing (Sahlins 1958:15–18). They also monopolized certain kinds of foods, though their food consumption was not qualitatively different from that of the rest of the population. Moreover, in order to maintain their position, they were obligated to distribute justly the foodstuffs that they collected. According to Malo (1951:62), the redistribution of food was a positive means of governing the population and of keeping the people "contented." However, the chiefs were not totally dependent on positive means of governing. Rather, they used their control over land and water to dispossess the means of subsistence from those persons who failed to contribute labor demanded of them, who failed to produce sufficient resources, or who secretly accumulated resources (Malo 1951; Sahlins 1958:14–16). More direct physically coercive sanctions were applied against commoners who committed criminal acts or misdeeds. Particularly severe sanctions were applied when misdeeds affected the paramount chiefs. According to Sahlins,

> punishment varied according to the status of the parties. Within this framework, coercive force was applied by the chief in punishing those who infringed his rights, especially if the transgressors were low in status. According to Ellis, Handy, Malo, and others, *people were slain by a high chief if they violated his economic or personal tabus, stole from, or committed adultery with his wife* (Sahlins 1958:19, emphasis added).

Thus Hawaii clearly demonstrates how coercive sanctions can be and are applied in the maintenance of a system of qualitatively different status differences.

The Zulu offer an example of secondary state formation in which the application and threat of violent coercive sanctions played a paramount role. The initial formation of the Zulu state came about as a result of the conquest and subordination of several hundred chiefdoms in southern Africa by the combined Mthethwa and Zulu chiefdoms (Walter 1969; Morris 1965). Once formed, the subsequent development of the Zulu state was characterized by widespread terror and wholesale slaughter of thousands of people at the instigation of the first two rulers, Shaka and Dingane. People were publicly executed for relatively minor criminal acts, and at times for apparently arbitrary reasons. Both these rulers governed for approximately ten years each before being assassinated. With the ascent of the third ruler, Mpande, the volume of slaughter decreased markedly and the Zulu lived in relative internal peace for the more than thirty years of Mpande's rule (Walter 1969:Chapter 6; Gluckman 1940; Morris 1965).

Service uses this basic sequence of events as a prime illustration of his assertion that government by force is ineffective and ultimately unsuccessful (Service 1975:111–16). He also cites Walter (1969) to support the assertion that the mass slaughter instigated by Shaka and Dingane was not aimed at coercing the populace but at impressing potentially rival chiefs (Service 1975:116, 285). However, an examination of the data and Walter's analysis reveals a markedly different picture from that painted by Service.

On an absolute scale it may in fact be true that Shaka and Dingane both ruled for relatively short periods of time. However, their combined despotic rule resulted in society's subjection to over twenty years of mass executions. In other words, the initial Zulu reign of terror lasted a full generation. Given a span of twenty years of terror, it would seem difficult to support a claim that the government of the first two Zulu rulers did not have a lasting coercive effect on the Zulu population. Walter makes this point very clearly:

> In the despotic system beginning with Shaka, as the intermediate authorities – fathers, elders, headmen, chieftans, chiefs – lost their autonomy, they were still respected, but the ruler became a magnified center of fear and awe. As the frequency of violence increased beyond measure, the people's fear not only augmented in degree but also changed qualitatively – the emotional climate was a compound of servile, inhibiting fear, preventing the desire to resist or even the thought of doing anything new (Walter 1969:188–9).

Walter does demonstrate that the violence of the first Zulu rulers was a political device aimed at their subordinate chiefs. However, he never underestimates the tremendous effectiveness of that violence in maintaining the subservient position of the rest of the population. The application of violent sanctions was by no means aimed strictly at impressing potential rival leaders as claimed by Service.

Furthermore, the data also show that the application of violent sanctions did not come to an end with the assassination of Dingane. There are numerous examples of the succeeding ruler, Mpande, ordering executions for offenses, ranging from conspiracy to thievery to wearing one's hair too long (Walter 1969:211–17; Gluckman 1955:40). According to early observers, the primary reason Mpande did not employ even greater violence is that he was prevented from doing so by the Boers and British, who by this time exercised a degree of colonial control in the area (Walter 1969:214–15). Walter points out that under Mpande, "[t]he despotic system had contracted, but terroristic rule, considerably limited in scope, remained. Generally regarded as the mildest of Zulu rulers, Mpande still declared flatly to Sir Theophilus Shepstone, Chief Native Affairs Commissioner of Natal, *'The Zulus are only ruled by being killed'* " (Walter 1969:218, emphasis added). Walter also states that although at no time was violence the only means used by the Zulu rulers to govern the population, it was always a critical component of the governing process, even under Mpande. "The system of power included other methods as well — authority, economic redistribution, rewards, persuasion, magic, and other techniques familiar to legitimate rulers. The pattern of violence, however, reacted to fundamental conflicts and it inhibited resistance. It made government possible . . ." (Walter 1969:218). As a whole, the development of the Zulu state serves to illustrate how violent coercive sanctions can be used to keep the majority of a population in a position of subordination. The rule of Mpande also illustrates how the threat of violence, accompanied by only limited application, is an effective element in long-term stable government.

Turning to the archaeological record of the early prehistoric states in the New World, one can make an initial empirical investigation to determine whether or not the rulers in those first states used forceful sanctions in governing their respective populations. Archaeologically, manifestations of coercion may be exhibited in skeletal remains and/or in iconographic representations. Skeletally, physically coercive sanctions may be seen in consistent patterns of violence inflicted on persons of lower social or economic status. Artistic evidence of coercion might include actual representation of the application of sanctions or the results of such application.

As was the case when looking for skeletal evidence of stratification, the analysis of human remains from early New World states has not been sufficient to tell us whether or not individuals were subject to the application of physical sanctions. From Mesoamerica there is some indication of decapitation among the burials at the late Formative site of Chupícuaro in western Mexico (Porter 1956). However, there is not enough information available to rule out the possibility that these persons were beheaded in the context of warfare. The pictographic evidence from Mesoamerica is also highly ambiguous. There are Olmec artworks that show elaborately clad individuals holding other unclad or semiclad individuals by a tether around the neck (Gay 1967; Covarrubias 1957:Fig. 29). There is also an Olmec carving that depicts a nude man, tied, and being confronted by masked individuals bearing clubs (Wicke 1971:18–19). The latter carving is interpreted as representing a sacrifice. Stone sculptures have been recovered from the Formative occupation of Kaminaljuyú depicting kneeling male figures, with ropes around their necks, and their hands and ankles tied behind their backs (Borhegyi 1965).

Again, these appear to be sacrificial victims, who are not particularly willing to participate in the upcoming event. From such limited kinds of pictorial evidence, it cannot be concluded that physical sanctions were being regularly and widely applied in the early states of Mesoamerica. It might be argued that scenes of high status individuals sacrificing war captives are visual demonstration of the ability to apply physical sanctions. On the other hand, it might equally be argued that if physical sanctions were being regularly applied they would be depicted more often in the various art forms. To settle this argument, we must have access to the information locked up in the skeletons of prehistoric Mesoamerica.

Indications of the application of violent coercive sanctions in South America also come exclusively from artistic representations. No substantial skeletal populations from early states have been subjected to any kind of intensive analysis. South American art, however, provides a more fertile and less ambiguous data base than that found in Mesoamerica. Of particular importance is the highly realistic Moche ceramic art. On Moche ceramic vessels there are a number of different representations of coercive sanctions being applied in circumstances that do not appear to be related to warfare. A number of individuals are depicted whose noses and/or lips have been cut off in a consistent pattern of mutilation (Benson 1972; Larco Hoyle 1938, 1945b; Kosok 1965:112). On other vessels individuals are shown bound to a stake or in stockades. In some cases these bound individuals are being attacked by carnivorous birds; in others they have been partially flayed (Donnan 1978:Figs. 137, 147, 148; Larco Hoyle 1945b; Kutscher 1950:200; Lanning 1967:123). Other individuals are shown with amputated limbs or genitals (Larco Hoyle 1945b; Kosok 1965). Direct representation of coercion is manifested in scenes in which scantily clad individuals are herded in a line by other individuals brandishing whips (Lumbreras 1974:103). The inference that these different depictions of coercive sanctions do not represent the treatment of war captives is based upon other scenes that explicitly depict the capture and treatment of prisoners of war. In these scenes prisoners are shown being exchanged for other prisoners (Lumbreras 1974b:105) or they are shown being sacrificed. In the latter cases, the sacrifice consists of either the prisoner being decapitated or having his throat slit and heart removed (Kutscher 1950:199–201; Donnan 1978:Figs. 239b, 240, 242). Thus the disfigurement, mutilation, and torture of individuals in some ceramics do not appear to be analogous to the treatment of prisoners of war shown in other ceramics. In the Moche ceramic arts, then, there is at least one clear line of evidence pointing to the regular application of forceful coercive sanctions against members of an early New World state population.

In reviewing the archaeological literature from Mesoamerica and Peru for manifestations of stratification, internal conflict and the use of force, I have undoubtedly missed both major and minor pieces of relevant data. At the same time, it has not been my goal to prove or disprove definitively the validity of the conflict model in the New World. I have intended to show how the conflict model can be tested archaeologically and what limited kinds of data are actually available to test it. I have also tried to place Service's rejection of the conflict model in an empirical perspective. It would appear that, in fact, there is no empirical basis for this rejection. Although the basic premises of the model, at best, can be confirmed only tentatively in the New World, there are virtually no data that directly or indirectly refute them. Relevant kinds of data have rarely been collected or extracted through analysis, but when they have, they correspond to the conflict rather than to the integration model offered by Service. Overall, there is simply insufficient relevant information at hand to carry out a satisfactory test of either model. With few exceptions, archaeologists have directed their research efforts in other areas and have not provided the kinds of data we need. Until more rigorous field- and laboratory work is carried out, with an awareness of "political" kinds of data, statements about the integrative or conflict nature of early states in Mesoamerica, Peru, and other parts of the world cannot rise much above the level of intuitive interpretation.

PART III

Environmental factors in state formation

4

The ecological basis of New World state formation: general and local model building

MARK N. COHEN

There is a long-standing controversy in anthropology concerning the relative merits of general evolutionary models and particularistic historical models in the explanation of culture change. Recent approaches to explaining the origins of pristine states tend to reflect this controversy as some scholars search for major parallels in the formation of various early states while others deny the existence of such parallels (or perceive them only at fairly high levels of abstraction) as they describe and analyze the process of the formation of individual states.

Both approaches contain something of value, and a good interpretation of culture history will need to contain a judicious mix of the two. But I believe both are now suffering from misuse in their application to the problem of the origin of the state(s): on the one hand, those searching for parallels are looking in the wrong place and perhaps seeking more pervasive parallels than really exist; on the other hand, those favoring particularism have dismissed the generalist position prematurely and for the wrong reasons. Both sides have failed to grasp some of the essential features of the problem. I believe that we must reorient our focus to identify the proper domain and proper contribution of the generalist and particularist perspectives.

A brief mention of some of the more general of modern theories of state formation—and the backlash against these theories—will serve to make the point. The modern archetype for general models of state formation is probably Karl Wittfogel's suggestion (1957) that irrigation (and the managerial class that irrigation stimulates) has played a role in the pristine evolution of despotic governments. In proposing such a theory, Wittfogel postulates, in effect, both common environmental incentives and parallel institutional responses on the part of societies in the process of evolution toward statehood. In the last two decades a number of other hypotheses have been offered suggesting a similar role for numerous other features of the environment or for various events and institutions thought to be generally conducive to statehood: warfare (defense or conquest), population growth, class differences, trade and symbiosis, regional environmental heterogeneity, and so on. Perhaps the most widely respected and discussed general theory is that of Robert Carneiro (1970), suggesting that population growth and warfare in "circumscribed" areas are features common to the early states that distinguish their histories from those areas where state formation did not occur.

These general theories have stimulated considerable controversy and research, but otherwise have "failed" as explanations to varying degrees because localized research has failed (1) to confirm the existence of the postulated common element in areas of state formation; (2) to demonstrate its absence in other areas; or (3) to confirm its postulated role in the evolutionary process. Thus recent syntheses of the origins of the state have generally failed to support consistently either Wittfogel or Carneiro or to find other postulated concrete similarities of environment or history in the formation of the early states (cf. R. Cohen 1978b; Service 1975; Flannery 1972; Wright and Johnson 1975; Claessen and Skalnik 1978). This failure has led scholars of a particularistic bent largely to reject general theories. Many recent studies have displayed skepticism about process, displaying greater tolerance of historical relativism in their description of individual sequences while recognizing parallelism only at abstract levels of analysis. Associated with the greater relativism of the new approach has been a tendency to dismiss "simple" or "monocausal" theories of change and to replace them with a greater appreciation of the interplay of various elements or actors, or groups, in complex social systems.

Flannery (1972), for example, has argued persuasively that the regularities of process that unify the histories of the early states should be sought in universal processes and mechanisms by which social systems evolve rather than in common features of the environment, ecology (in the narrow sense), or history. He argues that environmental features are only stressors that help induce and select for changes in social systems. These stressors differ from instance to instance; the parallelism exists solely in the universal nature of the system's common response abstractly defined.

Similarly, Wright and Johnson (1975) maintain that the evolution of the state represents the growth of an information-processing system that evolves in response to the demand for heightened processing capacity, a demand that may be created by various combinations of circumstances. Ronald Cohen (1978b) has argued that states represent the evolutionary convergence of social systems responding to a range of environmental stimuli, a convergence structured by the system's own nature. On a slightly different tack, in reacting not only to general models but to the overuse of systems theory, Herbert

Lewis (1978) has suggested reexamination of the process of state formation in terms of the flow of events and the actions of individuals and interest groups within particular societies. Thus varied recent literature seems to reflect a swing in the direction of more particularistic, local studies.

The need for a limited general theory as part of a two-tiered analysis

If existing general theories have proved too confining, however, and have not been confirmed, the reaction against them has moved too far in the direction of relativism, for it has failed to take into account one of the essential features of the problem: the temporal parallelism observable in the evolution of the various early states. Charles Reed (1977) has pointed out that the problem in describing the origins of agriculture is not merely explaining why it happened but in explaining why it seems to have occurred in so many parts of the world within a short time span. The problem here is similar: not merely "why did states evolve" but "why did states (or preferably, all forms of institutionalized central government including chiefdoms) evolve in so many parts of the world within such a short period?" In fact, as I pointed out in reference to the agricultural revolution, and in response to Reed's inquiry (M. Cohen 1977), *the general phenomenon of widespread selection for a new mode of adaptation (rather than the particulars of the evolutionary pathways in each particular case) is the significant issue to be resolved and the issue most likely to be susceptible to systematic analysis.*

When the issue is stated this way, apparently, no matter how local our focus or how complex the systems envisioned, we must search for at least one common selective element in the various evolutionary histories. Unless we recognize a common element we are forced to accept the notion that a number of social systems, evolving independently, converged on statehood (or on centralized government in general) simultaneously, largely by chance. The coincidence defies credibility.

Probably, moreover, despite Flannery's arguments, the common element is most likely to be something external to each of the evolving systems (i.e., an attribute of their common "environment" in the largest sense of the word). Otherwise we must assume that political centralization is an inherent part of social-system evolution and that the pace of that evolution in each system is internally regulated at a speed comparable to that of other systems. Such a common element would need to be relatively "simple," despite systems theorists' denials. It could hardly be the type of complex concatenation of events or circumstances that they tend to propose, but which would necessarily be highly idiosyncratic.

If we imagine a particular social system operating with a multitude of inputs and feedback loops (or in Lewis's terms [1978] if we imagine it as a complex of individuals and interest groups) and can identify a point or period in time when that system shifts out of one relatively steady state and enters a period of transition, then we are justified in trying to identify one or more new or altered factors or conditions that have changed the condition of the system or shifted the balance of power between competing components or groups. (Thus identifying a particular circumstance as triggering or selecting for a change in the state of the system is neither a contradiction of the idea of "system" nor a denial of complexity.)

To take a concrete and relevant example, imagine a society with a complex mixture of forces tending to induce greater political centralization—the ambition and charisma of would-be leaders, need for corporate action or defense, or security of mutual economic dependence—and of factors tending to oppose centralization—strong rivalries, an egalitarian or individualist ethic, a tradition of resolving social or economic stress by group fission and movement, and so on. If a society with such a mixture of opposing pressures first existed for a long time in a basically decentralized condition, without formal leaders or boundaries or defined membership, and then began to form a central government, we would be justified looking for one or more altered circumstances that shifted the balance or "selected for" increments in the new direction. Such an altered circumstance would not be a mystical "prime mover" but might be a single, relatively simple alteration of circumstances, no matter how complex we assume the social system is.

More important, suppose there are several such systems acting independently but all tending to maintain themselves in a decentralized condition. And let us assume at or about the same time, many of them begin to shift in the direction of greater formal centralization. Under those circumstances it seems we are justified in searching—or must search—for some common factor(s) whose alteration has helped shift the balance in each of the systems. As suggested, not to look for such a common factor would imply a belief in extraordinary coincidence.

Yet this is exactly what the archaeological record displays. Until about 6,000 years ago, decentralized human systems ("egalitarian" bands or loosely structured "tribes") were nearly universal. Shortly after, more centralized societies appear to emerge independently in numerous regions (Flannery 1972; Carneiro 1970; Service 1975). Even if we allow for the fact that societies affect their neighbors and therefore not all these systems (or even most of them) evolved independently, the level of coincidence is enormous. Scholars commonly discuss six primary areas of state formation (cf. Service 1975), evolving largely independently of one another, but remarkably parallel in time (in comparison to the length of the archaeological record of modern man). There is some dispute about the independence of individual cases, and some scholars would argue for more or fewer "pristine" states: but to my knowledge, none of those central to the present debate would propose that the distribution of early states could be explained entirely, or even primarily, by diffusion.

The coincidence is more striking if one looks not only at the occurrence of pristine states but at the occurrence of chiefdoms or of politically centralized societies in general, whose worldwide distribution emerges within the same limited time span. I am inclined to agree with Service's (1975) emphasis on the evolution of chiefdoms as the significant event in political evolution. Whether one agrees with his assumption that chiefdoms are a step in the formation of states or accepts others' arguments that they represent a separate evolutionary outcome is, for now, immaterial. The coincidental evolution of formal central political institutions seems to be the primary problem. I suspect that our major task lies in defining the *general* conditions that selected for the emergence of these institutions over so broad a geographical distribution within so short a time. Once this problem is dealt with, we can then try to explain the special evolution of particular pristine states to see whether there is any common evolutionary trajectory that they share and that distinguishes them, as a group, from that of chiefdoms.

Thus it should be noted that searching for a common element contributing to the evolution of otherwise diverse and independent systems is not at all similar to postulating a common evolutionary trajectory. That search merely postulates that the various trajectories undergo some selection in a common direction. If, for example, we accept Flannery's concept of environmental events as "stressors" acting randomly on social systems, then the common element need only be some common condition that acts generally to increase the sensitivity of diverse systems and to promote parallel responses to diverse stressors. Hence identification of such a common selective element need not contradict otherwise highly particularistic interpretations of individual culture sequences. After all, both the modern theory of biological evolution and what may be the most successful attempt to define cultural evolution in analogous terms (Campbell 1965) suggest that the *creative* processes of evolution are highly idiosyncratic; that order is only secondarily imposed by the channeling effects of natural selection.

I propose a two-tiered analysis of the origins of the state paralleling the analysis that David Harris (1977) and I (M. Cohen 1977), working independently, have offered for the origins of agriculture. I have argued that the parallelism exhibited by so many food economies in their evolution toward agriculture demands recognition of common selective pressures operating on all those systems, suggesting that the common element in the various systems was population pressure. Harris, starting with population pressure, but recognizing that it operated in a variety of cultural and ecological contexts, argued that different cultures responded to their common problems in different ways or followed "alternative pathways." Some cultures developed full domestication of resources, whereas others failed to develop it as a result of a variety of identifiable, but often historically unique combinations of circumstances. In sum, human societies had in common the need to obtain greater total productivity from limited space. But by virtue of local variables of environment or culture this common stimulus provoked a variety of responses, some of which converged on what we now define as "agriculture." Our task here, I suggest, is first to define those common problems that stimulated the parallel evolution of politically centralized societies and then to explore the "alternative pathways," determining if various alternatives are susceptible to further explanation or are themselves as idiosyncratic as some of the pathways to agriculture seem to have been.

A hypothesis to explain the general stimulus to political centralization

I suggest that the common incentive to centralization was the saturation by hunter-gatherers of the earth's usable environments. Further, sociocultural systems in many parts of the world were shifted from a condition in which centrifugal political tendencies predominated to one in which centripetal, centralizing tendencies predominated by a common shift in their ecology–the shift from the flexible, expansionist, presaturation ecology of hunter-gatherers to the kind of localized adaptations that emerged when hunter-gatherers had saturated all available space.

I have argued elsewhere (M. Cohen 1977) that agriculture began or, rather, was stimulated throughout the world by the pressure of human populations on wild resources and the saturation of hunting and gathering environments. Moreover, a review of archaeological sequences in the Old and New Worlds showed that agriculture was adopted widely after human populations had expanded geographically to fill the globe, simultaneously expanding into new biomes and infiltrating niches previously unused while exploiting a broadening range of secondary foods. I propose, now, that the rise of central governments was an indirect result of this same process.

Briefly, the argument developed as an explanation for agriculture was as follows: under conditions of relatively low population density, Middle Pleistocene hunter-gatherers enjoyed a fair degree of selectivity in their food economy while obtaining a nutritious and relatively reliable food supply at relatively low labor costs. Such populations throughout the Old World showed a broadly similar subsistence economy focused relatively heavily on the hunting of big game and centered on the kinds of environments (mainly open grasslands, savannas, or open forests) where game was comparatively abundant. Economic choices could be optimized for most populations—and periodic shortages minimized—by informal group mobility in which group members either individually or in concert periodically shifted their base camp. The slight tendency of such groups to outgrow this strategy was absorbed by the simple mechanisms of group fission, combined with availability of open frontiers and less-used space between group ranges. These groups then expanded to populate the world, both pushing to new latitudes in the Old and New Worlds and simultaneously infiltrating a number of secondary or suboptimal environments (e.g., denser forests) at each latitude.

As the population grew, the possibility for its absorption by outmigration diminished as did the possibility of maintaining the existing living standard by group mobility. Increasingly, other groups would have impinged on the frontiers or even on the annual range of each group. At the same time, certain resources became more and more scarce and incapable of supporting humans because either the resources were degraded (by overexploitation or deterioration of the physical environment) or they were now called upon to feed larger numbers of people. Consequently, the human reaction was to begin to exploit a variety of secondary resources such as aquatic foods and vegetable starches that were less preferred but capable of providing for human needs in times of want or of responding to human attention with increased productivity. As preferred foods became less adequate to provide seasonal nutrition, these calorically productive foods were consumed beyond their initial season of availability, resulting in attempts to store foods chosen more for their seasonal abundance and storability than for their palatability. Heavy reliance on such stores, combined with increasing human investment in food production—as well as the increasing propinquity of other groups—ultimately forced humans to settle in the vicinity of their most plentiful and storable resources.

Apparently, this process was very widespread. In the first few thousand years of the Holocene period enormous populations widely scattered through the world became sedentary, based on the exploitation of a number of food sources (wild and cultivated), which their ancestors a few millennia before had hardly exploited (M. Cohen 1977).

This model of the expansion of the human economy is highly generalized, both because it is attempting to see the broad parallels in the adaptive trends of different regions rather than in the local variations and because, by virtue of their generalized ecology and open social systems that minimize cultural drift, hunter-gatherers before the Mesolithic period *were* probably more susceptible to generalized description than are contemporary populations (M. Cohen 1978). The model has been dismissed by some critics (most recently Weiss 1978) as being untestable, that is, untestable *as a whole* if confined to searching for new digging strategies to test it. However, various parts and assumptions can be tested formally or informally against our general knowledge of human habits and economies–for example, comparative labor costs and the technical competence and food preferences of non-Western peoples. In terms of the Principle of Parsimony it is by far the simplest explanation available that accounts for the general flow of events in prehistory prior to the geographically diffuse origins of agriculture (which can be interpreted in light of modern ethnographic observations). Also, it has the virtue of accounting for the very widespread subsequent emergence of central governments.

Once human societies were forced, primarily by population pressure, to adopt a sedentary adaptation, a variety of conditions conducive to political centralization (and occasionally to actual state formation) would have emerged, implying further population growth and further buildup of population pressure. Significantly, various aspects of the new adaptation apparently tended both to speed the rate of population growth and to stimulate the aggregation of populations into artificially high densities. Alterations in diet and nursing practices accompanying sedentary agriculture were said to have stimulated birthrates in the Neolithic (cf. Lee 1980; M. Cohen 1980). Moreover, the changing marginal utility of additional workers may have helped promote cultural choices favoring large families (Hassan 1980) while a variety of new strategies may have come into use by local groups to acquire additional members by means other than new births. R. Cohen (1978b, see also Althabe 1965) has suggested that sedentism promoted a number of strategies, such as adoption, bridewealth, polygyny, clientage, and even capture, resulting in nucleation of settlements and artificially high local population densities.

It is important to note, however, that the evolution of central governments may have resulted equally from any of a number of processes set in motion by the problems of the new adaptation – processes that need not have implied continued population growth or pressure and which may not have been the same in different locations. Moreover, once set in motion, such processes may have received both their form and momentum from the social or political system in the manner postulated by Flannery or R. Cohen. In any case, the attractiveness of the saturation concept is that it would have triggered a number of new adaptive challenges paralleling many of the conditions already considered by various authors to have been conducive to political centralization and state formation. In fact, saturation of the type described is prerequisite to, and implicit in, most of the other theories of the origins of the state that have been offered.

Perhaps the most essential point is that some combination of environmental and social "circumscription" (Carneiro 1970; cf. King 1978) would have become a significant part of the adaptive milieu of many, if not most, human populations so that results paralleling those postulated by Carneiro would have been relatively common. Groups of people would now be less able to flee or dissolve in response to political pressures from adjoining groups because neighboring space would more likely have been occupied; moreover, sedentary populations committed to stored resources or to a relatively heavy investment in sowed fields would be vulnerable to conquest rather than to military defeat. Also, inequalities in the productive potential or special resources available to different groups, once resolvable by group mobility, would now be a likely cause for strife.

Awareness of this vulnerability on the part of each population may have helped shift the balance between forces tending to promote the hegemony of "big men" or to lengthen the tenure of chiefs and forces tending to undermine their power (Webster 1975). Thus both conquest and its threat are apt to have increased and contributed to conditions conducive to state formation.

The pattern of saturation described may also have contributed to the danger of warfare and conquest (and indirectly to the formation of states) in another way. Once settled patterns for sedentary populations were crystallized, a new kind of environmental niche would have been created—that of pastoral populations dependent on the sequential use of resources once used by mobile hunter-gatherers but no longer efficiently exploitable by sedentary groups. The military potential of such pastoral nomad groups is widely recognized, although their actual role in the formation of the early pristine states has been questioned (cf. Service 1975; Carneiro 1970).

Similarly, a new kind of social vulnerability must have emerged with sedentism, because by virtue of both crowding and investment, the people could no longer move away from their own squabbles. This kind of internal strife may have helped promote the judicial role of central authorities (cf. the discussion by Lee, 1972, of the role of central authority in the maintenance of large gatherings of Kalahari San). Internal strife may also have been exacerbated by further population growth, which, in the absence of outlets for migration, has been shown to lead to heightened competition for land, more formal definition of ownership, and inequality in access to resources with concomitant increases in social strife (Netting 1972; Boserup

1966; Fried 1967). Such strife can in turn contribute to the growth of centralized government.

Finally, such circumscription could stimulate groups to invest in corporate projects, like irrigation, for the purpose of either absorbing further population growth within a bounded area or buffering local resources against climatic fluctuations rendered increasingly dangerous to a population by virtue of its size and immobility.

All the conditions described may represent "alternative pathways" by which centralized government was stimulated once saturation had occurred or may represent factors that in different combinations contributed to this process in any particular region.

I suspect, however, that the most common adaptive problem underlying the evolution of complex societies in various parts of the world was the loss of economic buffers, the failure of old systems of ecological homeostasis that occurred as hunter-gatherers were forced to adopt sedentism. I suggest, following a number of contemporary scholars (cf. the discussion of chiefdoms by Service [1975] and of states by Isbell [1978] and by Gall and Saxe [1977]), that a major common feature of centralized governments and the role for which they were primarily "selected" is that of buffering human populations against ecological disasters—replacing natural buffers lost when saturation of usable space necessitated sedentism. I have suggested elsewhere (M. Cohen 1978) that the Mesolithic/Neolithic period of incipient sedentism (or the comparable Archaic culture of the New World) represents a watershed between two distinct homeostatic strategies of human populations: The first, or hunter-gatherer strategy—relatively simple socially but possible only before saturation occurs—involves adjusting the distribution of people to that of resources. The second— socially far more complicated and appearing to be most efficiently carried out by *governments*—involves adjusting the distribution of resources to that of people.

By reviewing the ecology of hunter-gatherer populations as they approach sedentism and adoption of agricultural strategies, we can suggest a decline in the capacity of human populations to buffer themselves, a decline resulting from both the increases in the risk factor in the environment itself and the gradual loss of social mechanisms for responding to such a risk. My argument parallels the concept of "niche breadth" developed for anthropology most fully by Hardesty (1978, 1979). Basically, niche breadth is a measure of the diversity of resources used or conditions tolerated by any population. A broad niche, providing a range of alternate resources, is well buffered because populations can respond to fluctuations in the availability of one or a few resources by shifting to others; it is optimal in an uncertain environment. Dense population and increased competition tends, however, to produce nonoverlapping, specialized adaptations in competing populations (i.e., competition leads to narrower niches), which, as Hardesty has pointed out, has accompanied population growth in human prehistory (see also Gall and Saxe 1977).

It is possible that for certain populations at certain times and places, more catholic tastes and exploitative strategies helped temporarily to reduce environmental risk. If, as I have argued, however, new resources were added only as preferred resources were exhausted or otherwise became inadequate or unreliable, then the extensions of the range of foods eaten regularly really represent the fact that human populations were coming to use as staples—to rely on—those things that had previously been their emergency supplies. Whether the risk factor would have increased or decreased early in this process of expansion is moot. Clearly, a late stage of this expansion, as the saturation point for hunting and gathering strategies was approached, the real breadth of the niche available to each population would have declined significantly. Each population would have had a smaller geographical range to exploit; many populations would have had only "marginal" ranges; and high population densities would have meant that relatively few of the resources available could be counted on as staples. Such high density and narrow geographic range would mean that fluctuations in the availability of resources over time or patchiness in their distribution in space would become increasingly threatening. As Sanders and Webster (1978) have pointed out, population growth in an environment otherwise relatively risk free can produce risk by causing greater dependence on more and more marginal or degraded resources or by reducing the size of the individual or group landholdings.

This problem would be exacerbated by the adoption of agriculture, which I believe was a necessary response to the need to intensify the production of calories in limited space. Farming is a calorically productive but relatively narrow niche (Hardesty 1978; Gall and Saxe 1977; M. Cohen 1977). A farming system is one designed for maximum energy turnover through a relatively small number of species, resembling a very early stage of ecological succession in creating an unstable community not well buffered against environmental fluctuations (Gall and Saxe 1977). Moreover, if, as is often true, agricultural staples are imports, not preselected for local survival, the risk factor is even greater. To assume that vulnerability was simply a function of farming is a mistake. The previous arguments suggest that it is high population densities and geographical confinement that primarily create the problem. Agriculture merely exacerbates it. It is interesting to note that problems of periodic critical food shortage have been identified and implicated in the formation of buffering systems suggestive of the beginning of centralized authority among densely populated and relatively sedentary hunter-gatherers such as the Indians of California and the Pacific Northwest (King 1978; Bean and King 1974; Chagnon 1970; Piddock 1965). Hence the sociopolitical parallels between such groups and agricultural populations may reflect their common vulnerability to fluctuations in resources.

This increasing ecological vulnerability would have been exacerbated by the loss of some of the adaptive mechanisms available to hunter-gatherers under conditions of low density—the loss of physical mobility and the loss of social mobility. Increasing both competition for resources and investment in local resources would have meant a declining tolerance of exploitation of resources by outsiders: an increase in the formalization of local group ownership if not of private property. In addition, increased investment and competition as well as the need for corporate projects would all have tended to increase the nuclear clustering of population and the formality of group definition, thereby reducing or eliminating the mechanism of simple group flux (informal group fission and re-alignment) by which hunter-gatherers adjust population densities to those of resources (Turnbull 1968; M. Cohen 1977). Moreover, social networks of reciprocal exchange obligations, once a major buffer of hunter-gatherer economies, may initially have declined in scope or at least in geographical range as density increased and sedentism emerged.

The combination of increasing environmental risk and a decline in traditional buffers would have provided selection in favor of the development of new homeostatic mechanisms. (Selection here has two meanings, referring both to the competitive success of systems that rapidly developed new buffers and to the incentive provided to individuals and groups to cooperate in the formation of such systems.) A number of such buffers potentially linkable to the evolution of centralized authority can be identified in the archaeological record beginning with Mesolithic or Archaic sites.

One of the most obvious, and earliest, responses to this problem appears to have been the development of storage systems that smooth out temporal irregularities in resource production (Earle and D'Altroy 1979). Hill and Dean, cited in the unpublished study of Schiffer, demonstrated (for certain circumstances) a correlation between stochastic variability in subsistence production and increased storage volume. Physical storage systems are well documented among early agricultural populations, particularly those harvesting seeds, but it is noteworthy that such facilities also occur in a variety of semisedentary or sedentary late preagricultural contexts (M. Cohen 1977). As Earle and D'Altroy (1979) point out, such storage, in addition to its buffering function, also plays a role in the evolution of complex organization by helping to finance corporate activities. A rapid expansion of this second function, they indicate, characterizes later stages of political evolution.

Similarly, interregional trade has been both characterized as a significant force in buffering populations against unpredictable events in localized ecosystems (Gall and Saxe 1977; Chagnon 1970; Dalton 1977; Wright and Zeder 1977) and also commonly implicated in the evolution of centralized governments. Hardesty (1978) cites studies suggesting that there is a correlation between the scope of certain interregional trading networks and the frequency of locally destructive natural events. Thus it is interesting to note that interregional trade networks begin to appear in the archaeological record in various regions when enforced sedentism became the rule. Webb (1974), in reviewing the archaeological literature on trade networks, notes that the evidence of such exchange is rare prior to the end of the Upper Paleolithic (imported objects generally being so rare and of such nearby provenience that it is difficult to establish foreignness, let alone the existence of a trade network). He suggests that regular long distance movement of materials appears to emerge just prior to the establishment of stable Neolithic economies in various parts of the New and Old Worlds (although again their occurrence among densely populated hunter-gatherers such as occurred prehistorically on the western coast of North America belies the notion that it is agriculture per se that stimulates the pattern). And as Webb further observes, the development of regional exchange economies is a common characteristic of the "formative" stages of many of the world's oldest pristine civilizations.

Some of the demand for trade emerges, of course, simply because sedentary groups, surrounded by other sedentary groups claiming territory, have less direct access to a range of resources, particularly raw materials, than do mobile populations. But it is noteworthy, too, that much of the early trade is in luxury goods (minerals, feathers, shell) for which there seems to have been little demand previously, as well as in goods such as obsidian whose utilitarian value does not always appear sufficient to justify its widespread distribution. Various scholars (cf. Chagnon 1970) have argued that such luxury trade primarily serves as a kind of "Kula Ring" function of the type described by Malinowski (1922) among the Trobriand Islanders, creating alliances and opening channels for the emergency trade of subsistence resources on those occasions when the latter became necessary. (Because the sporadic flow of these emergency rations is unlikely to be identifiable archaeologically, this dual function is hard to prove in prehistory.)

Wright and Zeder (1977) argue (following Rappaport 1968; see also Webb 1974) that the role of such luxury goods is also to create an open-ended or unlimited demand, which helps to stimulate continuous production and regular flow of more necessary goods for which the demand, more finite and irregular, cannot always be matched against reciprocal demand for other utilitarian objects or substances. Webb (1974) affirms that the growth of religious or civic monuments and of ceremonial activity can be explained in part as a means of creating precisely this kind of open-ended demand, thereby ensuring the continuous flow of utilitarian goods (ensuring that emergency trade channels for subsistence resources remain viable). As various people have indicated (Rappaport 1968; Suttles 1966, and others), prestige itself, generating more truly unlimited demand than almost any other commodity, plays a similar role as a stimulus of exchange and as an adjuster of both short- and long-term inequalities in the "real" value of goods exchanged. It may be significant that prestige, which could help to boost a central figure from the role of "big man" to that of chief, is most likely to accrue, at least in this circumstance, when trade is most imbalanced or irregular.

Finally, the organization of redistributive exchange systems in response to the irregular distribution of goods and subsistence resources in time and space has been cited by many scholars as a factor in the emergence of centralized governments. Elman Service (1975) in particular has argued that the growth of government results largely from the voluntary participation of people in centralized political systems among whose primary functions is that of centralized economic redistribution. He states explicitly that chiefdoms evolved fairly widely throughout the world primarily as a function of the role of centralized redistribution in equalizing the distribution of products generated in various parts of a heterogeneous environment—in the creation and maintenance of economic symbiosis. Service's conclusions have been criticized and qualified by others. Sanders and Webster (1978) question whether environmental heterogeneity or redistributive function are as universally important in the evolution of central governments as Service seems to imply and note that in some of the cases under their study, such as that of the Olmec chiefdoms, competition may be more important than redistribution in selecting for hierarchical organization. Similarly, Earle (1977) in discussing Hawaiian chiefdoms notes that sociopolitical units at this level do not crosscut heterogeneous environments in quite the manner postulated by Service and that redistribution may have served more to support the operation of the political superstructure itself than to buffer the population. Nonetheless, awareness of environmental risk at the local level and of the role of central authority in providing economic security looms large in both discussions. Earle, for example, notes that Hawaiian irrigation systems are vulnerable to flooding and tidal waves, random events creating crises beyond the adaptive capacity of local populations, whose effects therefore had to be buffered by some sort of supralocal exchange system. Even if Earle is correct that Hawaiian redistributive systems functioned more to support the political hierarchy than to buffer the people, it seems likely that the willingness of people to function in such a system owes at least something to the awareness of risk and acceptance of the provision of a homeostatic umbrella at the cost of high taxation.

In any case, Service's model—or at least the assumption that minimization of risk and heterogeneity by redistribution is one significant element in the formation of central hierarchies—gains much credence if we step back from such individual studies and return to the more general question—why do many independent human populations began to organize themselves hierarchically at about the same time after so many millennia of egalitarian structure. It seems that whatever the particulars of the Hawaiian case, or of the Olmec, this general phenomenon demands recognition of some common incentive to change, which could have operated in various environments but only briefly. I suspect that heightened risk and loss of preexisting buffers that accompanied crowding and sedentism is the common incentive and redistribution, the common vehicle.

Explaining the alternative pathways

If the *general* phenomenon of a worldwide movement in the direction of centralized, hierarchical governments can thus be explained, there still remains the real question of why, given this common incentive, some populations achieved early and pristine statehood and some did not, and the related question of whether this problem can be approached through comparative, as opposed to purely historical, analysis—whether states are the result of similar processes or are epiphenomena to be individually described and explained. I propose two alternative approaches: (1) viewing the state as a regular end product of political evolution in particular environments and (2) considering the state as an epiphenomenon, a random outcome of the general selection for centralization.

Explaining the special evolution of pristine states: hypothesis #1: the state as a function of special environments

The general model previously described suggests at least one direction in which we might search for regularities in state formation. If increasing vulnerability to environmental fluctuations is a primary stimulus to political evolution, we might expect that the process of centralization would have proceeded furthest in areas (1) where the vulnerability was greatest; (2) where large populations could build up (because there is considerable agreement that whatever else it is, the state is a mechanism for organizing relatively large numbers of people) but where, once accumulated, such populations would have a greater than average need for a system of environmental buffers on a fairly large scale; (3) where, for example, populations were confined or "circumscribed" most severely such that there was comparatively little potential for spatial adjustment as suggested by Carneiro; (4) where fluctuations in the physical environment were severe and of a frequency appropriate to political counteraction (i.e., neither so frequent that they simply discouraged population buildup nor so infrequent that the incentive to maintain readiness to respond was dissipated; and (5) where environments were sufficiently varied, yet complementary, over a fairly large geographical scale that incorporation within a single centralized political system was both feasible and profitable within the limits of available communication. Quantifying these factors is an empirical question that has so far defied analysis.

There have been various attempts, though only partly successful, to apply arguments similar to these to both of the New World centers of early state formation, Peru and Mesoamerica (cf. Service 1975). Recently, Isbell (1978) has argued explicitly that the early state in Peru was an "energy averaging" system that functioned appropriately in the Andes because of marked altitudinal and latitudinal variation in environments and the vulnerability of individual, often highly circumscribed territories to climatic fluctuations.

In a somewhat more detailed analysis, Sanders and Webster (1978) have attempted to develop a model of multilineal evolution of complex societies in Mesoamerica, with specific reference to variations in some of the postulated conditions. Noting Flannery's (1972) argument that *regularities* in the process of state formation result from universal processes and mechanisms in the evolution of sociopolitical systems, they suggest that *variations* in that evolution result systematically from variations in the physical environment. They propose that several evolutionary trajectories are possible, some of which converge in the evolution of the state, but some of which end in the production of chiefdoms. (In contrast to Service, these authors view chiefdoms as an alternate adaptive form rather than as a stage in the formation of states.) They suggest that these trajectories are dictated primarily by three kinds of variations in the natural environment: the degree of risk inherent in the environment; the diversity or heterogeneity of a region; and the size and productivity of an environment (more or less the same major variables already considered). High risk and high diversity are associated in their model with pristine state formation.

The identification of these variables as dictators of state formation as I have recommended, or as attempted by Isbell and by Sanders and Webster, is, however, problematic. For one thing, if such diversity and risk arguments seem applicable to the two New World centers of early state formation, their applicability to other centers of civilization in the Old World is harder to see. Service (1975) has pointed out that the nuclear areas of Mesopotamia and Egypt, at least, are much more homogeneous than those of the New World, and he notes both the uniformity and the predictability of the Egyptian environment tied to the regularity of the Nile floods. It may be possible to develop a risk-related argument appropriate to Egypt, noting both the very sharply delineated boundaries of the exploitable areas–a clear case of "circumscription"–combined with variations in the size of the annual Nile floods (Janssen 1978). This uncertainty may have required a storage and redistributive system long before the same problems suggested the employment of irrigation. But, this problem is moot.

There is, however, a more serious problem with any environmental explanation of alternate trajectories to statehood. Betty Meggers's (1954) description of "environmental potential" and its effect on cultural evolution in South America was criticized because she failed to provide an objective assessment of the environments in question independent of the presence or absence of prehistoric civilizations. A similar problem occurs in the evaluation of Carneiro's "circumscription" hypothesis. It is one thing to find conditions of circumscription in hearths of early civilization; but it is quite another to demonstrate satisfactorily that circumscription, objectively assessed, is more pronounced in areas where early states emerged than in areas where they did not. Similarly, it is a weakness of Isbell's discussion of environmental risk and diversity as of Sanders and Webster's and of mine, that we lack such independent evaluation of these variables. Sanders and Webster, who suggest specific criteria in the form of regional rainfall and periodicity of cycles of frost and agricultural pests, come closer to meeting the requirements for independent measure than do the other discussions but apply their criteria only within Mesoamerica. There is neither evidence that these features distinguish Mesoamerica as a whole from other environments where early states did not arise nor a sufficient number of cases of each of their separate trajectories within Mesoamerica to establish a correlation, let alone a causal relationship with the variables they discuss. R. Cohen (1978b), summing up the problem very well, points out that despite various recent discussions of risk, no study exists that has made a truly detailed analysis of early states (and nonstates) in areas with and without regular food shortages, using specific and measurable indicators of stress.

In sum, the application of environmental or ecological principles to explain the *specific* evolution of states as opposed to nonstates appears moot, although there appears to be ample justification for recognizing a common set of adaptive problems as underlying the more *general* emergence of centralized governments.

Hypothesis #2: the state as epiphenomenon

As an alternative hypothesis, I suggest that early states—pristine states at least—may *initially* have been epiphenomena, that is, specific outcomes of a more general selective pressure favoring centralization that can only be explained at the level of historical analysis. In short, the *distribution* of the *earliest* states may reflect the random creative processes of evolution rather than the more systematic selective processes whose effects are visible only in the spread, rather than in the origin, of the state as a political form. Perhaps for this reason previous attempts to formulate a general theory that focuses on the earliest states themselves, rather than on the broader trend toward centralization, have come to grief.

If one considers how random the creative forces of evolution have been; looks at the complexity of the variables involved in state formation (cf. Lewis 1978); looks at the difficulties that various scholars have encountered in describing the common elements in the evolution of pristine states or even in the definition of such states (R. Cohen 1978b; Claessen and Skalnik 1978); accepts R. Cohen's (1978b) definition of statehood as a convergent evolutionary category; and particularly accepts his argument and that of Webster (1975) that states are to be distinguished from chiefdoms largely on negative grounds (the inhibition of a natural tendency to collapse through fission); then it seems most likely that the earliest states are indeed epiphenomena whose special evolution (as distinct from their common evolution with chiefdoms or the later spread of the state as an adaptive type) is really not susceptible to systematic analysis except in a highly particularistic manner.

The problem, clearly, is an empirical one. The "alternative pathways" must be explored further with an eye not toward concrete and detailed similarities in actual sequences of events but, rather, toward the more general parallels that would be promoted by common selective processes of the type discussed. Given the complexity of individual actions and of environmental events, it is not surprising that comparative analysis fails to find similarities of detail. Wright and Johnson's (1975) conclusion that certain key elements are absent from certain archaeological sequences *at particular points in time* should not dissuade us from searching, more generally, for the role of common key elements operating in various forms and combinations in the parallel evolution of early states.

5

The transition to statehood as seen from the mouth of a cave

RICHARD S. MACNEISH

Introduction

As is generally known, my interests and specializations have rarely brought me in direct contact with the problem of the transition to statehood, either in my archaeological endeavors in Mesoamerica or in those in the Andean area (MacNeish 1978). In fact, even my life-style is in opposition to such things as urban life, civilization, and regulatory bureaucratic states. Although I am trying to be a scientist, I am at heart a nomad. I like small groups (bands) of compatible colleagues and prefer "wild" red meat and garden-grown vegetables cooked over an open fire. Yet civilization and statehood are all around me. I cannot escape them in my archaeological endeavors any more than I can in my day-to-day existence, for there are all those top layers in my caves, laid down by civilized people, as well as big ruins surrounding my shelters (MacNeish et al. 1975). Further, as a scientist I know that there are generalizations to be made about "the transition to statehood," just as there are about the rise of village agriculture or even the beginning of plant domestication and agriculture itself (Flannery 1972). I also know that my basic assumptions concerning culture and causation and my general methodology are roughly the same for any of these sets of problems but that in each case true "laws" about cultural change will be hard to come by (MacNeish 1978). In fact, I believe that as the structure of society becomes more complex in the movement toward statehood, and as the amount of data increases, the drawing of hypotheses – often multivariable ones – and the adequate testing of these hypotheses with comparative data in order to make generalizations become increasingly difficult. Thus, although some may think that my attempts along this line on the problem of the origins of agriculture and the concomitant rise of village life have not been very good nor provided valid generalizations, I guarantee you they are much better than any I may make about the more complex problem of the rise of pristine national states in the New World. Nevertheless, addressing this problem is definitely worthwhile in that although we may not reach a synthesis or bring forth any validly tested generalization to explain this cultural development, we may have some stimulating discussions, hear of some relevant, new hypotheses or even data, obtain some better definitions relevant to the problem, and perhaps even define the problems that confront us more acutely (i.e., devise "strategies for model building"). Thus with these hopes and limitations in mind, let me give my interpretations of the transitions to pristine statehood. But first, it behooves me to say a word about my goals, my assumptions concerning culture and causality and my methodology and terminology.

Terminology and methodology

As stated elsewhere, I have hopes that archaeology may become a science and as such may "discover and formulate in general terms the conditions under which events of various kinds occur, the generalized statements of such determining conditions serving as explanations of all or most corresponding happenings" (MacNeish 1976). Events that most often concern archaeologists are past human activities, which we hope can be discovered through studying products of these activities, such as arts, artifacts, or modifications of nature that result from human behavior. It is assumed that such reconstructed activities are part of a more encompassing system, which might be called a "cultural system." By *system* I mean "a complex of elements or components related to some others in a more or less stable way at any one time" (Odum 1971). In a cultural system there are various components or subsystems. These would include the so-called value or ideational subsystem, involving ideas and information in people's minds, which they relate or communicate to each other; the social subsystem, consisting of the institutional behavior that relates groups of people to each other; and the subsistence and technological subsystem, consisting of the human activities that interrelate in terms of energy flow with both each other and those of the other subsystems, as well as with the ecosystem. Further, all these interrelated subsystems exist within an ecosystem in which the natural entities are interrelated in terms of physiochemical flow. Cultural systems, however, differ from ecosystems in that they tend to be more open. That is, the various entities tend to relate in an unstable manner or in a positive feedback situation, causing one system to develop into another; whereas ecosystems, when unconnected with humans, tend to be more closed, with entities in a stable relationship to each other, creating a negative feedback situation between the elements. Obviously, these positive feedback relationships in cultural systems are the "sufficient conditions" under which one system develops into another. Thus one may discern causes or sufficient conditions for change by studying the lifespan of a cultural system, often a cultural

Table 1. *Developmental Periods for Highland Mesoamerica, Based on Radiocarbon Dates*

Period	Dates	Example
I(H)	earlier than 25000 B.C.	Diablo
II(H)	25000–10000 B.C.	Valsequillo
III(H)	10000–8000 B.C.	Early Ajuereado subphase
IV(H)	8000–7000 B.C.	Late Ajuereado subphase
V(H)	7000–5000 B.C.	El Riego
VI(H)	5000–3400 B.C.	Coxcatlán
VII(H)	3400–2300 B.C.	Abejas
VIII(H)	2300–1500 B.C.	Purrón
IX(H)	1500–900 B.C.	Ajalpan
X(H)	900–100 B.C.	Palo Blanco
XI(H)	100 B.C.–A.D. 700	Teotihuacán
XII(H)	A.D. 700–1521	Aztec

phase, and determining, often late in the life of the system, what positive feedback situations or other factors bring about its change into a new system. The necessary conditions, or prerequisites for change, may be determined by comparing two developing systems to see what conditions occur and are basic in the descendant types that were already present in the ancestral types but which were not a basic ingredient of the earlier system itself.

Now let me say a word about my methodology. Basically, I have attempted first to define a series of sequential events, the developing systems or cultural phases, for the Tehuacán Valley (MacNeish 1964). These represent ten sequential systems. Comparative data from nearby highland Mexico indicate that there were two still earlier phases (Aveleyra Arroyo de Anda 1964; Irwin-Williams 1967), so in total I propose twelve developmental periods (I–XII) for highland Mesoamerica. These periods are dated in radiocarbon years in Table 1.

I believe that each of these archaeological phases or subphases represents a hypothetical cultural system that has wide implications. Thus I tested these phases by comparing them first with other sequential phases from Mesoamerica, then with the sequential phases of the other areas where pristine national states evolved: The Andean region, the Near East, and the Far East. From these comparisons it became apparent that the sequence of systems held true not only for other highland regions of Mesoamerica but also for similar ecological regions of the Andean area and the Near East although the dates of the developmental periods were different.

Therefore my hypothetical types of systems did seem to be validated, and I gave them a series of names emphasizing not only their very apparent settlement and subsistence pattern features but also their sociopolitical organization. Let me add from the outset that the terms used for the later phases, such as band, tribe, chiefdom, and state, were derived from social anthropological and ethnographic studies. It has been suggested that they are analogous to stages in our archaeological sequence leading to the pristine national state (Sahlins and Service 1960). However, let me point out that for major portions of the sequence there are no ethnographic analogies: No hunters live in a lush environment like that of the Pleistocene; no bands are just undertaking incipient agriculture; no tribes or chiefdoms exist except on the peripheries of great states and nations; and we have few ethnographic descriptions of these becoming states. In fact, these ethnographically derived "evolutionary" types of sociopolitical organizations are but hypotheses to be tested and modified by the archaeological data, and it is not surprising that many of our archaeological examples of bands, tribes, and chiefdoms have features not found in the ethnographic record (Flannery 1972). At best, these types are general models that may sometimes be of assistance in reconstructing our archaeological systems: nothing more, nothing less. The sequence of systems for Tehuacán and other, similar highland areas is listed in Table 2 as I(H) through XII(H).

The next step was to analyze each of these systems in the manner just described to determine why each changed into the next. That is, what were the necessary and sufficient conditions for systemic change?

Besides comparing these sequences to others in similar highland ecological zones in order to derive systemic types and the conditions for change of each, I also compared them with sequences in dissimilar ecological zones in the same nuclear area. It immediately became apparent that although the end products, pristine national states, as well as the three earliest types were the same in the different ecological zones of each area, many types in between were different. A highland–lowland dichotomy was then posited. Analysis and comparison, again starting with our Mesoamerican data, revealed the lowland sequential systems, shown in Table 2 as I(L) through XII(L).

Further study revealed that the conditions of change for these lowland stages were different from those in the highlands. Even the initial change from specialized hunting camps, III(L), to seasonal collecting-hunting camps, IV(L), had different necessary environmental conditions from the analogous shift to seasonal hunting camps, IV(H), in the highlands, whereas the change from sacred city states, XI(L), to pristine national states, XII(L), saw even more different and complex reasons for their development than the change from secular city states, XI(H). Thus I gradually developed a complex, dichotomous model to explain the rise of pristine national states. Obviously, one reason for its complexity is that the hypotheses

Table 2 *Comparative Developmental Period Sequences in Highland and Lowland Mesoamerica*

Highlands		Lowlands	
Period	Cultural type	Period	Cultural type
I(H)	Unspecialized collecting (band) camps ("Diablo")	I(L)	Unspecialized collecting (band) camps
II(H)	Specialized collecting (band) camps ("Valsequillo")	II(L)	Specialized collecting (band) camps
III(H)	Specialized hunting (band) camps ("Early Ajuereado")	III(L)	Specialized hunting (band) camps
IV(H)	Seasonal hunting (band) camps ("Late Ajuerdo")	IV(L)	Seasonal collecting-hunting (band) camps
V(H)	Seasonal collecting (band) camps ("El Riego")	V(L)	Semisedentary (base) camps ("Conchita")
VI(H)	Horticultural (band) camps ("Coxcatlán")	VI(L)	Collecting (band) hamlets ("Palma Sola")
VII(H)	Agricultural (macroband) base camps ("Abejas")	VII(L)	Tribal collecting villages ("Palo Hueco")
VIII(H)	Tribal agricultural hamlets ("Purrón")	VIII(L)	Tribal horticultural villages ("Santa Luisa")
IX(H)	Tribal administrative villages ("Ajalpan")	IX(L)	Tribal templed towns ("San Lorenzo")
X(H)	Chiefdom administrative centers ("Palo Blanco")	X(L)	Priestdom civilized centers ("Olmec")
XI(H)	Secular city states ("Teotihuacán")	XI(L)	Sacred city states ("Tikal")
XII(H)	Pristine national states ("Aztec")	XII(L)	Pristine national states

have been tested and modified by "real" data (meager as it may be) from independent areas that evolved into civilization. I have not tried to test my hypothetical models with analogous ethnographic data (Sahlins 1968). This would be testing hypothesis with hypothesis, which more often than not leads to neat theoretical speculation, not scientific generalization (Fried 1967). My generalizations may still be invalid, but this is because my testing data are inadequate, not my methods.

Here, all too briefly, I have touched upon a basic analytical technique for determining hypotheses about causes or conditions of change, whether it be the change from preagricultural band to agricultural village-type cultural systems or that from prestate to state cultural systems. In terms of general methodology this type of study is but one part of a whole chain of studies. Basically, one must start with data collection. Description of chronologies and cultural contexts must then follow in order that a synthesis of "historical – cultural integrations" (Willey and Phillips 1962), including a sequence of cultural systems, may be made. All or part of this may then be analyzed in the manner previously described to derive hypotheses about conditions that bring about change. Then one must test these hypotheses by the comparative method – that is, compare the conditions of change of one independent but similar cultural – historical integration with that of another in order to revise the hypothesis into a generalized statement of determining conditions. These conditions then serve as explanations of all or most corresponding happenings (all the cultural changes of similar cultural – historical integrations).

Having given this superficial sketch of my assumptions, methods, and terminology, let us now consider the problem at hand, as I see it: Why do pristine national states occur? I would define pristine national states as those first developing (pristine) cultural systems that had the following characteristics: (1) a hierarchy of stratified classes with the rulers at the apex of the heirarchy, concentrating the political and economic power, as well as other resources, in their hands; and (2) an organization of such groups and their states along territorial lines. These territories, including a number of regions and often a number of cities, tended to expand so as to maintain (3) a favorable balance of trade as well as to obtain tribute, which was also concentrated in the hands of the ruling group; (4) a group that was assisted by a bureaucracy of full-time specialists, middle-class traders, craftsmen, specialized food producers, and others, who often lived in cities or were oriented toward them; and finally, (5) this expanding system was controlled and maintained by a monopoly on the use of force by the rulers, usually in the form of a controlled but expanding military (Fried 1967; Harris 1968).

This is the type of cultural system in our final developmental period of this study, and the causes of the change to this system are to be found in the cultural systems that exist in the eleven periods that precede it. In this chapter I will consider in some detail the seven stages immediately preceding the final stage, which I believe are the most relevant to the rise of pristine national states.

The part of the world under consideration is the New World, where only two culture areas, Mesoamerica and the Andean area, developed pristine national states. Obviously, relevant areas in other parts of the world would be the Near East and perhaps the Far East. Although these areas are out of our present realm of discourse, for purposes of comparison and the testing of hypotheses I cannot help but refer to the former, where much data relevant to this problem have been amassed. I might add that I do not include Egypt or the Indus Valley as having seen pristine state development, for I consider these two areal developments secondary to those of the Near East.

It might also be added that all of these areas had a number of general characteristics in common that might be considered necessary conditions not only for the rise of statehood but even for an agricultural village way of life (MacNeish 1978). These common features were:

1. In each area there were a number of plants and animals that, due to their genetic makeup, were susceptible to domestication and could be the basis of a successful, surplus food-producing economy; each area had as well, other natural resources, such as salt, obsidian, metals, flint, and gems, which allowed for technological expansion.

2. All the developments occurred in warm temperate to tropical climatic zones.

3. Across all these nuclear areas there had been only one major environmental change preceding our final cultural development; this occurred at the end of the Pleistocene, when the overall biomass was greatly reduced and the ecozones shifted and expanded in number.

4. The various ecozones of each region or subarea within each of the nuclear areas differed seasonally one from the other, so that certain foods had to be obtained in different microenvironments during different seasons.

5. Moreover, not only did the ecozones of a single subarea have features that allow for beneficial exploitation but also the subareas had different resources that if exploited would benefit not only the subarea in which they occurred but also all subareas with which they interacted; these interdependencies thereby lead to an areal cultural symbiosis.

6. All the microzones or subareas had easy communication
with each other, thus allowing the subareas or zones to
form a similar interaction sphere throughout all the periods under consideration here – that is, the last eight of the
twelve cultural stages.

7. And, finally, the subareas within the major areas where
pristine national states developed fell, generally speaking,
into two dichotomous types. The first was a highland zone
with few wild foods readily available and with a tendency
for microenvironments to be stratified with regard to ele-
vation. Gradually these microenvironments merged by a
series of transitional subareas into the second dichotomous type, the lowland zone, which in terms of food resources was lusher or richer than the highland zone, and
whose microenvironments were arranged so that one had
to exploit them in a radial manner.

We should remember that not only the two dichotomous subareas
but also all the areas in between have had sightly different cultural
developments and often different causes of development throughout most of the periods under consideration. However, they have
always had some sort of stimulating interaction among them. I might
add here that this interaction may be one of conflict just as much as
one of cooperation or mutual benefit. Ideally, full understanding of
the cultural developments in all the pristine areas requires complete
cultural sequences in each of their various subareas, and this we do
not have for Mesoamerica or the Andes (or, for that matter, for the
Near East or the Far East). Further, even if we did, it would make
this article too complex and too long for our present purposes.
Therefore I will just present the sequences for the two dichotomous
subregional sequences for Mesoamerica and then Peru, with but a
brief mention of the possible comparable data from the Near East
and Far East. However, let me emphasize that it is the interaction
within *all* subareas, not just in two dichotomous ones, that led to the
rise of civilization and national states.

The developmental periods in Mesoamerica

Highlands
Obviously, much of the Mesoamerican highland data will be based
on the region I know best, Tehuacán (MacNeish et al. 1975). I am
forced to supplement these data in the final period, XII(H), by
materials from Puebla and the Valley of Mexico (Sanders and Price
1968), for Tehuacán never developed a true national state.
Tehuacán's few city states are actually characteristic of Developmental Period XI(H), as is the penultimate period of the prehis-

toric sequence in Oaxaca and the Valley of Mexico. Going from most recent to earliest we seem to have the following stages or developmental periods in highland Mesoamerica.

Developmental Period XII(H). Examples of this stage would be the Aztec (Aztec I–IV) and the Mixtec (Monte Alban V), possibly the Zapotec (Monte Alban IV), as well as the Toltec (Mazapan and Coyotlatelco phases). Dates would range from about A.D. 700 or A.D. 800 to the time of the Spanish Conquest (Carrasco and Broda 1978). These I would consider to have been representative of pristine national states, as all had the characteristics already mentioned. For brevity I have nicknamed this the "Aztec" system. Although much archaeological and ethnographic study has been done on these cultural phases or systems, secure evidence for each of my stage characteristics is difficult to find in the archaeological record and much of it is debatable. However, bad as it may be, these interpretations, thanks to ethnohistorical studies, are, generally speaking, better than those from earlier stages or periods.

Developmental Period XI(H). Examples of this stage, whose cultural system I call secular city states, nicknamed the "Teotihuacán" type, would have been in the Valley of Mexico, Teotihuacán phases I through IV (Millon 1967), and in Oaxaca, Monte Albán II, IIIa, and IIIb (Winter 1974), all dating roughly from a century or so before the time of Christ until about A.D. 600 to 750. I would also include Venta Salada from the Tehuacán Valley in this stage and type, even though it was slightly later in time (A.D. 700 to 1530) (Sisson 1973, 1974). Here, we have evidence both from archaeology and ethnohistory for deriving the characteristics of this stage. The characteristics include a hierarchical class structure with a ruling class (dynasty) that controlled the political and economic system by the use of force. Those under the control of the ruling class were the full-time specialists, who lived mainly in the urban or town center, and the food producers, whose surpluses were redistributed by the ruling class and their bureaucracy along with other products, including those traded into or out of the region under their control. Again, more acute analyses are needed to define better the stage or culture's systemic characteristics. The kind of study most sadly lacking is an analysis of this type of cultural system to determine why secular city states developed into the type of Period XII(H). I will attempt this analysis, but it is at best just a start, perhaps even a false start.

Developmental Period X(H). I have called the cultural system in the highland subarea of Mesoamerica at this stage the chiefdom administrative center system, the "Palo Blanco" type for short. Obviously, a major characteristic of this stage was redistribution by a set of ranked chiefs or heads of some sort of a conical clan arrangement. They often had their headquarters in towns or centers that had some craft specialists, as well as many agricultural specialists (often irrigation) and a few specialized long-distance traders. Soldiers or police may have existed in order to keep the chiefs in power and the hierarchy, including an incipient bureaucracy, going and to maintain the expanding redistributive system. However, the emphasis was on reciprocity and equitable redistribution of surplus from intensive (irrigation?) agriculture rather than on the use of raw force. By the end of this stage a sort of "middle class" of specialists – which is not a characteristic of most ethnographic chiefdoms – seems to have developed. Many of the cultural phases of the Late Formative of the Valley of Mexico, such as Cuicuilco, Ticomán, and perhaps Zacatenco or Atoto, Totolica, and Iglesia (Tolstoy 1975), as well as San José, Guadelupe, Rosario, and Monte Albán I of Oaxaca (Drennan 1976) would be examples of this stage. All of them existed roughly during the millennium before Christ. In Tehuacán, much of Late Santa María of the same time period might belong to this stage, as well as Palo Blanco of a later time period (MacNeish et al. 1975). Again, good evidence of the stage characteristics from the archaeological materials is highly interpretative and has not been well analyzed, nor has the determination of the conditions that forced this type of system to change into that of Stage XI(H) been well thought out.

Developmental Period IX(H). The chiefdom type of system seems to have developed out of a still earlier type, which I would call the tribal administrative village type, or the "Ajalpan" type. Here, in place of the hierarchical situation of the later stage, was a much more egalitarian arrangement, with the masses having over them a few shamans or priests, often of cults, or leaders of sodalities or clans (kin-aggregate groups). These leaders were located in village centers along with some of the farmer population; most of the latter were found in a series of sedentary hamlets, oriented toward these ceremonial or administrative centers. Long-distance exchange was often carried out through socioceremonial exchange systems, whereas local exchange occurred in informal, Palta-type markets in the village centers. However, throughout this stage there was the development of a pochteca-like long-distance exchange system with a specialized trading class. Examples of this type of system would be Ajalpan of Tehuacán (MacNeish et al. 1975), Tierras Largas of Oaxaca (Drennan 1976), and perhaps Nevada, Ayotla, and Manantial of the Valley of Mexico (Niederberger 1976), all dating roughly from 1500 to 1000 B.C.

Developmental Period VIII(H). The system of this stage might be called the tribal agricultural hamlet type, or the "Purrón" type, for short. Although the archaeological evidence for the stage is very slim, I would speculate that its system would be characterized by sedentary farmers with subsistence agriculture; small hamlets; a tribal type of social organization; leadership in the hands of the heads of lineages or kin-aggregate groups; few, if any, full-time specialists; limited ceremonials; and the making of the first crumbly pottery. This is perhaps the most poorly defined of any of our stages for highland Mesoamerica, with the Purrón phase of Tehuacán, dating from 2300 to 1500 B.C., being the only manifestation uncovered so far (MacNeish et al. 1975). It continually amazes me, particularly in light of the bragging of the "new archaeologist" saviors, that with all the money they spend on their digging and surveying in Mexico, we still do not have more examples of this stage (Blanton 1972). Perhaps a few lessons from old archaeologists in archaeological reconnaissance techniques might help?

Developmental Period VII(H). The agricultural base camp, or "Abejas" type, is only slightly better defined, and our best example, again from Tehuacán, is the Abejas phase, dating from 3400 to 2300 B.C. (MacNeish et al. 1975). Zohapilco from the Valley of Mexico (Niederberger 1976) and some of the latest preceramic layers from Texcal Cave in Puebla (García Moll, 1977) may also be examples, but both are so poorly defined that it is difficult to tell. Obviously, a semisedentary way of life based on subsistence agriculture was a major characteristic of this cultural system type, as were base camps, a lineage type of social organization, and the lack of pottery.

Developmental Period VI(H). The validity of including this stage, called seasonal horticultural band camps, or the "Coxcatlán" type, in a discussion of the transition to states is open to question. This, however, was the period during which domesticated and cultivated plants were first extensively planted and used; and, of course, statehood could not have come into being without this development (MacNeish 1971). Coxcatlán of Tehuacán, 5000 to 3400 B.C. (MacNeish et al. 1975), Playa I and II of the Valley of Mexico (Niederberger 1976), and the Zone D remains of Cueva Blanca of Oaxaca (Flannery 1970) are all examples of this type.

Developmental Period V(H). Equally difficult to justify as relevant to this discussion is the type called seasonal collecting camps, or the "El Riego" type, but this was the period when the first cultivars and domesticates, so necessary to statehood, came into being. El Riego of Tehuacán and Puebla, dating from 7000 to 5000 B.C., and Gheo Shih and Guila Naquitz of Oaxaca, (MacNeish 1964; Flannery 1970) of about the same period, are the examples on which this type is based.

Developmental Periods I(H)–IV(H). The earliest four stages were characterized by specialized hunting and collecting macrobands with relatively little seasonal scheduling. Period IV(H), seasonal hunting camps, is represented by late Ajuereado, 8000 to 7000 B.C.; Period III(H), specialized hunting camps, by early Ajuereado, 10000 to

8000 B.C.; Period II(H), specialized collecting camps (MacNeish et al. 1975), by Tlapacoya of the Valley of Mexico and Valsequillo of Puebla (Irwin-Williams 1967), 25000 to 10000 B.C.; and Period I(H), unspecialized collecting camps, is perhaps represented at Tequixquiac (Aveleyra Arroyo de Anda 1964), at more than 25,000 years ago. All these phases are not really germane to the present discussion, so I will say no more about them. However, it should be pointed out that all but the latest occurred during the Pleistocene and that at this time and stage of development the same sort of cultural systems probably existed in both the highland and lowland dichotomous subareas.

Lowlands

Developmental Period XII(L). During the final period the highland and lowland zones had similar traits for much of Mesoamerica, thanks to conquests in the lowlands by the Aztec. But even unconquered subareas in the lowlands, such as the Yucatán peninsula, Tabasco, Chiapas, much of the Mexican Pacific coast, Guatemala, and Belize, culminated during the period from A.D. 1000 to 1500 with similar pristine national state cultural systems (M. Coe 1966). The question now becomes, Did the lowland subareas have cultural systems similar to those of the highlands or systems that could be classified into the same type of cultural system during Period V(L) through XI(L) as well? My answer to this question in *no*.

Developmental Period XI(L). For the Maya lowlands this period would have been characterized by the so-called Classic period, and much investigation has been undertaken on these manifestations. The more I read about these finds, particularly the magnificent project that was undertaken at Tikal (W. Coe 1967), and the more I compare it with the new findings made at Teotihuacán and Monte Albán of the same period, the more I become convinced that the cultural system of the highlands, the so-called secular city state type, was not the same as that which existed in the Maya lowlands. Granted, both had a hierarchical class structure with ruling dynasties, and both may have used force to maintain their systems, although it is only in the last part of the Maya Classic (during Period XII(L)) that we have much evidence that the force was military. Further, I think that even then the force was mainly of a sacred nature and oriented more internally than externally. Second, although lowland rulers may also have had power over the political and economic system, much of this power was religious in nature and used to build more complex religious structures and to carry on greater and greater ceremonial undertakings rather than to control imports and exports. Also, the craftsmen were intimately connected with religion, and the bureaucracy comprised some sort of religious group or lower-echelon priesthood, which redistributed food and other items via religioceremonial mechanisms.

The evidence suggests, therefore, that although the highland and lowland cultural systems were similar enough for both to be called city states, they were different enough to be classified as different types. In the lowlands the period is called sacred city states, or the "Tikal" type, as opposed to the secular city state, or "Teotihuacán" type, of the highlands. I might add that other Classic manifestations of the coast, such as Tajín I–II, Huastec III (Pithaya), and IV (Zaquil and Tamuin), Remojadas of Veracruz, Jaina of Tabasco, and some of the Guatemala and Chiapas Classic cultural phases, seem to fit better into this sacred city state type than they do into the secular city state type of Monte Albán, Teotihuacán, early Xochicalco, Cholula, Venta Salada of Tehuacán, and so on. Kaminaljuyú of highland Guatemala, which may have been a "colony" of the Teotihaucán secular city state, fits into this latter category, although most highland Guatemalan Classic manifestations do not (Sanders and Price 1968). Obviously, much more research is needed to clarify this situation, and the differences previously mentioned are worthy subjects for debate.

Developmental Period X(L). Further, it would seem that those two slightly different cultural systems developed out of even more different cultural systems, for rather different reasons, in stage X(L), the Late and Middle Formative for the two areas. Perhaps the finest example of the lowland cultural type, so different from the highland one called chiefdom administrative center, or "Palo Blanco" type, X(H), would be that found in the Olmec area at such sites as San Lorenzo and La Venta (M. Coe 1968a). This spectacular type I would call the priestdom civilized center, or "Olmec" type. Here, the heads of a class (not ranked) system were the priests (not chiefs), and redistribution was carried out by subpriests by means of ceremonial mechanisms. In fact, there could very well have been a system of conical cults, rather than conical clans. Crafts and trade functioned to obtain ceremonial or "sacred" objects for priests, their ceremonies, and the ceremonies of the temple; wealth was not for the storage bins of chiefs. Although soldiers or sacred police may have exercised the power that kept the system going and may have seen to the building of the grand structures, these were sacred, not secular, practitioners. Food surpluses may have occurred, but they did not come from any sort of secularly administered irrigation system. More often they were the result of a neat exploitation of a number of food production systems in slightly different, contiguous ecozones. Again, the definition of this culture system is far from complete, and differences between the contemporaneous highland and lowland culture systems are well worth discussing further.

Developmental Period IX(L). The highland and lowland cultural systems were slightly less different in this preceding stage or the period of the Early Formative, from 1500 B.C. to at least 100 B.C. However, even here I do see some differences that, allow me to classify the two into slightly different kinds of tribal societies, with slightly different subsistence systems and settlement patterns, different ranking systems, and very different religious organizations. Unlike the contemporary system in the highlands, the lowland subsistence system was a highly unspecialized agriculture, heavily supplemented by the lush natural food resources. Settlements had as centers major religious towns with large monuments and structures, such as those found at San Lorenzo in Veracruz (M. Coe 1968). Obviously, these were run by priests and their assistants and their craftsmen all of whom were a cut above the lineage-oriented, farmer population. Initially, because of local wealth, this ruling group was not extensively involved in redistribution, but as population became more and more concentrated, some involvement in redistribution was bound to occur. This type I have called the tribal templed town or, for short, the "San Lorenzo" type. Examples of this type would be the earlier levels of San Lorenzo at Veracruz and La Venta (M. Coe 1968), La Barra of Chiapas (Lowe 1975), and the Ponce-like levels at Santa Luisa in central Veracruz (Wilkerson 1976). Contemporary highland groups with the tribal administrative village, IX(H), or "Ajalpan" type system, although in contact with lowland groups, often by socioceremonial exchanges, were sort of "country cousins," who did better farming with fancy hybrids.

Developmental Period VIII(L). This period is as poorly defined in the lowlands as its contemporary is in the highlands. Perhaps the best examples come from the Santa Luisa site on the Tecolutla River in central Veracruz, which dates between 1800 and 1400 B.C. (Wilkerson 1976). The Pox pottery layers from near Acapulco (Brush 1965) and Swasey of Belize may be other examples of this cultural type (Hammond et al. 1979). The slim evidence we have suggests that there were major village centers, with mounds and central plaza areas that were surrounded by a series of hamlets. The mounds, of course, suggest some sort of small, elite, religious ruling group, but there is little evidence of craftsmen or full-time specialists. Figurines and linear arrangement of houses or structures along waterways suggest some sort of lineage social organization with sodalities. Limited numbers of grinding stones, manos, and metates, and large numbers of netsinkers, fish bones, shells, and animal bones suggest a highly specialized collecting subsistence system, perhaps supplemented by limited domesticated plant food grown in small garden or "infield" horticulture. The time period seems to be roughly from 2500 to 1500 B.C., and some of the newly discovered Swasey early ceramic remains from near Orange Walk in Belize may turn out to be relevant to the definition of this cultural system (Hammond et al. 1979). Obviously, our knowledge is very limited, and we need more data. However, even the little we have suggests that we are dealing with a cultural system that I have called the tribal horticultural village or "Santa Luisa" type, which is far different from the contemporary highland tribal agricultural hamlet, VIII(H), or "Purrón" type.

Developmental Period VII(L). Again, the best evidence for this period, with its distinctive cultural system, comes from Wilkerson's preceramic Palo Hueco levels in his excavations at the Santa Luisa site on the Tecolutla River in central Veracruz (Wilkerson 1976). The Chantuto phase from coastal Chiapas (Voorhies 1976), Nogales-Repelo from the Tamaulipas coast (MacNeish 1958), and the Ostiones preceramic phase from Puerto Marquéz on Pacific coastal Guerrero (Brush 1965) may also pertain. The time period is roughly from 3500 to about 2000 B.C., contemporaneous with the agricultural base camps, VII(H), or "Abejas" phase, in the interacting highlands. However, meager as our remains are, it would appear that this coastal cultural system was far different from the contemporary highland one. I have dubbed it the tribal collecting village, or "Palo Hueco" type, for short. Here there appear to have been large sedentary villages without evidence, or even hints (no true metates), of agriculture. Again, there is from Chantuto a suggestion of hamlets or base camps oriented toward the villages, and there are hints of ceremonial leaders (and perhaps mounds) from Palo Hueco. Further, from coastal Tamaulipas and Chile near Tampico are the Nogales-Repelo sites, which show a series of small hamlet sites or microband camps oriented toward larger, more sedentary base camps, hamlets, or villages, with little evidence of agriculture but good evidence of intensive collecting. Whether their social organization was some sort of lineage system or composite band system is unknown, but I suspect it was the former.

Developmental Periods VI(L) and V(L). The next two relevant stages from the lowlands are even more poorly defined, but they still seem to have had different cultural systems from those in the highlands during the same time period. The latest of these is represented by surface collections from the huge Palma Sola site on the central coast of Veracruz (MacNeish 1967) and perhaps the nine Nogales sites from coastal Tamaulipas (MacNeish 1958). Although most of these data are from the surface, there is a hint that these sites represented large groups of macroband or composite band, specialized collectors, exploiting rich catchment basin regions from sedentary bases or hamlets. I have called this period in the lowlands the collecting hamlet, or the "Palma Sola" type, in contrast to the contemporary horticultural (band) camps, VI(H), or "Coxcatlán" type, in the highlands.

Earlier than this we have only the single Conchita manifestation excavated by Wilkerson (1976) near Zamora, whose radiocarbon dates reveal that it had been roughly contemporaneous with El Riego in Period V(H) in the highlands. Shells and bone materials as well as the site's location suggest that these people may have belonged to semisedentary (base) camps, or a "Conchita" type cultural system, as opposed to the seasonal collecting camps, or "El Riego" type, in the highlands. Again, the evidence is meager, and my types are more hypothetical, if not downright speculative.

Developmental Periods I(L)–IV(L). However, poor as the types for Periods VI(L) and V(L) may be, there are at least hints as to their characteristics. For the earlier stages we barely have even this, unless one counts the Lerma and Diablo region from peripheral Tamaulipas and the newly discovered remains from the Loltún site in Yucatán. In any case, however, these periods are outside the scope of this chapter.

These, at the present time, comprise the lowland sequence. They are far from complete but, even so, there is little doubt that the lowland sequence of cultural systems was different from that of the highlands. This is particularly true of the last four periods, VIII(L)–XI(L), which developed directly into the pristine national state type.

The developmental periods in the Andean area

When one compares the dichotomous developmental phenomena within the Mesoamerican interaction sphere with that of the Andean area, one cannot help but be struck by how well this Mesoamerican hypothetical development is confirmed by the Andean data (see Table 2).

Developmental Period XII. Although there are some obvious differences in terms of the five basic attributes among the empires of the Aztec, Toltecs, and Mixtecs of Mesoamerica compared with the Inca, Chimu, and Wari of the Andes, the latter can also be classified as belonging to the same pristine national state type of almost the same time period, A.D. 600 to 1540 (Lumbreras 1974b).

Developmental Period XI. Also, in the preceding stage or developmental period, there is evidence of city states with all the characteristics mentioned previously for the same type in Mesoamerica. As in Mesoamerica, the lowland or coastal city states, such as Moche-Gallinazo, Nazca, and perhaps Lima, have a much more religious bent, with priest-kings and craftsmen connected with religious phenomena, art depicting the supernatural, an emphasis on sacred rather than on secular power, and great urban capitals that are primarily religious centers (Lumbreras 1974b). Certainly these may be classified as sacred city states. They contrast with the more warlike and urban administrative states, such as those found in Huarpa and Huancayo in the central Andes (MacNeish, Patterson, and Browman 1975), Pucara and Tiahuanaco in the southern Andes (Ponce Sanquines 1971), and perhaps Recuay and Cajamarca in the northern Andes. The Andean cases are all good examples of secular city states, and I might add are not very well studied. This time period in the Andes dates from roughly 300 B.C. to A.D. 600, a century or two earlier than its equivalent in Mesoamerica.

Developmental Period X. In this developmental period it is more difficult to see a sharp separation between the highlands and lowlands of Peru, due to the all pervasive influence of the religious phenomenon known as the Chavín cult. So, although there are more administrative than civilized or sacred centers in the highlands, the real distinction between the chiefdom and priestdom is difficult to make. Yet there was a tendency in this direction, with highland Chupas and Rancha of Ayacucho (MacNeish, Patterson, and Browman 1975), and Kotosh-Chavín on the east slopes of the Andes (Izumi and Terada 1972), as well as with Kuntur Wasi and Cajamarca in the northern Andes having a secular emphasis; whereas Paracas on the south coast, Ancón-Supe and Cerro Sechín on the central coast, and Guanape and Cupisnique on the north central coast (Lumbreras 1974a) had a more sacred emphasis. This period dates roughly from 800 to 300 B.C. Obviously, more study and data are needed; here is a worthy subject for discussion.

Developmental Period IX. The lack of distinction between highlands and lowlands of Period X does not occur in the earlier Stage IX, for now early Wichqana of Ayacucho (MacNeish, Patterson, and Browman 1975), Kotosh-Kotosh (Izumi and Terada 1972), and the like in the highlands are easily classified as the tribal administrative village, or "Ajalpan" type. Garagay and Curayucu (Lumbreras 1974), on the other hand, are easy to classify as the tribal templed town, or "San Lorenzo" type. This period, dating from 1400 to 800 B.C., is when agricultural villages, albeit regionally different ones, came into being in the Andean area.

Developmental Period VIII. The next earlier stage also sees sharp contrasts between the highlands and lowlands. Relatively small villages with full-time agriculture and some sort of water control occurred at Andamarca in Ayacucho (Lumbreras 1974b) and Wairajirka in Huanaco (Izumi and Terada 1972); they represent the tribal agriculture hamlet, or "Purrón" type. In the lowlands Las Háldas and La Florida (Lumbreras 1974b) are good examples of villages with horticulture rather than with true agriculture (i.e., the tribal horticulture village, or "Santa Luisa" type). This period dates from 1850 to 1400 B.C.

Developmental Period VII. The contrasting highland-lowland division that we see in Mexico at the end of the preceramic also occurs in Peru. Cachi of Ayacucho and Mito of Huanaco (Izumi and Terada 1972), with hamlets and base camps with agriculture as well as with herding, would be good examples of the agricultural base camp, or "Abejas" type (MacNeish, Nelken-Terner, and García Cook 1970), whereas earlier El Paraíso or Gaviota, Rio Seco, and Culebras of the coastal lowlands (Lumbreras 1974b) would all be examples of the tribal collecting village, or "Palo Hueco" type. This period occurs in the Andes from 3000 to 1850 B.C.

Developmental Periods VI and V. These two developmental periods are again similar in both Mesoamerica and the Andes. They are just barely germane to our discussion because during this period plants became domesticated and some people did become sedentary. Chihua of Ayacucho, dating from 4400 to 3000 B.C., saw the beginning of horticulture that used a number of plants, such as corn, beans, quinoa, lucuma, cucurbits, and potatoes, and a macro-microband way of life. This is a good example of the horticultural (macro-microband) camp, or "Coxcatlán" type, of Developmental Period VI(H). This period is preceded by Piki, dating from 5800 to 4400 B.C., a good example of seasonal collecting camps, or the "El Riego" type, of Developmental Period V(H) (MacNeish, Nelken-Terner, García Cook 1970). These two developments of sequential types in the highlands would contrast with the lowland sequence, with the Canario and Luz phases, dating from 5500 to 4000 B.C. – representing the collecting hamlet, or "Palma Sola" type, of Period VI(L) – and Arenal – representing the semisedentary band camp, or "Conchita" type, of Period V(L) (Patterson 1971).

Developmental Periods I–IV. Again, the earlier stages, best represented by the sequence in Ayacucho, with Period IV represented by Puente-Jaywa, Period III by Huanta, Period II by Ayacucho, and Period I by Paccaicasa, are outside the scope of this chapter (MacNeish 1971a).

The developmental periods in the Old World

Before passing on to an analysis of why these various systems develop one into another, I should mention the comparable material from the Old World (see Table 3. Adams R, McC. 1966).

Developmental Period XII. In the Near East the end product of the process, the pristine national state, seems to be represented by the late Uruk or Dynastic Sumerian phase, dating from about 3500 to 2500 B.C. (Redman 1978), whereas in China it would be the Chou dynasty, dating from 1100 to 220 B.C. (Chang 1963). This is when both culture areas were unified under one empire.

Developmental period XI. This period, that of the city states, would see a clear dichotomous split in the Near East, with Late Hacilar and Tepe Gawra, in the highlands, dating from 5500 to 3500 B.C., having a more secular orientation, whereas Eridu and Ubaid 1 – 4 in the

Table 3. *Comparative Sequences in Four Nuclear Areas of Pristine National State Formation*

Developmental period	Subarea	Type		Examples in nuclear areas			
				Mesoamerica	Peru	Near East	Far East
I	Highland	1.	Unspecialized collecting camps	Diablo	Paccaicasa	Lower Paleolithic	Soan
	Lowland			San Isidro	?		Choukoutien
II	Highland	2.	Specialized collecting camps	Valsequillo	Ayacucho	Mousterian	Ordos
	Lowland			?	Red zone?		Fenho
III	Highland	3.	Specialized hunting camps	Hueyatlaco	Huanta	Baradostian	Sjara-osso-gol
	Lowland			Loltun	Chiwateros	?	?
IV	Highland	4a.	Seasonal hunting-collecting camps	Itzapan	Puente, Jaywa	?	?
	Lowland	4b.	Seasonal collecting-hunting camps	Lerma	Arenal, Luz	Kebaran	?
V	Highland	5a.	Seasonal collecting camps	El Riego	Piki	Palegawra	?
	Lowland	5b.	Semisedentary base camps	Conchita	Canario	Kebaran A	?
VI	Highland	6a.	Horticultural band camps	Coxcatlán	Chihua		?
	Lowland	6b.	Collecting hamlets	Palma Sola	Encanto	Early Natufian	?
VII	Highland	7a.	Agricultural base camps	Abejas	Cachi	Zawi Chemi	?
	Lowland	7b.	Tribal collecting villages	Palo Hueco	Gaviota	Late Natufian	?
VIII	Highland	8a.	Tribal agricultural hamlets	Purrón	Waira-Jirka	Usiab	?
	Lowland	8b.	Tribal horticultural villages	Santa Luisa	La Florida	Mureybit	Yang Shao
IX	Highland	9a.	Tribal administrative villages	Ajalpan	Wichqana	Jarmo	?
	Lowland	9b.	Tribal templed towns	San Lorenzo	Garagay	Jericho	?
X	Highland	10a.	Chiefdom administrative centers	Palo Blanco	Chupas	Hacilar	Liang Shu
	Lowland	10b.	Priestdom civilized centers	La Venta	Sechin	Hassuna	Liang Shu
XI	Highland	11a.	Secular city states	Teotihuacán	Huarpa	Tepe Gawra	Shang
	Lowland	11b.	Sacred city states	Tikal	Mochica	Ubaid	Hu-Shu
XII	Highland	12.	Pristine national states	Aztec	Inca	Sumerian	Chou
	Lowland						

lowlands would have a more sacred one (Redman 1978). In China the case is not so clear, but is it not possible that Shang in the interior and to the north represents the secular facet, whereas the coastal Hu-Shu in the lower Yangtze represents the more sacred one (Chang 1963)?

Developmental Period X. This period, when the chiefdom-priestdom centers dichotomy occurred, might very well see the former represented by Middle-Late Hacilar and Late Çatal Hüyük, whereas the latter would be represented by Hassuna, Byblos, and the like (Redman 1978). In China the division is less clear. Is classical Lungshan in the interior representative of a chiefdom type and coastal Liang-Chu or T'an-Shih-shan of the priestdom type (Chang 1963)?

Developmental Period IX. In China the earliest relevant phase so far found would be the Yang-Shao. This, however, may provide only half the picture, representing the tribal administrative village type, whereas the dichotomous tribal templed town type may still be undiscovered or at least undefined. However, in the Near East we do seem to have both the lowland tribal templed towns being represented by Jericho PPNA, and the like, whereas the highlands tribal administrative village types would be represented by Jarmo, Early Çatal Hüyük, Early Hacilar, Aşikli Hüyük, and the like

Developmental Period VIII. This period would see the contrast between the tribal horticultural village type in the lowlands, as represented by PPNB at Beidha, Jericho, Mureybit, and Bus Mordeh, and the highland tribal agricultural hamlet type of groups found at Cayonu, Asiab, Karim Shahir, Upper Ganh Dareh, and the like (Redman 1978).

Developmental Period VII. This period would see the agricultural base camp type as seen at Zawi Chemi in the highlands, contrasting with the tribal collecting village type represented by late Natufian in the lowlands.

Developmental Period VI. During this period Natufian would be representative of the collecting hamlet type, which contrasts with the horticultural (macro-microband) camp type as represented by Zarzi (Redman 1978).

Developmental Period V. This period might see the contrasts of semi-sedentary base camps in lowland Keberan A with seasonal collecting camps in highland Palegawra, similar to the dichotomies in Mexico and Peru.

Developmental Periods I–IV. The earlier four stages would again not seem very relevant to the present discussion.

Thus, although archaeologists are prone to emphasize the uniqueness of the remains they uncover, there are many general similarities in the dichotomous sequences in the key areas where pristine national states appeared. Now the question arises, What are the conditions that cause the types of systems of the various periods to develop one into another? And here we move into an entirely different level of speculation, for the data necessary to give definite answers are just not available at the present. Nevertheless, let us at least set up some testable hypotheses, even if we cannot presently test them adequately.

Cultural causality

Before we review the crucial stages from agricultural villages (Period IX) to empires (Period XII), let us first consider the data for the earliest stages, which led to plant domestication, then to agriculture and/or villages, and finally to agricultural villages. Figure 1 schematizes the discussion that follows.

Intensified food procurement and sedentism

From many standpoints the entire process, with its dichotomous implications, began at the end of the Pleistocene and at the shifts from Period III to IV and from Period IV to V. Here the basic triggering causes were the changes in the biomass, specifically the diminution of herd animals and other megafauna that were hunted. This occurred at about the time that humans had developed an entirely new series of subsistence options, such as seed collection, seed storage, leaf and berry picking, trapping, and seafood collecting. These changes shifted the emphasis from a nomadic way of life, consisting of living in family groups and depending mainly upon hunting for subsistence, to a collecting way of life, with a seasonally scheduled subsistence system and a settlement pattern with group size fluctuating from microband to macroband with each season. This latter is the way of life that in the New World is often called the Archaic.

Environmental factors. Exactly what kind of Archaic way of life developed was in large part governed by environmental factors, necessary conditions, if you will. Those who moved into harsh areas with steeply stratified ecozones and great seasonal variation formed seasonal collecting camps or "El Riego" types, whereas those who moved into lusher areas with catchment basin types of ecozones formed semisedentary base camps, or "Conchita" types. Thus by Developmental Period V different culture systems or types were exploiting different environmental zones. Although these were interacting with each other, major evolutions in each subarea were to continue to take place for rather different reasons.

The El Riego type, or seasonal collecting camp, perhaps represented by El Riego in Tehuacán, Piki in highland Peru, and Pal-

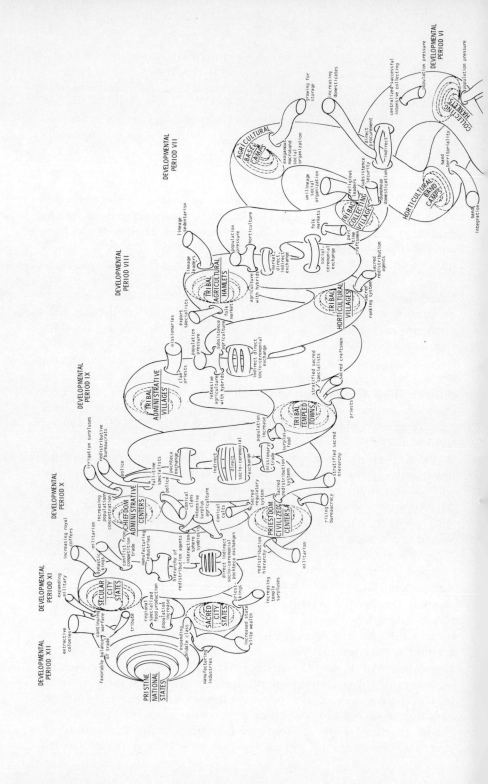

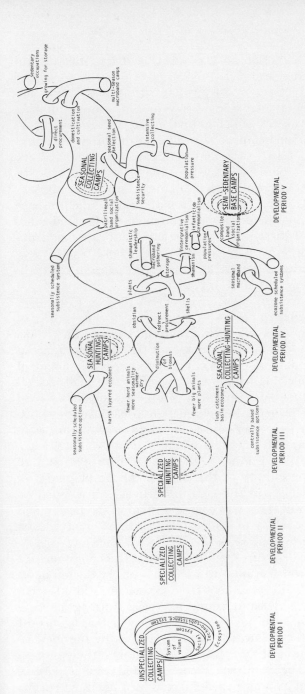

Figure 1. Model of the evolution of cultural types leading to pristine national states

egawra in hilly Iraq, experienced a positive feedback situation. Increasing seasonal seed selection led to the planting of domesticates and cultivars, and increased use of this new subsistence option and food storage led to increasingly longer stays and increasing numbers of macroband encampments, which in turn led to an increasing need for ceremonialism and shamanism as an integrating force to control these larger groups. These sufficient conditions occurring in the highland zones led to the development of the "Coxactlán" type, or seasonal horticultural (macro-microband) band camp. The necessary conditions for change in these highland zones included the presence of more plants that could be domesticated than in the lowland zones and the distribution of these plants such that domesticates and cultivars were exchanged with other similar zones where people were using other kinds of domesticates. Here were the reasons for highland development from Period V to VI.

Because of the rather different environments, again a necessary condition, the semisedentary (base) camp, or "Conchita" type, of lowland culture developed into the collecting hamlet, or "Palma Sola" type, for rather different reasons than did the simultaneous highland shift. Here intensive collecting and the development of increasingly better collecting techniques, as well as seasonally scheduled exploitation from a base camp, led to a more sedentary way of life. This in turn led to increasing population in base camps, which caused more intensive collecting, and so on. Here were the sufficient conditions, very different from those of the highlands, that made a positive feedback situation leading to the change from Period V to VI. Perhaps the best example of this shift is the development of Canario to Encanto-Chilca in the central Peruvian coast. Furthermore, the shift from Kebaran A to early Natufian in the Levant and perhaps that from Conchita to Palma Sola on the Veracruz coast took place for much the same reasons.

Highlands. Now let us set up hypotheses about the conditions for or causes of change from Period VI to VII in both the dichotomous zones. In Tehuacán the development from Coxcatlán, with its horticulture (macro-microband) band camps, to Abejas, with agricultural base camps, seems to have been caused by the increasing use of domesticates that diffused into the area, as well as by the increasingly efficient production of food from the planting of these domesticates or cultivars. These sufficient conditions started a positive feedback characterized by a more sedentary way of life due to growing for storage, leading to population increases. These factors in turn led to more and better use of imported domesticates and/or cultivars, which led to a more sedentary way of life, population increase, and so on. However, I should point out that the exchange system and the increased horticultural food production were the causes or sufficient conditions in these highland situations; the population factors were the consequences of these and were in themselves, in turn, necessary conditions for change, along with such other factors as the potential of some of the domesticates or cultivars to give increasingly greater yields. This process seems also to have occurred in the development from Zarzi to Zawi Chemi in highland Iraq, from Chihua to Cachi in highland Ayacucho, and perhaps also in the development to Mito in nearby Huanaco.

Lowlands. This is very different from what seems to have occurred in the contemporary dichotomous zones in the lowlands. In Mexico, population pressure in the lowlands once again was a sufficient condition for change and was linked with the rise of sedentary life in the "Palma Sola" types or collecting (band) hamlet, which developed into the "Palo Hueco" type, or sedentary tribal collecting village. Thus there was a shift from hamlets to villages, which led to increasingly more efficient collection and perhaps even to plant domestication via the dump heap mechanism, as well as to diffusion of domesticates from the highlands. Both these factors acted in a positive feedback loop along with a changing social organization of composite bands, which led to some sort of lineage type of social organization with strong ceremonial leadership. This allowed not only for better social integration but also for better planning of food production. Again, the necessary conditions were the environmental factors, which permitted these developments from Period VI to VII on the coast. Again, I feel that this was the sort of process that was occurring in the Levant between early and late Natufian, as well as in the development from Encanto to Playa Hermosa, Gaviota, and the like, on the central Peruvian coast.

The next shift in the lowlands, from the "Palo Hueco" type, or tribal collecting village, to the "Santa Luisa" type, or tribal horticultural village, at the transition from Period VII to VIII was paralleled by the shift from Playa Hermosa and Gaviota to cultures such as those of Paraíso and Rio Seco of Peru. Again, a major necessary condition for change was population pressure, but now it was coupled with increased planting of domesticates and a ranked type of social organization with strong religious leadership.

The causes of the contemporary shift in the highlands from "Abejas," with its agricultural base camps, to "Purrón," with its tribal agricultural hamlets, were similar to those in the lowlands. For the first time in the highlands, population was the major factor in the positive feedback chain that included subsistence agriculture and led to greater sedentarism, which in turn led to population increases, the need for more and better food production, and so on. However, there were differences in this process for the highlands, for there were none of the social conditions for change, such as ceremonial or religious leadership, which were so important in the coastal development. This also seems to have been true for the shift from Cachi to Andamarka and Mito to Waira-jirca in highland Peru and Zawi Chemi to phases such as Asiab, Cayonu, and so on in the Near East.

Toward complex political organization
Thus we come to the threshold of the stages leading to the rise of pristine national states. In each of the areas the shifts from Period VIII to IX were similar. However, the shift in the highlands from tribal agricultural hamlets to tribal administrative villages also had new factors as sufficient conditions for change besides those of population and food production with new and better hybrids. These included increasing organizational and religious influence from the lowlands, a lineage social organization, a market exchange system, all of which acted in a positive feedback manner. Purrón to Ajalpan in Mesoamerica, Asiab to Jarmo in Iraq, Andamarka to Wichqana in Peru, and Waira-jirca to Kotosh on the east slope of the Andes may be other examples where this same process was taking place.

For the lowland shift from tribal horticultural villages to tribal templed towns, the factors of population and food production were still major sufficient conditions for systemic change, but again social factors involving redistribution and a shift from an egalitarian to a ranking system of social organization, linked with a shift from lineages to some sort of sodalities or kin-aggregate groups, were involved in a positive feedback situation. Again, much research is needed to work out the details of the exact relationships among these positive feedback loops. Nevertheless, although we see the picture very poorly, this may be the sort of thing that was happening in the shift from PPNB to PPNA in the Levant, Bus Mordeh to Ali Kosh in lowland Iraq, El Paraíso to La Florida on the Peruvian coast, and Santa Luisa to San Lorenzo on the Veracruz coast. Now we have a base for considering the rise of national states themselves, so let us get to the nitty-gritty of our discussions.

Highlands. The first question is, How and why does the tribal administrative village, or "Ajalpan" type, develop into the chiefdom administrative center, or "Palo Blanco" type, in the highlands? The former had a village lineage-type social organization, simple leadership, simple, two-tiered ranking system, exchanges on a relatively direct basis, few, if any, full-time specialists with the exception of shamans, and a subsistence agricultural economy. The latter type had a conical clan type of social organization, three (or more) ranked hierarchical classes, much exchange based on a redistribution system, a middle class of full-time specialists (both bureaucrats and craftsmen), and a subsistence system yielding surpluses.

Fortunately, we have much fine data on just this period of the transition from Ajalpan to Palo Blanco from Tehuacán. Some of this information comes from the fifteen stratified zones at Coatepec, each roughly fifty years apart, from 1050 to 50 B.C. Some of these data come from survey, but the most crucial data come from the Purrón dam area (Spencer 1977). Here we have not only the ten stratified layers from Purrón Cave, dating from 1300 B.C. to A.D. 400, with abundant foodstuffs, giving us information about sustenance and subsistence in the crucial period, but we also have Woodbury and Neely's study of the five periods of dam building from 800 B.C. to A.D. 200 and of water control of the same time (Woodbury and Neely 1972). More recently, we have Spencer's intensive testing, survey, and mapping to determine changes in population, the social stratification system the redistribution system and craft production from the period from 800 B.C. to A.D. 400 in terms of four to six periods, each about two hundred years long. A study of these shows how each of eight characteristics changed; namely, social organization, leadership, social stratification, exchange, specialization or division of labor system, settlement pattern, population, and subsistence subsystem (C. Spencer 1977). But it is more important to align these changes in chronological order, to determine which ones occurred before the others, thus giving a basis for hypothesizing those sufficient conditions or trigger causes for the other elements in the system to change later.

Now let us look at the evidence. What is very clear is that in Early Santa María times surplus food began to be grown by irrigation. Hand in glove with this comes our first evidence of ranking: Five of the stone platform houses of the total fifteen to twenty contained almost all the prestigious obsidian and figurines and also had more bowls than ollas. These two conditions seem to have triggered several positive feedback situations (Wittfogel 1957). The irrigation or water control that had slowly developed for millennia led to greater food production in Early Santa María, which led to more irrigation in the form of dam stages II and III, which led to still larger population in the Late Santa María, which led to dam Stage IV, which led to the towns such as Tr73 in Early Palo Blanco. The second factor seems to show that the surpluses from irrigation were being immediately redistributed by the upper echelon group living in the stone houses of Early Palo Blanco, first to more houses in their villages or hamlets, then to downstream villages, and eventually to a middle class in the town centers, as well as to villages in the satellite communities. Another factor was that the system of social stratification and leadership had changed, but with each change were necessitated further increases in food production via improved irrigation. Perhaps also the stone house people became the top clan in a conical clan arrangement. In addition, in Middle Santa María they dammed up water, resulting not only in two crops per year but also in about four times as much food as was needed, including more fruit than could be eaten. Immediately thereafter, in Late Santa María and Early Palo Blanco, we have evidence of blade making, pottery making, and cotton weaving by craftsmen or full-time specialists living in stone foundation houses just below the elites on the mounds. This, of course, meant that more distribution agents were needed as well as more food: another positive feedback situation. Thus the redistributing elite became richer and richer as they skimmed off some of the cream of each redistribution undertaking.

In sum, *if* a tribal administrative village type of society is characterized by certain necessary conditions, then the three or four positive feedback situations mentioned previously will arise, causing the chiefdom administrative center type, with the characteristics already discussed, to develop. These necessary conditions are (1) the potential for great food surplus, (2) the possibility of exchanges, and (3) gradual population increases – with the sudden development of (1) an irrigation system to provide food for more population as well as to produce a food surplus so that more specialists and craftsmen may arise to form a middle class (Wittfogel 1957), (2) a social organization with an ability to increase the mechanism of redistribution via (3) an increasing middle class, (4) more surplus, and (5) the increased power of the elite. This, then, is my hypothesis for change from developmental period IX to X in the highlands. It also seems to explain the shift from Tierras Largas–San Lorenzo to Monte Albán I in Oaxaca. Is this not the sort of process that took place in Ayacucho in Peru in the development from Andamarka–Wichqana to Chupas–Rancha or Kotosh–Kotosh to Kotosh–Chavín, as well as from Jarmo-like cultures to Hacilar in the Near East or from Yang-Shao to Lungshan in the Far East? This is where more analysis is needed to test this hypothesis.

Lowlands. Now, do these same conditions bring about the contemporaneous change in lowland Mesoamerica from the tribal templed town type to the priestdom civilized center type? My answer is *no.* Here, I believe that expanding population, due to sedentary life in part based upon subsistence agriculture and specialized collecting with surpluses, led to an increase in both these subsistence options, which led to population increases, which led to more and more agricultural production to maintain surpluses, and so on. Going hand in glove with this development was the increasing wealth of the priests who controlled this surplus and who redistributed it via ceremonies and other mechanisms to their assistants and craftsmen, as well as to the peasant farmers. Furthermore, the more often both these situations occurred, the larger was the number of classes below the ruling, priestly elite, the greater was the activity of the elite building of public religious structures, and the greater was their web of exchange to obtain goods for the craftsmen to work or the various privileged classes to own. Was this not the sort of process that was happening between Santa Luisa and Trapiche, or Ojite to La Venta in Veracruz, or La Barra to Ocos in lowland Guatemala? Also, is this not the sort of process that was going on from Las Háldas to Sechín or Cupisnique in lowland Peru, or from Jericho PPNA to Hassuna or Byblos in the Near East?

Toward city states

Highlands. Now, what about the shift to city states? In Tehuacán this was the shift from Palo Blanco to Venta Salada, a secular city state. Again, populations were increasing and food surpluses were grown but, as before, they were necessary conditions for change, however, not sufficient ones. A number of new factors or sufficient conditions working in a positive feedback manner seem to be of key importance in the change from chiefdom administrative centers to secular city states. The following includes the most important: (1) Stratified classes continued to develop, with increasing power and resources centering in the hands of chiefs who in time become kings of dynasties, the apex of the hierarchical class system. (2) Further, these leaders controlled the ever increasing crafts and industries, not only for redistribution internally but also for export, as was the case with salt. This export trade brought other resources, mostly raw materials such as cotton, into the hands of the elite or kings. These were sometimes in turn used in local industries, such as weaving. The products of such industries could be exported as well as locally redistributed, which in turn made for more specialization. (3) However, because many local neighboring dynasties or chiefdoms were exporting very similar or even the same products, there was increasing competition and conflict. (4) Further, this external redistribution, as well as (5) internal redistribution and the cultural system itself, were maintained by the use of force by the elite, who had a monopoly on this use of force because of their development of military–police groups.

Not only was this development taking place for these reasons or conditions from Palo Blanco to Venta Salada, but it seems to have been what was happening in Oaxaca in Monte Albán I, leading to the state in Monte Albán II, II–III, and IIIa, and might have been what happened from Ticoman to Teotihuacán in the Valley of Mexico. It may have been what happened in the development from Chupas Rancha phases to Huarpa with its city states in highland Peru and also during Hacilar times in Turkey and in the shift from Lungshan to the

Shang dynasty of China. If so, then our hypothesis based on Tehuacán data will have been tested and on its way to becoming a generalization. Again, this matter needs much discussion.

Lowlands. The shift from Developmental Period X to XI in the
lowlands – that is, from priestdom civilized centers to sacred city
states – seems to occur in a slightly different manner and for different reasons. The necessary conditions – population increase, food
surpluses, and foreign exchange – also occurred as they did in the
highlands, but the sufficient conditions seem to have been slightly
different, although they still involved the use of force to maintain
the sacred city state system. In the lowland case this appears to have
come into being because of problems concerning internal redistribution. Increasing construction of sacred buildings and more ceremonies to obtain more crops to feed an increasing number of sacred
supported craftsmen put increasing pressure on the proportionately
shrinking number of peasant food producers. To stop revolt or
slowdowns in food production and to continue the building pro-
grams, the elite priest-kings increasingly had to use force to control
the peasant class and workers. Also, as craftsmen received less food
and products, highland invaders threatened the local systems and
local trade became more competitive. Increasing force had to be
used by the priests, who held a monopoly on both secular and sacred
force, to control these groups as well. This is what I believe happened in the shift in the Petén from Chicanel to Tzakol. In coastal
Peru this may have been what occurred from Paracas to Nazca and
Cupisnique to Moche. Could this be what was happening in the early
development in Ubaid 1 to 4 leading to the city state in the Uruk or
the Late Ubaid period in the Near East? Did something similar occur
on the south coast of China during Shang times? None of this has
been very well worked out, but it is time to consider these matters.

Toward pristine national states
And now we come to the development of the pristine national states.
Here the causes seem to have been about the same whether we are
dealing with secular or sacred city states and therefore were the same
for both highlands and lowlands. Obviously, many areas became part
of national states because they were conquered by them, but what
about the others? What drove them on to be the conquerors? Population pressure may still have been a necessary condition, but food
surpluses were not. In fact, the proportional diminution of food surpluses grown internally may have been a driving force leading certain
states to expand and conquer others that did have food surpluses.
Hand in glove with this was an expanding exchange system with the
need for a favorable balance of trade, not only to feed the increasing
masses but also to feed and supply the growing middle class of bu-

reaucrats and craftsmen or industrial workers. Both foreign conquest and the maintenance of a continually expanding favorable balance of trade required the increased use of force by the elite, resulting in a well-established military. Further, the military had a tendency to increase the warfare continually to ever widening regions so that the military became greatly overexpanded and warfare became chronic. Other factors may also have been important, for now we are dealing with very complex and large cultural systems.

In conclusion

Thus we do have some testable hypotheses about the rise of the first city states as well about pristine national states. I have attempted to test them with the data from Mesoamerica and the Andean interaction sphere and have even suggested that the first states from the Near East and Far East developed in the same way for the same reasons. Obviously, we need more data and analysis to make these hypotheses into valid generalizations, but at least we have made a start.

What about cultures that obviously did not develop as I have outlined? Why did not other chiefdoms develop into states? Why did not Carneiro's Amazon chiefdoms become states (Carneiro 1970)? What about the Central American, Venezuelan, and Colombian warlike chiefdoms? What about those of New Guinea, the Polynesian Islands, the Iroquois, and the Northwest Coast (Sahlins 1968)? Many were certainly warlike; some felt population pressures, and many were in circumscribed regions: Carneiro's reasons for their becoming states. It would seem that his conditions are not the real sufficient conditions and that we must add those I have suggested. Let me point out that most of the ethnographic chiefdoms previously mentioned were not in interaction spheres with dichotomous developments. Most did not have subsistence systems producing large food surpluses, and most were not chiefdoms with a developing class system and a competitive, well-organized exchange system striving for a favorable balance of trade. Without these sufficient conditions, the pristine national state does not develop. The necessary conditions of population pressure and warfare alone are not sufficient. Further, circumscribed territories do not seem to be a sufficient condition at all, for many of our first highland states did not have such confining conditions, whereas many long-term chiefdoms in other areas that did not develop states were circumscribed.

Thus it is my belief that Carneiro's (1970), Service's (1962), Fried's (1967), and other theorists' hypotheses about the origins of states must be modified and supplemented. This paper is a step in that direction. Is it not time for us to test my hypotheses with further analysis of the chiefdoms just preceding the first states, not only in the Andean area and Mesoamerica but also in the Near East, Far East, and perhaps even in the secondary states of the Indus Valley, Egypt, and Africa? Let us consider again what kinds of data we need to test or modify these hypotheses. How do we collect and analyze them? What new definitions and methods are needed? Let us do something, not just talk. These are problems that are not unsolvable, just unsolved.

PART IV

Ideological factors in state formation

6

Religion and the rise of Mesoamerican states

MICHAEL D. COE

And the devil said unto him, If thou be the Son of God, command this stone that it be made bread.
And Jesus answered him, saying, It is written, That man shall not live by bread alone, but by every word of God.

Luke 4.4

We know from the works and opinions of early Spanish missionaries how deeply religious the native peoples of Mesoamerica were on the eve of the conquest. All the early accounts make it clear that much of the beliefs and behavior of the early sixteenth century Aztec, Maya, and other groups were concerned with the supernatural – and that this concern was found on every social level, from the rulers down to the common people and slaves.

It is puzzling, therefore, and perhaps even ironic, that an entire generation of archaeologists has chosen to ignore a facet of Meso-american culture that the people themselves would have viewed as the most important in their universe. In New World archaeology, and increasingly in Old World prehistory, material-determinist views of the past have come to hold exclusive sway in archaeological analysis, to the almost total exclusion of ideological factors. While taking up the challenge of Binford's 1962 cry for "Archaeology as anthropology," the "new" archaeologists ignored the fact that religion has been a central concern to the science of anthropology since the days of Sir Edward B. Tylor. Even some social anthropologists have been gripped by the grim hand of material-determinism; as an extreme example, one might point to Harner's (1977) claim that Aztec human sacrifice was instituted as a remedy for widespread protein deficiency in central Mexico.

But the pervasiveness of the material-determinist school, which of course holds economic factors such as the relations of production to be the "prime movers" in social and cultural evolution, can be found throughout the contemporary Mesoamerican literature. One would be hard-pressed, for instance, to find any serious treatment of religion or mental systems in *Mesoamerica: The Evolution of a Civilization* by Sanders and Price (1968), let alone the most cursory treatment of these subjects in the average site report. To take another example, I doubt if one would be able to discover from Richard MacNeish's magnificent work on the prehistory of the Tehuacán Valley, which to a large extent is based upon cave excavation (MacNeish et al. 1975), that the primary use of caves in Mesoamerica is today – and surely was in the distant past – for ritual purposes. These rituals are related to the common belief that caves are entrances to the Underworld and therefore to the world of departed spirits (for a discussion of caves in Mesoamerican thought, see Heyden 1975).

The problem, of course, stems from the fact that archaeologists are dealt a bad hand by the past; the very nature of the remains, unless writing or a representational art style has been found, calls for a material-determinist explanation, because the thought systems of prehistoric peoples are very difficult to recover. But we should all remember Edmund Leach's admonition to archaeologists, that in real life most of what "native" people talk about consists of religion and politics and hardly at all of subsistence and modes of production (Leach 1973). In Mesoamerica this state of affairs has produced a dichotomy of scholarship with, until recently, little chance of dialogue or synthesis between the two sides. On the one hand, we have a majority of "dirt" archaeologists, determinedly material-determinist whether they call themselves paleoecologists or something else; and on the other hand, a minority of "traditional" scholars who work with codices, native accounts, pre-Spanish art, and other documents testifying to the nature of native Mesoamerican thought and religion. Like two darkened ships in the night, these two schools seem to proceed on their journey unaware of each other's existence.

In the past decade, however, a small number of scholars have become interested in bridging this gap, and I am gratified to say that included in this group are specialists on the Olmec, Zapotec, and Classic Maya civilizations. In this respect, a particularly important paper is that by Flannery and Marcus (1976b), suggesting how the Zapotec world view has constrained and influenced the Zapotec past. In this, they are adopting an approach that has been used by a few North American specialists, particularly historical archaeologists; here I am thinking of the demonstration by Deetz and Dethlefson (1967) of the effect of a religious movement (the Great Awakening of eighteenth-century New England) on material remains (stylistic variation in carved tombstones) and Leone's explorations of Mormon landscape and architecture as channeled by Mormon theology and philosophy (Leone 1973).

This chapter does not aim to establish religion in place of economics as the prime mover in the development of civilization; in fact, I remain an unbeliever in the prime mover approach. What I would like to do, more modestly, is to suggest that religion, and especially world views, are important variables to consider in social change, including the move toward state society; that religions have been creators and maintainers of stability as well as destroyers of the status quo and that different ways of viewing the universe have nourished, in the Weberian sense, widely divergent forms of social, cultural, political, and even economic life. Mesoamerica is very definitely different from ancient China or Mesopotamia in all these respects, and its religious system must have had something to do with it.

Religion and society

Archaeologists, if they deal with religion at all in its relation to society, tend to see its effects in terms of social differentiation, emphasizing cleavages between groups and enhancing status with symbolic prestige, almost as if religion consisted of nothing but sumptuary laws. Flannery's (1968) paper on the nature of the Olmec presence in Oaxaca illustrates this point. The two greatest students of religion and society, however, Emile Durkheim and Max Weber, saw religion as something infinitely vaster than this. Durkheim (1915) saw religion as an extensive symbolic system that makes social life possible by expressing and maintaining the sentiments or values of a society. Lessa and Vogt (1958:1) take this one step further when they say that religion is concerned with the explanation and expression of the ultimate values of a society. To Durkheim, the ultimate function of religion and its "collective representations" is to enforce social solidarity on its members; he thus would have appreciated Oscar Wilde's adage, "Man created God in his own image," for in the Durkheimian view, by worshiping God, society was in effect worshiping itself.

Durkheimian theory has had an enormous effect on anthropology, particularly on British functionalism and French structuralism, and is probably largely correct. But if system maintenance – social stability – were its only function, then religion could have little influence on social change. It was Max Weber in his landmark essay of 1905, *The Protestant Ethic and the Spirit of Capitalism* (Weber 1930), who tried successfully to answer the problem of "whether men's conceptions of the cosmic universe, including those of Divinity and men's religious interests within such a conceptual framework could influence or shape their concrete actions and social relationships, particularly in the very mundane field of economic action" (Parsons 1963:xxi). By showing, through the comparison of several civilizations, that only a Calvinistic Protestant ethic could have led to modern capitalism, Weber was not really pitting "ideal" against "material" in the question of causation, but showing, in contrast to Marxist theory, that at various times in history, either one could be the *independent,* and the other, the *dependent* variable. In the evolution of society Weber gave "prime causal significance to the factor of 'religious orientation' as an initiating factor and as a differentiating factor in the process." However, he treated this factor as " 'actualizing itself'. . . [only] through highly complex processes of interaction with other factors . . ." (Parsons 1963:LX).

According to Weber (1956:209), religious ethics penetrate social institutions in very different ways. The decisive aspect of the religious ethic is not the intensity of its attachment to magic or ritual or the distinctive character of the religion generally but, rather, its "theoretical attitude towards the world." An ethic that rejects the world, such as Theravada Buddhism, is going to lead to a very different form of society than one that accepts it as it is (i.e., Confucianism).

Ever since the days of James Mooney, anthropologists have devoted a great deal of study to religions whose vowed intent is to overthrow the establishment and to replace it with a new order. Wallace (1956) has called such religions "revitalization movements." These are usually responses to real and/or perceived cultural deprivation and often take the form of messianic, millenarian, and rejectionist ideals. We are familiar with such religions in the recent imperialist past, such as the Ghost Dance of the Plains and the cargo cults of Melanesia. We are even familiar with such cultures in the more distant past, for instance, the rise of Christianity and extreme Jewish cults as a response to Roman imperialism. One wonders whether such initially destructive religious movements arose in the even more remote past, such as during the rise of state societies and the consolidation of the power of elites. With one possible exception, the testimony of Mesoamerica is mute on this subject.

Finally, we should touch on the subject of state religions, because these are what finally came to be in most areas of Mesoamerica. In his study of the sociology of religion, Joachim Wach (1944) was one of the few religious theoreticians to deal with this subject. Based upon comparative data from archaeology and ethnography, he proposed an evolutionary sequence of three stages. Stage 1 is marked by the identity of secular and religious groups, with a state integrated by common exclusive worship of representative deities and by a ruler who both governs his subjects and intercedes with the gods on their behalf. Stage 2 sees a fuller development of government and a cultic organization with relatively greater independence or even autonomy for the latter. The head of the priestly organization now has great importance, and the religion is still ethnic and even tribal in character, with no claims to universality. Often there are dual centers, one secular and the other sacred. In stage 3 there is a high degree of political development, coupled with claims of universality on the part of the religious community; by suggesting that a religious group can even, in a sense, "conquer" the state, I presume that Wach is thinking of the Roman Empire under Christianity or what happened to Near Eastern states under early Islam.

In terms of Mesoamerica, as we will see, stages 1 and 2 certainly existed and perhaps even coexisted, but there is no evidence for stage 3 for any Mesoamerican peoples on any level of development.

The Mesoamerican religious system

Thanks to the efforts of native intelligentsia and the early Spanish friars, we have an immense body of data on the religious system of the Aztec, and even on their philosophy and ideals. We have considerably less information on the Maya and only the spottiest accounts for other peoples like the Zapotec, Mixtec, and Tarascans. Nevertheless, bolstered by epigraphic and iconographic research on the Maya, it has become increasingly clear that in spite of local specializations (such as tutelary deities), there was something like a pan-Mesoamerican religious system with roots in the distant past. Opposing such a view in favor of partial or total discontinuities in time and space are George Kubler and Tatiana Proskouriakoff, but this is now a minority standpoint (Nicholson 1976). By positing such a grand system, I do not wish to imply that this was in any way a universal religion, for the Mesoamericans never seem to have made any effort to proselytize elsewhere, and there was never any element of messianic fervor in their beliefs and rituals.

The integration of time with space is one of the most important concepts in this system: The contemporary Zinacantan Maya wending his way among hilltop shrines in accord with the dictates of his calendar is carrying on an ancient tradition. The basis of the calendar is a sacred count of 260 days, consisting of twenty day names permutating with the coefficients 1 through 13. The day names represent animals (like jaguar), plants, and natural forces, such as wind, death, and darkness. Each day name had its own presiding deity, its own fortune, and, most importantly, its own association with a color and cardinal direction, preceding in a counterclockwise fashion, thus automatically linking space with time. Intermeshing with the sacred count is the approximate solar year of 365 days, divided into eighteen months of twenty days each and a final, unlucky period of five days. Among both the Aztec and Maya, great public rituals (and private ones for segments of society like the so-called merchants) were geared to both kinds of calendar.

The Mesoamerican universe can be looked at in one way as a space–time continuum. There are the four cardinal directions previously described, intimately linked with the 260-day count, specific colors, and world trees. This concept is widespread not only in the New World but also on the other side of the Pacific basin and probably has a common origin. A fifth world direction is the Center, with a great "World Tree of Abundance" standing there rising up through the heavens. Two further directions, making a total of seven, are the Zenith and Nadir. Looked at another way, the universe is layered, probably like an onion, in Ptolemaic fashion. There is the earth's surface, probably conceived of as the back of a gigantic saurian floating in a pond or ocean. Above us are the thirteen layers of heaven, each with its appropriate celestial body, force, and presiding deity; below are the nine Underworlds or "Places of the Dead." Although the souls of those who had died by some special form of death, such as childbirth or drowning, proceeded to the heavens, the ultimate destination of everybody else was the deepest, uttermost hell; in the pessimistic Mesoamerican outlook, the fate of all but the elite was to suffer extinction there.

This universe came into being through successive acts of creation, and the idea of movement through time and space of everything is implicit in the creation stories, as is the notion of cyclicity, which the Mesoamericans shared with the ancient Greeks and Hindus. A dualistic creator deity, conceived of as an aged male–female god–goddess, resides in the thirteenth heaven; they mate and begin the process; thus creation equals procreation. From this union spring four young divinities, each assigned to a specific color-direction. Between two of these, one the patron of the warriors and the other the patron of the priests, begins a cosmic struggle for supremacy that both creates and destroys successive worlds. There have been four such universes in the past, the last one annihilated by floods. Our own universe, the fifth, is destined to end by earthquakes. This world outlook is, of course, profoundly pessimistic, because everything we know and love is destined, like ourselves, for universal destruction. Such a philosophy and ethic are bound to have resulted in ways of dealing with the world, which were profoundly different from those in the progress-oriented society that has existed in the West since at least the beginning of the Rennaissance.

The continued motion of the heavenly bodies – the sun, the moon, and Venus were the most important – is a sign that our own creation is not yet going to end. Each day the sun rises in the east, borne by the Fire Serpent, an avatar of the old male–female creator pair. As it reaches the noon sky, five malevolent women, the souls of those who had died in childbirth, rise up from the west and bear it down on its journey into the Underworld. To ensure that the sun would rise again from its period of temporary death, it has to be nourished with human blood, either that drawn from one's own body or from human sacrifices. The Aztec creation myth explicitly states that human beings were brought into existence at the start of the fifth universe so that they might make war upon each other and provide the necessary sacrificial victims for the nourishment of the sun.

There is little question that the Mesoamericans truly believed that the ultimate fate of the world as we know it was destruction. It so happens that the apparent cycles of the sacred count, the sun, and Venus coincide every 104 vague solar years, and the Aztec, at any rate, held the endings of such "centuries" to be critical moments, with special ceremonies ensuring the continued movement of the heavens at that time. For the Maya, it is likely that they thought such destructions would occur at the end of their 13 baktun cycle, a period somewhat larger than 5,000 years.

Nicholson's (1971) magnificent synthesis of central Mexican religion has demonstrated that the bewildering multiplicity of Aztec deities can be simplified in several ways. First, many or most supernaturals can be seen as having quadripartite natures, in line with the color-direction principle in Mesoamerican thought. Second, there is the concept of youth and age: the very sexual young moon goddess, for instance, has a somewhat malevolent and aged avatar who functions as a patroness of weavers and curers, both surely symbolizing the waxing and waning moon. Third, there are entire complexes of deities whose aspects and accoutrements may blend into each other: The lunar goddesses just described may include other female supernaturals connected with water, salt, sweat baths, confession, and illicit sexuality. Several supernatural complexes were surely associated with agriculture and the natural forces ensuring its success; these include a rain god and his consort, a goddess of water who runs across the ground. After the holocaust of the Spanish Conquest, it is these agricultural cults that have survived in peasant form.

If Durkheimian theory is correct, state religions should closely reflect the inequalities of a highly stratified society, and this is surely true of Aztec and Classic Maya religion. It has been my good luck to discover that God K, the so-called "mannikin scepter god" of the Classic Maya — the most common divinity of elite power displays on the Maya monuments — is cognate to the great Aztec god Tezcatlipoca. We know from prayers recorded in Book VI of Sahagun's encyclopedia that the latter was the patron of the royal house, invoked at coronations, and that he was thought of as the offspring of the male–female creator god–goddess. Thus the Mesoamerican rulers aligned themselves with the central axis of the universe and with creation itself, setting themselves off symbolically as a race apart from ordinary humankind. Lesser groups within Mesoamerican society had their own divinities and rituals, such as the "merchants" and the priests, and in fact the complexity of these advanced societies was closely reflected in the supernatural division of labor expressed in these elaborate pantheons. Apparently entire cities or ceremonial centers had their tutelary divinities, of which one of the great Aztec divinities, Huitzilopochtli, who guided them to Tenochtitlán, is the most renowned. There has been some debate about what the emblem glyphs peculiar to each Classic Maya center really stand for, some favoring place names, others, lineage names; but given the central Mexican example, these could well be the tutelary divinities of the place.

As Miguel León-Portilla (1963) has made clear in his great work on Aztec thought, although all the people were deeply religious, there was a group in Aztec society that specialized in deeply philosophical questions, such as the meaning of life and death and the destiny of humankind after death. This class of thinkers probably existed among the elite of all Mesoamerican state societies, and perhaps at even a simpler level of social development. For instance, among the Navajo of southwestern United States, some curing specialists are persons of deep esoteric and even scientific knowledge, and such "men of high degree" are known around the world from supposedly simple, tribal societies. With a people like the Classic Maya, such specialists must have been formidable indeed.

In accordance with the grim cyclicity of their cosmology, these great thinkers were prophets of universal doom, an outlook that finds expression in some of the greatest poetry of the Nahuatl language. But León-Portilla points up another aspect of their philosophy: an ingrained dualism that often approaches a Hegelian dialectic. To the thinkers, the entire universe in all of its bewildering complexity was but an emanation of the basic principle of duality and all of the supernatural world as well as the natural was encompassed in the persona of the old male–female god–goddess of creation. This almost Manichaean dualism can be seen throughout Aztec, and by extension, Mesoamerican life: male versus female, youth versus old age, life versus death, the heavens versus the underworlds, the priesthood versus the warrior orders. The cosmic struggle between Tezcatlipoca and Quetzalcoatl, resulting in multiple creations, brings to light the Hegelian nature of the Mesoamerican dialectic: that movements through time and space result from the synthesis of opposing forces.

This, then, in capsule form is the Mesoamerican world view; although based largely upon Aztec data, I have presented nothing that, in my opinion, cannot be found among the Classic Maya as well. It will be noted that there is no doctrine of personal salvation, no idea of progress, no claims of universality. The idea of sin and expiation was definitely present but in a different form from that given to us by the Judeo-Christian tradition, and even different from the *kharma* of Buddhism. In all sources, sins seem to have been restricted to transgressions, sexual and otherwise, of the rather rigid behavioral ethic of the Mesoamericans, but there were no rewards or punishments in the afterlife or in future lives for one's actions in this world. Excepting always the ruling caste, the pessimistic Mesoamerican philosophy saw total extinction as the end of the road for all, whether good or bad.

The archaeological record

It is unfortunate that the earliest complex society of Mesoamerica, the Olmec, has left no written records. Not only does this make it difficult to talk about the relation between religion and Olmec society, but it is virtually impossible to decide whether Olmec polities were chiefdoms or states. Frankly, I do not think that the latter distinction is important. What *is* important here, however, is that we have the first fully stratified societies in Mesoamerica, with political, economic, and religious power in the hands of an elite, which probably was hereditary. From our work at the site complex of San Lorenzo Tenochtitlán, we have gathered a great deal of evidence to show that the move toward sociopolitical complexity, beginning some time before 1200 B.C., followed the lines of Carneiro's "circumscription theory" (Carneiro 1970). In fact, the process must have followed the same scenario for the middle Amazon chiefdoms, with restricted river levee lands of immensely high productivity being co-opted by one or more lineages through success in war. In this case, if one has to look for prime movers, then the factors invoked by Carneiro fit the case very well, indeed.

If one does not look at San Lorenzo Olmec sculpture and ceramics, this picture is indeed satisfying from the material-determinist point of view. But we have some sixty-five basalt monuments from San Lorenzo alone, plus another ten or so from outlying sites. These bear the stamp of a highly complex, codified religion, with a highly diversified pantheon, probably cognate with that of later Mesoamerican religions (Joralemon 1971:1976). It used to be thought that all Olmec religious representations could be reduced to a were-jaguar divinity, product of a mystical union of jaguar and human mother, and that this was some sort of "rain god." There probably was a rain god, but the high differentiation of supernatural representations in this and other Olmec sites of the "heartland" (southern Veracruz and Tabasco) suggests that Olmec iconography reflects the social and economic division of labor within a complex, stratified society.

What puzzles me is that there is virtually no real iconography, or any real art at all, prior to the Olmec explosion of 1200 B.C. We have earlier occupations at San Lorenzo going back to about 1500 B.C., and pre-1200 B.C. levels have been excavated in many other areas of Mesoamerica. Where are the gods? Prior to 1200 B.C., all one has are baked clay figurines, such as those of the Ocós culture of Chiapas and Guatemala, and these provide no hint of anything resembling god images. The possibility exists, however, that a few Olmec sculptures of aberrant form, which were deposited in the destruction levels of San Lorenzo about 900 B.C., come from pre-1200 B.C. contexts. These are rude columns with low bas reliefs, one of which exhibits the face of some kind of Olmec deity.

Both ecological and art historical data from San Lorenzo imply, therefore, that the rise of stratified society and the evolution of the visibly expressed Mesoamerican pantheon happened at an extraordinarily fast rate and went hand-in-hand. This is in strong contrast to ancient Peru and the Near East, where the evolution of religious structures and art seems to proceed along more conventional lines, at a slower rate. Was there a Weberian "religious orientation" that preceded the quantum jump in societal and religious development that we see at San Lorenzo? Did the Mesoamerican world view that I have outlined already exist? If we had written documents, these questions could be more easily answered. Clear-cut split-face dualism is present in masks from Olmec-influenced burial offerings at Tlatilco in the Valley of Mexico, a site that is largely contemporaneous with the San Lorenzo phase. Human sacrifice is more than suggested by cannibalized human remains that we found in San Lorenzo contexts. And there may have been dual capitals at that time in the Olmec heartland, for the poorly investigated site of Laguna de los Cerros, although only 55 kms. northwest of San Lorenzo, is at least as large as San Lorenzo itself and is its exact contemporary. The possibility suggests itself of a religious and a secular center, along the lines of Wach's classification.

Thus the evidence for the influence of religious thought and behavior upon the rise of Mesoamerica's first civilization is yet equivocal. We do not know, for instance, whether they even had the 260-day count, although this is likely because several later civilizations, ultimately derived from the Olmec, share this basic calendar along with names for the days that are completely cognate.

Although there is debate about whether or not the Olmec culture was a state civilization, there is no question about Classic Teotihuacán having reached that status. Situated in a small valley opening into the Valley of Mexico on its northeastern side, from the time of Christ until well after A.D. 600, it dominated the rest of Mesoamerica as a military, manufacturing, and mercantile power, with a population of well over 150,000 souls: a true merchant city. It would be convenient to be able to point out a long and slow development of urbanism in central Mexico culminating in this mighty city. The only trouble is that there is nothing like it until Teotihuacán itself appears. And according to the archaeological surveys and mapping undertaken by René Millon and his colleagues, it just about appears in full-blown form (Millon 1973). At about the start of the Christian era, what had been a large village or small town in the northwestern part of the city was suddenly totally transformed into a vast, planned city, laid out on a regular, grid pattern. This grid was oriented astronomically to a point about 15 degrees east of true north, and the metropolis was divided into four quarters by a pair of great avenues intersecting at the theoretical center of the site.

That this was a mercantile center of great importance is beyond question, with local obsidian being the main export. Millon estimates that more than 25 percent of the population was engaged in craft activities and more than five hundred workshops have been located, along with barrios occupied by foreign traders. Certainly tribute would have poured into Teotihuacán from its conquered provinces at a great rate.

But what led to the establishment of such an urban state? Sanders and his colleagues (1970) have made much of the great ecological potential of the Teotihuacán Valley, which has the possibility for limited irrigation. However, this rather restricted environment could never have been the raison d'être for its rise in this particular place. Here I think that we will have to look at the factor of "religious orientation," *à la* Weber. The mere fact of its odd compass orientation suggests a preoccupation with religio-astronomical matters, not practical matters. Several authors have noted the strange relationship of Teotihuacán to its topographical surroundings, particularly that of the Pyramid of the Moon at the end of the Avenue of the Dead, which seems echoed in the Cerro Gordo that rises up above it. And the division into four quarters calls to mind the four world directions of the Mesoamerican cosmological scheme.

The archaeological facts make it fairly clear that Teotihuacán, perhaps even before the Teotihuacán state had taken form, was planned and laid out as a tour de force by one man or a small group of persons. Where they acquired their knowledge of surveying is a mystery, but they were obviously skilled astronomers. Why did they put the city exactly there, as there are surely better locations for an urban center in the Valley of Mexico? One might think that a location nearer the Great Lake would have been more feasible. But in central Mexican mythology, Teotihuacán plays a major role in events leading to the final shape of the present universe, with the gods themselves performing acts of self-immolation in the successful effort to get the sun and the moon to move in the sky. I am convinced that this site was in some important way connected in their minds with the center of the world and the act of creation. Two additional factors reinforce this point. One is the discovery of a natural, cloverleaf-shaped cavern directly underneath the center of the Pyramid of the Sun, the greatest structure at Teotihuacán. As Heyden (1975) has shown, a cavern of this shape would have many associations, particularly as a womblike "place of emergence" from which the people would have come in the mythical past. The other is my hypothesis that the reliefs on the so-called Ciudadela at the very center of the city represent the initial creation of the universe from a watery void through a series of dual oppositions. Because this was probably the royal enclosure itself, the rulers of Teotihuacán established for themselves an identity with the dual creator divinity and the power emanating from him/her.

I do not argue that the Mesoamerican mind-set was the causal factor in the evolution of the central Mexican state. Certainly the proximity of abundant obsidian sources both in the Teotihuacán Valley and elsewhere helped in the process. But surely at the beginning, religious factors were interacting in complex and subtle ways with economic ones to produce this highly successful polity, which endured for over six centuries as the leader of Mesoamerica. In my estimation, the people of Teotihuacán believed that they lived at the center of the world, where our universe had been created, and this must have given them the feeling of certainty that they were destined to govern this universe. Much the same way in the much later Aztec politician Tlacaelel gave the Aztec tribe the feeling that they were destined to keep the universe going in time and space by providing a constant supply of hearts and blood as food for the hungry sun.

In examining the relation between state and religion in central Mexico, one has to tackle this question: Why, if trade and production were so important, did not a real merchant class arise? As is well known, there was a so-called merchant class among the Aztec, the *pochteca*. It is highly likely that these existed in Teotihuacán, too. Many have wanted to see this as some sort of rising middle class, gradually coming into competition with the hereditary nobility. But a reading of Weber's 1905 essay would show how completely improbable such a state of affairs would have been in pre-Spanish Mesoamerica, for the Mesoamerican ethic simply did not allow such traits of advanced mercantilism as the accumulation of capital (Sahagún [1959] is explicit on this), loaning at interest, and so forth. In fact, the merchants were heavily sanctioned and tabooed from the supernatural point of view and even had their own gods and rites. The state that the Spaniards discovered in Tenochtitlán in 1519 was far from capitalistic.

Finally, one should mention the Classic and Postclassic Maya, for here, in a totally different environment, we find states that had adopted alternative, somewhat nonurban ways of coping with complex sociopolitical life and large populations. For more than a century it has been argued that the ancient Maya were so religiously oriented that they were under the control of priests. Modern epigraphic advances show that there is not a shred of truth in this assertion. On the other hand, it is surely true that much of the public architecture at Classic Maya sites had a religious function; and although the figures carved on monuments are now known to be secular lords and ladies, they are covered with and surrounded by accoutrements that are virtual symphonies of religious iconography. Recent research has demonstrated that some, perhaps most of this iconography, is directly comparable to the pantheistic iconography of later central Mexico.

Several lines of inquiry have shown the extraordinary elaboration of the Classic Maya concern with the elite dead: richly stocked burials, funerary vessels with pictorial representations of the underworlds and their macabre denizens, funerary monuments built over the tombs in the manner of Egyptian pyramids, and posthumous dynastic records. All this testifies to a kind of ancestor worship involving the ruling elite. Deceased rulers and their relatives were, on death, identified with the gods and were worshiped as such. A Maya city, beyond its economic and political functions, was in a way a vast necropolis, a "city of the dead." One can infer over this a pattern of calendrical rituals and ceremonial circuits, perhaps even following an ideal four-way division as dictated by the Mesoamerican world view.

These seem to have been the major preoccupations of the elite in the stratified city states of the Classic Maya. It is difficult to determine how far back this goes, as earlier remains, covered by the burden of later constructions, are difficult to get at. There is reason to believe that the Classic Maya religious system was in full gear by the opening of the Classic by about A.D. 300, because at least some of the gods and even the funerary texts found on elite ceramics are somewhat earlier. But the evidence is less clear for the role of "religious orientation" in the rise of the Classic Maya state, although it must have been a powerful factor in the siting of cities and their planning and in bringing power into the hands of the elite caste.

At the other end of the Classic time scale one can see some interesting things happening to both religion and state. Beginning at about A.D. 800, and culminating around A.D. 900, the sociopolitical and religiouscoatt system of the Maya elite was annihilated throughout much of the lowlands, and most of the Classic cities were abandoned, probably through a combination of revolution and foreign invasions. In Postclassic Yucatán, as recorded by Diego de Landa, we see little statelets forming after a period of Toltec domination. In place of the pantheistic ancestor worship and intense funerary cult of the Classic Maya, we find a religion centering on the Feathered Serpent (Quetzalcoatl or Kukulcán), a god unknown among the

Classic Maya but ancient in the central Mexican highlands, particularly at Teotihúacán. Now this deity associated with the Mexican priesthoods, was far from the most important god in his homeland. On the other hand, he enjoyed a powerful cult, almost to the exclusion of other gods, in Yucatán, under the protection of upstart rulers of generally Mexican extraction.

In his homeland, the Feathered Serpent was considered to be a fair-skinned, bearded deity with a message of benevolence for humankind. He was supposed to have abhorred human sacrifice, to have brought the arts to people as a culture-bearer, and, through the machinations of Tezcatlipoca, the god of warriors, to have been expelled from his native land, to return some day. It is no surprise that some of the Spanish missionaries took him to be Saint Thomas, although they probably were really thinking of Jesus. To me, this peculiar and rather non-Mesoamerican cult among the survivors of the Classic debacle suggests a revitalization movement. Could the overthrow of Classic Maya society and the downfall of the old elite have been brought about by the introduction of a new cult? If so, it would be the only Mesoamerican instance of anything smacking of messianism.

Conclusions
Certainly the nature of the Mesoamerican religious system put its stamp on the final form of the Mesoamerican states or near-states that have been considered here. The state religions, with their elaborate, calendrically governed rituals, reflected these highly stratified societies along thoroughly Durkheimian lines. These reached their extreme form among the Classic Maya, with their obsession with ancestor worship and the deification of the honored dead. Given a knowledge of this system, such mysteries as why the Aztec rulers should have made a treaty for perpetual war with some of their neighbors, instead of for peace, can be readily answered. Even the very forms of cities and the reason for their location can, in part, be explained through the religious orientation of the Mesoamericans. I believe that religious considerations have been important factors in the rise of complex societies and in the formation and perpetuation of elites. In the case of Teotihuacán there is strong evidence that religious factors led a small number of elites in central Mexico to initiate urban civilization in Mesoamerica.

To deny that religious factors have intertwined with sociopolitical and economic ones throughout history and prehistory is to ignore the facts. These factors have often operated, however, in strange and unforeseen ways. Who could have predicted that the Spaniards under Cortés, with his white face and beard, would have arrived in Veracruz in A.D. 1519, in the very same named year in which the

Feathered Serpent was supposed to have been born? And yet, in view of this and given the Mesoamerican cosmological outlook, it was virtually inevitable that Motecuhzoma, the emperor, would have welcomed the Spaniards as gods and invited Cortés – bent only on Motecuhzoma's destruction – into his palace in the heart of the empire. The fatal pessimism implicit in the concept of universes condemned to destruction led Motecuhzoma to a logical conclusion: that the world of Mexico-Tenochtitlán was doomed and that these gods had been sent to effect its annihilation.

In searching for ultimate causalities, for prime movers, in the evolution of the state, we have perhaps overlooked the complexities of the situation. Archaeologists who think about these matters would perhaps be best off following Weber's lead, in examining all possible variables and keeping an open mind about which conditions might be independent and which dependent. Above all, we cannot afford to overlook that central concern of a century of anthropology – religion as an important factor in the development of all ancient societies.

7

The nature and role of religious diffusion in the early stages of state formation: an example from Peruvian prehistory

RICHARD W. KEATINGE*

In a recent article appearing in the journal *World Archaeology*, Joyce Marcus (1978:172) makes the point that among archaeologists "there is absolutely no agreed-upon theoretical or methodological framework for dealing with prehistoric religion." In confronting the general problem of the evolution of the state in prehistory, archaeologists find it difficult to ignore the wealth of data characterized as being of a religious or "ceremonial" nature. And yet the role of religion as an important mechanism in the development of increasingly stratified societies is often given short shrift by comparison to the interest shown in technoeconomic or sociopolitical variables. This seems particularly strange in light of the fact that there is ample evidence indicating that religion played a critical role in the cultural evolution of each of the six world areas where pristine states arose.

The purpose of this chapter is to examine the role of religious ideology in the development of the state by focusing on selected aspects of Peruvian prehistory. The major points reviewed will be the following:

1. The evolution of state society in Peru owed a great deal to the widespread influence of an early religious movement.
2. This religious movement was responsible in large part for the initial fostering of interregional trade and communications.
3. In general, religion provided a cohesiveness to Peruvian societies prior to the evolution of state sanctions based upon the use of coercive force.
4. The evolution of religious ideology, and to a certain extent even the temple buildings themselves, was intimately intertwined with the development of economic and redistributive systems.

*The author would like to acknowledge the insightful comments and editorial assistance of Elsie Begler during the preparation of this chapter.

5. The development of a more complex economic system, even though associated with the ascendance of political power and an increased secularization in the goals of society, does not necessarily imply that the role of religion was consequently diminished.

In my view, religion is best seen as an enabler or catalyst that provided an avenue for the manipulation of populations and thereby laid the foundation for control over strategic resources. In terms of cultural evolution it seems clear that religious ideology provided both the means and the sanctions for an increasing secularization in the goals of developing societies, goals whose emphasis became inexorably politicoeconomic. It thus comes as no surprise that the development of religion – and here I am referring generally to ideas as well as to physical manifestations such as buildings – within prehistoric state societies was associated with and, in fact, fostered the evolution of economic structures. In its ultimate format, this increasing politicoeconomic role of religious ideology eventually led to the use of religious sanctions to validate the prosecution of militaristic policies so evident in the late preconquest empires of the New World.

Although few would deny the importance of ecological or politicoeconomic variables, an argument can also be made that theories of cultural evolution must take into account belief and value systems as well (Willey 1962; M. Coe 1968; Flannery 1972). The grounds for this contention lie in the fact that these ideological systems may well have had a great deal to do with the actual regulation of humanenvironmental interactions (Flannery and Marcus 1976b). As Gordon Willey (1976:205), has pointed out, "it seems highly probable that, from early on, ideas provided controls for and gave distinctive forms to the materialist base and to culture, and that these ideas then took on a kind of existence of their own, influencing, as well as being influenced by, other cultural systems." One can, I think, argue that in dealing with prehistoric religion we are grappling with something more than simply "epiphenomena" and that, in fact, gods, goods, and politics are not at all incompatible. Let us now turn to some examples.

The Chavín phenomenon
In Peru the template for the role of religion in the development of state level societies is most graphically illustrated in the cultural manifestation known as Chavín, which is associated with the Early Horizon time period. Ever since Julio C. Tello (1943, 1960) discovered Chavín de Huántar, the so-called type site for the Chavín phenomenon, a considerable amount of effort has been expended by archaeologists attempting to define the nature of what has been variously referred to as the Chavín cult, religion, and art style. Be-

ginning between 1000 and 800 B.C. and continuing to sometime
between 200 B.C. and the time of Christ, Chavín solidified the trend
toward the religious permeation of prehistoric Peruvian societies
that was to continue until the time of the Spanish Conquest. As
exemplified in some twenty-five to thirty major temple centers as
well as in numerous minor ones, the Chavín cult has traditionally
been characterized as spreading rapidly into virtually all major environmental zones of Peru and as maintaining itself for upward of
1000 years (Tello 1923; Larco Hoyle 1941; Willey 1948, 1951; Carrion Cachot 1948; Bennett and Bird 1949; Rowe 1962, 1967).
Among archaeologists who have considered the question (see Benson 1971, for a recent review), it is generally thought that Chavín
was a religion spread by peaceful proselytizing missionaries, not unlike the spread of Christianity throughout the Mediterranean world
(Patterson 1971b:42–3). This rapid spread, the elaborate art style,
and the lack of associated fortifications have tended to support this
particular view. Such an interpretation, however, implies a certain
amount of centralization or theocratic unity, which close examination of the evidence suggests may be an oversimplification of a complex system of interaction.

   The type site for the Chavín art style is Chavín de Huántar, located on a tributary of the Marañón River in the northern highlands. The focus of this site is a large, stone-faced temple, which was
enlarged in several stages and is honeycombed with dark, narrow
internal galleries. Each of the major remodeling phases of the
temple follows a U-shaped plan, with the arms of the earlier U-
shaped structure encompassing a circular sunken plaza (Lumbreras
1977:11–14) and those of the later structure, a rectangular sunken
plaza. The use of this U-shaped plan in conjunction with sunken
courts is strongly reminiscent of the similar, in many cases, earlier,
structures on the central coast (Williams 1971, 1972). The most striking features of the site, however, are the many relief-carved monuments associated with the different construction phases of the
temple. Rowe (1962, 1967) has seriated these monuments into a
sequence tied to the Ocucaje ceramic sequence of the Ica Valley on
the south coast of Peru. Each of Rowe's phases is associated with a
different deity found carved on a major stone monument. The earliest of these major monuments depicts the Lanzón or Smiling God,
followed by the Tello Obelisk depicting a cayman, and, finally, the
Raimondi Stela depicting a Staff God. Other stone monuments at
the site are seriated on the basis of their stylistic similarity to these
three monuments. Ceramics from the site have been analyzed by
Lumbreras and Amat Olazábal (1969) and Lumbreras (1971, 1972,
1974b, 1977), producing a multiphase sequence based upon excavations conducted from 1966 to 1972. Burger (1978) has recently reex-

amined this earlier work and developed his own three-phase ceramic sequence. Because of the general lack of published ceramic information from many other Chavín-related sites, and in the absence of absolute dates, sites that manifest attributes of the Chavín monumental art style as known from Chavín de Huántar are chronologically placed on the basis of their similarity to one or more of the phases represented by the major monuments that provide the key to Rowe's sequence (e.g., Roe 1974).

Precursors of Chavín
Although Chavín de Huántar is an impressive site, both in its art works and in its monumental architecture, it nevertheless is not an anomaly either for its time or in terms of the social organization reflected in its size. Important premonitions of the rise of Chavín are amply available in the archaeological record for the preceding Late Preceramic (2500–1800 B.C.) and Initial periods (c. 1800–1000 B.C.). On the central coast, sites such as El Paraíso (Engel 1967), Aspero (Willey and Corbett 1954; Moseley and Willey 1973; Moseley 1975; Feldman 1977a; 1977b), Piedra Parada (Moseley 1975; Feldman 1977b), and Las Haldas (Engel 1957; 1970; Fung Pineda 1969a, b; Grieder 1975; Matsuzawa 1978), all indicate the existence of labor organizations capable of constructing large religious temples. Huaca La Florida (Lanning 1967:90–4; Patterson and Moseley 1968:119–20) in the Rímac Valley and, perhaps, Sechín Alto (Tello 1956:26–7, 79–83; Collier 1962; Thompson 1964; Fung Pineda 1972) in the Casma Valley attest to the considerable abilities of these pre-Chavín polities to construct elaborate ceremonial structures on a truly gigantic scale. Sechín Alto, which may well have construction phases dating to the Initial period, is estimated to be some fifteen times the size of the temple at Chavín de Huántar (Moseley 1978:521).

It is also of particular importance to note that these early temple complexes were often built in a U-shaped pattern accompanied by a sunken circular or rectangular plaza (Williams 1971; 1972; Ravines 1975:8). In the highlands, successively used Preceramic temples were constructed at the site of Kotosh (Izumi and Terada 1972) in the Huallaga drainage. Construction at the large site of Pacopampa (Rosas La Noire and Shady Solis 1970; Rosas La Noire 1976; Fung Pineda 1975) located in the Upper Marañón drainage may predate Chavín de Huántar by a considerable margin. In every case – and the possible examples have by no means been exhausted – the monumental constructions at these sites with pre-Chavín occupations are clearly directed toward a ceremonial purpose. In light of this fact, one would be hard put to conclude that the advent of Chavín was correlated with the introduction of some new form of control over the manipulation of labor. By the end of the Initial period, labor in the service of religion was already a long-established attribute of Andean society and neither the florescence of Chavín nor its demise, for that matter, changed this basic practice.

Regional variations in Chavín influence

The point to be made, then, is that although it seems plausible that during the 1000-year time span of Chavín influence a pan-Peruvian religious foundation was established, this foundation was itself based upon earlier, regional precursors. Moreover, as Willey (1951) pointed out some time ago, and as Burger (1978) has reemphasized more recently, the impact of Chavín varied greatly from region to region – at least as far as can be determined by examining similarities and differences in monumental art style and ceramics. In the highlands, after long periods of local development, both Pacopampa and Kotosh became dominated by Chavín artistic traits. However, at Pacopampa, although there is a clear desire to imitate Chavín de Huántar in both remodeled architecture (including the construction of a sunken rectangular plaza) and stone sculpture, the ceramics of the Pacopampa Chavín phase incorporate Chavín designs in a distinctive local fashion. This results in "a non-Chavín style, more closely tied to its local antecedents than to the ceramic style from where the new traits emanated" (Burger 1978:387). These changes have been interpreted as indicating that Pacopampa may well have remained an important and perhaps independent center in its own right (Burger 1978:343, 397). On the other hand, Kotosh and the Upper Huallaga region were completely overrun by the ceramic style of Chavín de Huántar and the traditional settlement pattern of the region was disrupted (Izumi 1971:67), prompting the assertion that the region may well have been subordinated to Chavín in terms of administration, religion, and social interaction (Burger 1978:397).

On the coast there are numerous sites showing varying degrees of Chavín influence, combined with a considerable amount of regional or local variation. One need only look at the elaborate murals of Garagay in the Rímac Valley (Ravines and Isbell 1975; Ravines 1975) or the adobe sculpture of Moxeke in the Casma Valley (Tello 1956) and Huaca de los Reyes in the Moche Valley (Moseley and Watanabe 1974; Pozorski 1975, 1976) to obtain an idea of this variation in stylistic attributes. Such a contrast in regional style can also be seen in the Paracas ceramics (Menzel et al. 1964) from the Ica Valley on the south coast and the Cupisnique style of the north coast (Larco Hoyle 1941, 1945a, 1948). As Menzel et al. (1964:258) have pointed out, "the maintenance of local specialties makes the Paracas style in general, and its Ica variants in particular, at all times a distinctive one, very different from the Chavín influenced styles in central and northern Peru." The Cupisnique ceramics can be viewed in a similar fashion, constituting a distinct regional style centered in the Chicama Valley with its own unique set of Chavín affiliations (Willey 1951: 116–17; Burger 1978:362, 365–6).

A region-by-region survey of the effect of Chavín would seem to indicate that the acceptance of Chavín artistic attributes was in many cases *highly* selective. Local or regional religions were well established by the late Initial period, prior to the florescence and spread of Chavín. Certainly the importance of Chavín de Huántar as *the* fount from which the Chavín phenomenon spread has been emphasized far beyond what the data can support (Pozorski 1976:289–90; Burger 1978:4). Chavín, as some sort of religious movement, may not have been so pervasive nor as unifying as one might think.

On the other hand, it may be that stylistic interpretations of the spread of Chavín are complicated or confounded by the fact that the portrayal of numerous traditional, local deities selectively took on specific artistic attributes with Chavín affinities. These local deities had roots not in Chavín but in their earlier precursors of the Preceramic period. The proliferation of these regional deities, which are distinct entities yet exhibit Chavín-related attributes, suggests certain relevant concepts from Hinduism in which divinities may take on a variety of aspects. As Leach (1962:85–6) has pointed out:

> Hinduism says that the cosmos embraces different deities whose functions are complementary... Even in Village Hinduism where the multiplicity of deities is a matter of homeliness rather than logical distinction the different members of the pantheon are not fully distinct from one another... In this way any Hindu deity can assume almost any role... Different aspects of deity are given emphasis in different kinds of context.

These different aspects of deity may well be what we see emphasized or modified from region to region throughout the area of Chavín influence.

On the other hand, the Ceylonese religious systems studied by Leach (1962) provide an example of religious syncretism that might serve as another model for the Peruvian situation during the Chavín era. This example of syncretism focuses on the elephant-headed Hindu diety, Ganesha, who is also worshiped by Ceylonese Buddhists. In the Hindu religion, Ganesha is the third son of Shiva (God) and his consort, the mother goddess Parvati. In this context, Ganesha is worshiped "as the doorkeeper of heaven, a trickster whose friendly help can clear all obstructions but whose enmity can cause disaster" (Leach 1962:80). However, among Ceylonese Buddhists, Ganesha is known by the name Pulleyar and is worshiped as the elephant lord of the forest. There is no cult to Shiva, no mother goddess, and Ganesha (Pulleyar) is viewed as merely a feudal dependent of the Lord Buddha. Yet the Hindu deity Ganesha is iconographically clearly recognizable in the Buddhist pantheon, though known by a different name and revered for distinct reasons.

This appearance of Ganesha in Ceylonese Buddhism can be explained by the fact that in Asia sectarianism is much less specific or restrictive than it is in Christendom. Following the belief that divinity has a variety of aspects, a Hindu follower of Shiva believes it is perfectly proper and normal to attend ceremonials of some other major deity. Such ceremonials will merely be reinterpreted by the Shiva follower in light of his own theological doctrine. For instance, followers of the Hindu deity Vishnu view Buddha as a manifestation of Vishnu; thus all Buddhist rites are also Vishnuite rites. This Asian attitude toward the nature of divinity makes it possible for Hindu, Buddhist, Moslem, and Christian pilgrims to participate together in religious festivals that primarily honor a deity of one of these religions, without feeling as though they are participating in heathen rites (Leach 1962:85).

The variation in regional manifestations of Chavín provides an example of the interpretive problem inherent in the iconographic analysis of prehistoric religions (Lyon 1978:97). In this case such variation may in part be attributed to religious syncretism, together with the fact that acceptance of the Chavín religious ideology was selective, varying by degrees from area to area. Furthermore, the evidence suggests that the Chavín religion may have been reinterpreted and combined with local belief systems, enhancing its level of acceptance by different regional audiences. At the least, the religious theology spread by Chavín must have been autonomously manipulated by the individual temple centers (Willey 1948:10). Such distinct religious manifestations do not automatically suggest a proselytizing missionary religion, which might be expected to produce a much more unified iconographic system. To the contrary, the evidence could also be interpreted as indicating a truly vast array of different temples or shrines that variously emphasized local or regional deities, incorporated specific Chavín deities into regional pantheons, or embellished local gods with differing degrees of Chavín-influenced attributes, and were tied, perhaps, in a loose fashion to a pan-Andean belief system.

Chavín influences upon later Peruvian religion

The Staff God
Whether through a truly unified religious movement or through the loose diffusion of ideas and symbolism, it nevertheless appears that within the 1000-year time span during which Chavín flourished,

something approaching a pan-Peruvian religious foundation was, in fact, established. Regardless of whether or not it emanated from a single, centralized source, this pan-Peruvian phenomenon can be seen as having a continuing effect on the evolution of later Peruvian societies (see Tello, 1923, for considerable elaboration on this theme). In support of this view it is perhaps important to emphasize that representations of the Staff God, which makes its first appearance as one of the central figures in the iconography of the Chavín cult, continued to appear long after the demise of Chavín. The Staff God was an important deity in the iconography of the highland Huari state of the Middle Horizon (A.D. 600–1000) and is found as far south as Bolivia where it occurs on the famous Gateway of the Sun at the site of Tiahuanaco, another important Middle Horizon center (Rowe 1962:21). Representations of this figure are also found among the north coast Moche and Chimú cultures, which cover the period from shortly after Chavín to just before the arrival of the Spanish. The fact that this particular figure continued to persist throughout the Peruvian area in the iconography of later, disparate cultures tends to support the pan-Andean nature of the religious foundation established during the Early Horizon. A similar though somewhat more abstract case has been made for the feline deity (Tello 1922, 1923).

Pilgrimage to oracle centers
Another feature of Peruvian religion whose ancestry may be traced to the Chavín cult is the practice of pilgrimage to centers of oracle worship. At the time of the Spanish Conquest in 1532, this practice was an important aspect of Inca religion (Rowe 1946:302), and there seems to be little doubt that it represents a long-standing tradition in Andean religion, predating the advent of the Inca by a considerable period of time. Evidence of the pilgrimage nature of Chavín de Huántar is provided in the form of exotic ceramics from a number of different areas (Burger 1978:116–24, 164–6, 236–9), including the Kotosh region, Cajamarca region, northern highlands, south central highlands, the Cupisnique area of the north coast (Lumbreras 1972:78), and possibly the central coast. There are also a number of other exotic shards whose provenience is as yet unknown. Furthermore, Chavín de Huántar has also produced evidence suggesting that it may have been the dwelling place of an oracle. This evidence consists of a room or passage located immediately above the gallery in which the carved figure of the Smiling God is located. The upper room and the gallery are connected via a small opening near the top of the Smiling God, and it is not too farfetched to suggest that voices coming from the upper room would be heard in the vicinity of the cult figure located below. There are also indica-

tions that oracles were an important element in the much later Huari state as well (Patterson 1971b:46).

When the Spanish arrived in Peru, the site of Pachacamac located
in the Lurin Valley just south of Lima was still functioning as a
major oracle center. Spanish chroniclers describing the situation record that the oracle at Pachacamac was so ancient and powerful that
even when the Incas conquered the coastal region they did not dare
destroy the site; they merely ordered that a temple to the sun be
erected alongside the much older temple housing the oracle (Cieza
de León 1959:329, 336). Archaeological research conducted at the
site (Uhle 1903; Strong and Corbett 1943) supports these reports on
the age of the site, indicating that Pachacamac was a functioning
center at least as far back as the Middle Horizon and probably earlier. The ethnohistoric sources also record that long-distance religious pilgrimages to centers of oracle worship were an ongoing feature of Peruvian religion at the time of the Spanish Conquest (Cieza
de León 1959:242). People making pilgrimages to religious centers
were allowed to pass through territory from which they would nor-
mally have been prohibited. Such a practice is in many ways similar
to what we know of situations in other parts of the world where
pilgrimage religions developed. An especially pertinent example is
provided by the city of Mecca during the early history of Islam (c.
A.D. 400–700). There the Koreish, a group of traders who were
instrumental in the development of Mecca as both a religious and
economic center, guaranteed the inviolability of pilgrims on their
way to the holy center through a special pact with other tribal
groups (Caetani 1905:165, cited in Wolf 1951:338).

That pilgrims traveled long distances to Pachacamac is indicated
by the following eyewitness account of Miguel de Estete who visited
Pachacamac in 1533 as a member of the first Spanish expedition to
reach the site:

> They come to this Devil, from distances of three hundred
> leagues [c. 1500 km] with gold and silver and cloth . . .
> from the town of Catamez [Atacames, on the coast of
> Ecuador], which is at the commencement of this govern-
> ment, all the people of this coast serve this mosque with
> gold and silver, and offer tribute every year (Estete
> 1872:82–3).

Estete also goes on to describe how Hernando Pizarro (the con-
querer's brother and leader of the expedition to Pachacamac) forced
his way into the temple in order to see the venerated idol (Estete
1872:82):

> It [the idol] was in a good house, well painted, in a very
> dark chamber with a close fetid smell. Here there was a

> very dirty Idol made of wood . . . and it was held in such
> veneration that only the attendants and servants, who, as
> they say, were appointed by it, were allowed to officiate
> before it. No other person might enter, nor is any other
> considered worthy even to touch the walls of the house
> [temple] . . . In all the streets of this town, and at its prin-
> cipal gates, and round this house, there are many wooden
> Idols, which they worship as imitations of their Devil.

Estete also records how the Indians believed that the idol could
destroy them if they offended it and that they were shocked when
Pizarro ordered the temple destroyed and the idol broken up, believing that the idol would destroy the Spaniards (Estete 1872:83).

The situation described for Pachacamac, where the cult figure was
housed in a secluded inner precinct accessible to a limited number of
individuals while representations of the diety were located in public
or exterior areas where they could be worshiped by people not admitted to the inner temple, is strikingly similar to what Rowe
(1967:85–6) has suggested for Chavín de Huántar. Rowe notes the
importance of a representation of the Smiling God, which is found
on a small flat sculpture located in the wall of a patio in front of the
old south wing of the temple. He argues that this particular sculpture provided a public focus for worship of the actual cult figure of
the Smiling God, which was housed in a dark gallery of the oldest
part of the temple. Rowe (1967:85) makes a similar argument for
the relief carved Staff God figure on the flat Raimondi Stela, suggesting that the slab was originally located on an exterior wall of the
temple "where worshippers who would not be admitted to the inner
sanctum where the original image was could see it." Thus the Raimondi Stela depicting the Staff God, like the previously described
representation of the Smiling God, was also a public representation
of another image worshiped in the interior of the temple. In this
case Rowe argues that the restricted location of the cult figure of the
Staff God – never actually recovered – would have been in a later
addition to the original temple housing the Smiling God, in the
section referred to as the "new temple." Pozorski (1976:285, 287)
has pointed out that central access systems consisting of passageways
and staircases, combined with single or multiple plaza systems are
found at many Chavín-influenced sites. Such systems arc undoubtedly correlated with restricted access to the most sacred areas of the
temples and, along with the public display of cult figure representations such as the adobe sculptures at Moxeke and Huaca de los
Reyes, provide a widespread analogous situation to that described in
more detail for Chavín de Huántar and Pachacamac.

The practice of maintaining distance from the source of supernatural power, embodied in this case in the secluded image of the cult figure, is not unique to Peruvian religious systems but is also widespread in both Eastern and Western religions. The aim of all religious activity is to obtain the aid of this ultimate source of sacred power, but direct approach by the common person is frequently thought to be fraught with danger. This belief is tied to the development of intermediaries in the form of priests who constitute a special, privileged group with respect to the deity. It is the priests who accept the tribute and offerings to the gods and who can intercede on behalf of the general population. The limitation of access to sacred precincts as well as the special nature of priestly privilege is amply documented in the Bible:

> So the Lord said to Aaron . . . and you and your sons with you shall attend to your priesthood for all that concerns the altar and that [which] is within the veil; and you shall serve. I give you your priesthood as a gift and anyone else who comes near shall be put to death (Numbers 18:7).

Nor is the fear of physical destruction from entering a restricted area or touching a sacred object a belief particularly unique to prehistoric Peru:

> no one who is not a priest, who is not of the descendants of Aaron, should draw near to burn incense before the Lord, lest he become as Korah and his company (who were swallowed up by an earthquake for attempting to burn incense in front of the altar) (Numbers 16:40).

In summary, the restricted nature of the priesthood, its power of intercession between humans and the gods, and a belief in the awesome sanctity of the temple are elements that may have been common to both Pachacamac and Chavín theologies and which are shared by other religions of the world.

The persistence of the Staff God and the feline motif, together with the evident importance of oracle centers, indicates that the religious legacy of Chavín may have established a situation not unlike that described by Childe (1951:143) for ancient Sumer. There the temple gods were not exclusively local deities but were common to the whole land, like many of the saints to which Christian churches are dedicated. In effect, Rostworowski has suggested just such a situation in the case of Pachacamac. On the basis of her ethnohistoric research, she presents evidence indicating that belief in the deity of Pachacamac was spread over considerable distances, possibly even to the tropical forest, through associated temples established in various regions (Rostworowski 1977:202–4). Evidence from the north coast (Keatinge 1977, 1978, in press) also tends to substantiate both the widespread influence of Pachacamac and a connection between different religious centers. There would seem to be no reason that such a model could not also apply to the earlier Chavín time level as well.

Pilgrimage, trade, and communication

It is not hard to imagine how a religion based upon widespread pilgrimage to oracle centers could help foster the development of long-distance trade and communication between different areas. An interesting ethnographic case that may furnish some insight into how Chavín influence was spread between neighboring regions is provided by the Ibo of eastern Nigeria. Among the Ibo, political integration was aided by

> the spread of agents of the Aro Chuka Ibo . . . The Aro represented a powerful oracle . . . and acted in the dual role of solicitor-merchants. They overcame local parochialism and hostility by traveling under the protection of their oracle, who was reputed to kill anyone harming its agents. A full roster of legal services and magical solutions was offered to clients who came from far and wide in Iboland . . . Colonies of Aro not only managed oracular consultations but carried on extensive trade in chickens, cloth, iron tools, palm products, and especially slaves (Netting 1972:231).

We already know from the example of Pachacamac that there were at least some Peruvian oracles endowed with considerable power. The case of the Ibo oracle demonstrates both the profitability inherent in the manipulation of that power as well as its utility for infusing a widespread population with a modicum of common identification. A similar argument can be made for Chavín. The expansion of the cult through selective diffusion or, perhaps in some cases, missionary proselytism, together with the development of pilgrimage centers in distinct environmental zones, provided the necessary bases for long-distance trade between widely separated areas, thereby laying the groundwork for later political integration.

Although the archaeological evidence is not altogether conclusive, I would posit that the rise of the Chavín cult served to intensify long-distance trade between different regions. Although this trade may well have emphasized the procurement of luxury items, other more basic or strategic resources may also have been included. Of particular importance would have been such items as coca from the *montaña;* tropical bird feathers, honey, wood, herbs, and, perhaps, hallucinogenic snuff from the tropical forest; minerals (gold, silver, and copper) and possibly wool from the sierra; and *Spondylus* shells, marine products, salt, shell beads, ají peppers, and cotton (possibly in the form of finished products as well as in its raw form [see Conklin 1978:7–8 for an insightful discussion of this whole question on the Early Horizon time level]) from the coastal regions (see Netherly 1977:254–71 for a recent discussion of interregional trade; also Murra 1972, 1975; Lathrap 1973a).

Moreover, Burger (1975, 1978:312, 345) has presented evidence from the trace element analysis of obsidian found in large quantities by Lumbreras and Amat Olazábal (1969:173) in their excavations in the galleries of the temple at Chavín de Huántar, which indicates that the majority of the obsidian was imported from the Quispisisa mine located in the Department of Huancavelica in the central highlands, more than 450 km. to the south. Chavín iconography itself indicates interregional contact. *Strombus* and *Spondylus* shells from the coast, the latter found in ritualistic contexts throughout Peru on virtually all time levels and unquestionably imported from the Gulf of Guayaquil more then 700 km. to the north (Paulson 1974), as well as tropical forest animals such as the cayman and the harpy eagle and primarily lowland plant species such as coca, ají peppers, bottle gourd, achira, and manioc (Rowe 1962; Lathrap 1971, 1973b, 1977) are all depicted in the stone carvings of Chavín de Huántar. It is easy to conceive of how a religious system based upon a guarantee of safe passage to the inviolable zones of sacred shrines would help to account for the development of extensive interregional trade. Julius Wellhausen describes just such a situation in the development of Mecca:

> Within the tumultuous confusion which fills the desert, the festivities at the beginning of each season represent the only enjoyable periods of rest. A peace of God at this time interrupts the continuous feuds for a fair period of time. The most diverse tribes which otherwise did not trust each other at all, make common pilgrimage to the same holy places without fear, through land of friend and foe. Trade raises its head, and general and lively exchange results ... The exchange of commodities is followed by an exchange of ideas. A community of ideological interest develops that comprises all of Arabia ... (Wellhausen 1884–99:183; cited in Wolf 1951:338).

Religion and political centralization
Analysis of the Chavín phenomenon during the Early Horizon tends to support a view of a society with an essentially religious orientation and an absence of coercive force (Willey 1948:10). Although the iconography, artifacts, and architecture at Chavín-influenced sites

located throughout much of Peru strongly suggest at least a limited sharing of common ideologies (Willey 1962:9–10), there is at the same time nothing that indicates overall political integration of these sites under a centralized government. How then, one might ask, were Peruvian societies of the Early Horizon held together? In answering this question, one might draw an interesting parallel between the Chavín situation and that of the Classic Maya chiefdoms of Mesoamerica as referred to by Webb:

> Chiefdoms, especially those whose size and complexity approach the maximum for the type, inevitably are theocracies . . . Perhaps as important to the strength of chiefly theocracies is the fact that religious ceremonies, in contrast to the "selfish" needs of the rulers or even public works, can be seen as of benefit to participants gathered from throughout the entire chiefdom. In addition, cult activities are likely to be strongly patterned and to reflect the established ways. Gods are not bound to time or space and "have been" from the beginning. Religion thus supports the society in the absence of political controls. Clearly, however, the strength of the cement which holds the system together depends basically upon the believability of the cult itself (Webb 1973:379).

I would add, however, that another feature of that "societal cement" may well have revolved around the association of religion and economy in the form of long-distance trade.

The immediate post-Chavín period from roughly 200 B.C. to the beginning of the Middle Horizon around A.D. 700 seems to have been dominated by regionally distinct polities typified by the Moche on the north coast. As during Chavín times, elaborate temple pyramid mounds continued to be built, perhaps in even greater profusion. Toward the end of this period large compounds are found associated with or attached to the temple pyramid structures, perhaps indicating bureaucratic expansion as a response to a developing economy based upon the extraction of tribute in goods and services. Somewhat later, palace or administrative structures in the form of completely separate compounds became a feature of expansionist empires. It thus seems clear that religion remained the cornerstone of society throughout a period during which population and agricultural production increased and irrigation systems became more extensive.

Not until the beginning of the Middle Horizon is there definite evidence for imperialistic expansion in the archaeological record. Warfare, previously characterized by clashes of neighboring chiefdoms finally became a means for wide-scale political and economic expansion. Yet even during the final period preceding the arrival of the Spanish, the expansionist states of the coastal Chimú and the highland Inca had divine rulers at their heads. Although the advent of militaristic policies clearly indicates that the goals of Peruvian society had become more secular, this does not mean that religion had in any way ceased to be a part of the central societal foci. As Paul Wheatley has so cogently put it:

> use of the term "secularization" is misleading, for kings no less than priesthoods subscribed to the all-pervading norms of religion. What distinguished the two power groups were their political goals, rather than the methods employed to attain them. Kings and corporate warrior groups tended to pursue aims not subsumed under, and indeed alien to, the values of kin-structured society. Whatever their precise relationship to the deity, they were prone to use religious authority not only as a means for consolidating their own social position, but also as a primary instrument for the achievement of autonomous political goals beyond the ethical conceptions of an ascriptively organized society, and for the validation of a concentration of power beyond that sanctioned by the moral order of a folk community. As such the importance of these groups lies not in a professed lesser intensity of religious conviction but in their willingness to extend the secular sphere of government operations, and to use their power in the prosecution of wholly secular aims . . . palaces and tombs, and many more besides, are eloquent testimony to the massive concentrations of social and political power commanded by monarchs invoking sacrally sanctioned authority in the pursuit of essentially secular goals (Wheatley 1971:315–16).

At no point in Peruvian prehistory is there evidence of a truly secular state, a state in which religious authority is completely divorced from the primary seat of political and/or military authority. The situation ascribed to Chavín seems to be not unlike that of the Classic Maya in which a heavy emphasis on religious ideology served to hold together a society that though pushing toward statehood, never surpassed the level of tenuously united theocratic chiefdoms. For centuries, religious ideology provided a primary means for the maintenance and growth of Peruvian chiefdoms through the promotion of long-distance trade and communications and by the stimulation of local tribute economies. Not until population pressure and consequent agricultural production had reached critical proportions does there seem to be any evidence for widespread, interregional warfare. And even then, militaristic expansion seems clearly to have been carried out under the auspices of religious sanctions.

The intent of this chapter is not to present a new model enshrining religion as the prime mover in the evolution of the state but, rather, an attempt to call attention to the importance of religion as something more than simply a candle on the techno-environmental-politico altar. In the absence of naked coercive force, religious sanctions provided a path toward the development of political centralization. The sheer size and numbers of the religious edifices found in the archaeological record leave no doubt of their social significance to the societies that built them. The amount of resources, both human and natural, expended on religion in the form of temple constructions and tribute must have had a profound effect on the configuration of early state economies as well as on the forms of political organization developed to organize and direct the exploitation of these resources.

8

Civilization as a state of mind: The cultural evolution of the lowland Maya

DAVID A. FREIDEL

Introduction

> As we examine the record for evidences of population growth, subsistence resources, warfare, and trade, there is a tendency to relegate ideology to an epiphenomenal position, to reject it as a significant causal force or "prime mover," but, leaving aside for the moment the question of initial or prime cause, there are indications that idea systems played an important part throughout the course of Maya development (Willey 1977b:416).

The study of cultural evolution is entering an exciting and potentially enlightening controversy of which this quote is but a signal reflection. On the one hand, there are the scholars who maintain that culture, defined as the shared conception and perception of reality in society, is strictly a consequence of social action. As social organization changes, be it through intrinsic dynamics (Flannery 1972) or as an accommodation to changing relationships with the environment, cultural reality will change. Culture and its reified forms, ideology and religion, constitute dependent variables; which are phenomena to be explained. They are not explanatory in and of themselves. On the other hand, there are scholars who suggest that cultural realities themselves are intrinsically dynamic, that social action is predicated upon cultural definition rather than the reverse, and that social organization will change as the cultural reality structuring it changes. This chapter will attempt to explore the largely unascertained theoretical potential of the latter position as a means of elucidating the evolution of complex society and ultimately the state among the lowland Maya of Central America.

The lowland Maya provide a suitable testing ground for the notion that religion and ideology can prove determinative factors in the rise of civilization and the state. Recently, several scholars have argued that the Maya progressed to this evolutionary stage as a matter of practical exigency and adaptation to stress (Webster 1977;

Ball 1977; Sanders 1977; Sanders and Webster 1978). Before the particulars of an alternative case for the lowland Maya can be argued, however, certain salient points in the following theoretical position are germane.

The primary principle of the view that culture may be a causal factor in human evolution is that the symbolic expression of shared realities is simultaneously a mental and a material phenomenon. Material culture is not a product of culture. It is culture in material form as Sahlins (1976:207) has cogently stated:

> At first glance the confrontation of cultural and material logics does seem unequal. The material process is factual and independent of man's will: the symbolic, invented and therefore flexible . . . But the error consists in this: that there is no material logic apart from practical interest; and the practical interest of men in production is symbolically constituted. The finalities as well as the modalities of production come from the cultural side; the material means of cultural organization as well as the organization of material means.

Social relations, subsistence practices, and technology (proposed prime movers in cultural ecological explanations) exist and affect society only as they are "symbolically constituted" within the shared reality of that society. The constraints of the real world as it exists rather than as it is perceived no doubt provide selective pressure. Nevertheless, just as adaptation does not provide sufficient cause to explain the workings of genetics in biological evolution but, rather, points to the necessity of its independence as a source of variation, so adaptation to material constraints cannot provide sufficient cause to explain the workings of cultural realities in human evolution. Instead, it points to the necessity of regarding the generation of culture as an independent source of variation.

The culture of complex society
It has become obvious that cultural diversity is not mechanically generated by environmental diversity. I suggest that this is true not only of culture content but of culture form or organization as well. People respond to their environments through their cultures (White 1959). If this axiom of evolutionary anthropology is valid, it follows that the shared reality defined as culture is itself adaptive or maladaptive. This conclusion is not so obvious because culture is easily confused with its products. In the matter of state level society, for example, take the following statement:

> It is the hierarchical arrangement of the members and classes of society which provides the actual integration in

states. The critical contribution of state religions and state
art styles is to legitimize that hierarchy, to confirm the
divine affiliation of those at the top by inducing religious
experience (Flannery 1972:407).

Here hierarchy stands as a factual and objective phenomenon accessible to observation. It is a phenomenon existentially independent of
religion or ideology. But hierarchy is simply an arrangement, albeit
a complex one, of social relationships. How does a member of such
an organization know that he is a part of it and where he stands
within it? He knows the former because he shares certain fundamental features of a reality with other members through the medium of
shared symbol systems like language. He knows the latter because he
has differential access to some other more specialized symbol systems, which are expressed through clothing, shelter, food, and
wealth, as well as to the nonmaterial symbol systems represented by
mannerisms, social etiquette, and ritual. Social hierarchy exists only
when these shared symbol systems exist.

To go a step further, what is a state religion but the reification and
codification of these complex symbol systems? From this perspective,
religion or ideology is culture made conscious and provides the public explanation of a culture to itself. It is a specialized system of
symbols within the larger system that is the total culture. Religions
and ideologies promoting hierarchy do not develop to justify a previously developed hierarchical social organization. Both state ideology and hierarchy are produced by the evolution of the symbol
systems we gloss as cultures. Because they derive from a single
source, these phenomena are interdependent and cannot bear a causal relationship to one another.

In fact, within hierarchical societies the symbols of cosmic and
world order that make up a state religion and ideology are often the
same as those that signify power relationships. Such central and
public symbols do not simply serve to justify extant relationships of
power. They also comprise a vital feature of their realization, for the
material bases of power, such as labor, land, and wealth, can only be
manipulated by means of symbolic denotation. In the last analysis,
state religion and ideology in archaic civilization constitute the codified and idealized reality of government.

The peculiarity of state societies and societies evolving toward state
organization is that they have not only centralized insititutions integrating a heterogeneous field of social segments but have also centralized conceptions of reality integrating a heterogeneous field of
subcultures. Insofar as complex societies are directed in their growth
by self-conscious governments, the policy of such organizations can
only be conceived of in terms of the potentials and limitations of the

symbol systems constituting their realities. Obviously, governmental realities vary substantially in their structure, geographic spread, and endurance. Sometimes regions are successfully integrated into civilizations, and sometimes they are not.

Following this line of reasoning, we see that the material expressions of religion and ideology are far from being epiphenomenal. They can be key monitors of the evolutionary processes occurring within governments that lead some to rule by law as states and that lead others to stabilize as chiefdoms structured by sanction. In the sections that follow an attempt will be made to show that the varying potentials and limitations of the centralized integrating symbol systems among Preclassic societies in southeastern Mesoamerica determined that the primary locus of civilization and the state would be in the relatively uniform lowlands rather than in the resource rich, diversified highlands.

Ecological approaches to the problem

Long-term research in the mountainous regions of the Maya highlands has revealed a rich and complex culture history prior to the time of Christ (Lowe 1977; Sharer 1978; Sanders and Michaels 1977; Lowe and Mason 1965; Borhegyi 1965; Shook and Kidder 1952). Although the Early and Middle Preclassic origins of complex society in the highlands are still being investigated, it seems clear that major centers were being constructed in various parts of the highlands by Middle Preclassic times (1000–300 B.C.) and that social life and public art reached a peak during the Late Preclassic period (300 B.C.–A.D. 100) (See Figure 1). Life in this area subsequently stabilized into a mosaic of small polities characterized by local art styles during the rest of pre-Columbian history. In contrast, the lowland Maya first began building major centers with public art during the Late Preclassic period and went on to establish one of the great and enduring civilizations of the ancient world. Why did not a unified regional civilization flourish in the highlands during the Classic period rather than in the lowlands?

There have been several recent attempts to answer this question. In a general review of the ecological determinants of the evolution of Mesoamerican civilization Sanders and Webster (1978) suggest that both the highlands and lowlands of southeastern Mesoamerica constitute low risk environments not conducive to the development of social stratification and the state. They go on to contrast the highly diverse environments of the highlands with the uniform environments of the lowlands. The precocious economic integration found in the highlands, they reason, is inspired by diverse resources but eventually levels off because of the absence of risk in the environment. The lowlands, however, go on to develop state level insti-

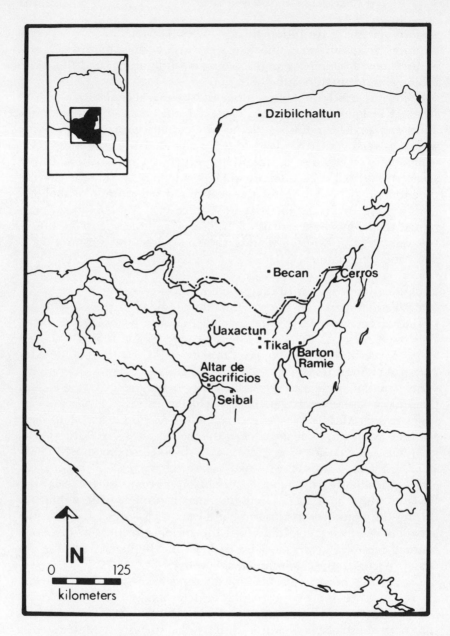

Figure 1. Map of the Maya lowlands with known Late Preclassic period centers

tutions during the Classic period, "as a response to an extremely unusual productive potential – perhaps unmatched in other tropical forest zones – which allowed populations to increase still further, causing continued change in the lowland system." (Sanders and Webster 1978:294). Their scenario, however, begs the question of why equivalent population pressure did not exist in the highlands. Here the authors must fall back on the empirical notion that unimpeded population growth did not occur in the highlands:

> Evidence from a number of agricultural studies reveals that the deep soils of the volcanic ash basin of the highlands have very high natural fertility even under intensive cropping. This would suggest considerably greater demographic capacity than the archaeological data indicate and that the contemporary population is considerably larger and agriculture much more intensive than in the past (Sanders and Webster 1978:284).

Yet there is every reason to believe that the populations responsible for the great centers like Kaminaljuyú were as substantial as those found in contemporaneous lowland centers during the Late Preclassic period. Unless subsequent population growth is considered to be peculiar to the lowlands, and therefore not of general explanatory value, there is no foundation for this argument. The environmental contrasts pointed out by Sanders and Webster merely exacerbate the problem because resource diversity would presumably favor greater social complexity in the highland region.

In a comprehensive discussion of Preclassic Chiapas, Lowe (1977) offers a more complex explanation of the situation. Granting that environmental factors no doubt played a role in the differential development of highland and lowland regions, Lowe suggests that cultural factors, such as ethnic rivalry between lowland pioneers and the established societies of the highlands, helped to weld the lowland Maya into a cultural unity. Before dealing in detail with Lowe's innovative attempts to employ culture as an explanatory factor, we must consider some of the environmental and geographical arguments he brings to bear.

In the case of Chiapas, Lowe suggests that a combination of environmental and geographical factors operated to inhibit further social advancement during the Classic period. At the great center of Izapa, however, environmental limitations were evidently not the problem because this area is particularly rich in resources and even at the time of the conquest was well populated. Here Lowe suggests that a combination of shifting exchange networks and a geographically exposed position undermined Izapa's economic and social organization. The particular shift Lowe has in mind is from exchanges based upon cacao to exchanges based upon obsidian. Although Izapa dominated a region rich in cacao, it is not strategically located to service the obsidian trade. Even though this argument explains the available data, neither cacao nor obsidian are necessities of life. Discussion of shifting exchange mediums like these must ultimately be based upon cultural factors, such as the political manipulation of exotics in international trade and the resultant shift in value attached to wealth objects, rather than upon the natural distributions of these resources.

Moving from economic to geographic arguments, Lowe goes on to suggest that, "Finally, constant exposure of the isthmian peoples, in their crossroads position across communications routes, to repeated exterior interference dealt the death blow to possibilities for steady cultural evolution" (Lowe 1977:245). It is unusual to see it argued that location on a geographically strategic communications route would actually inhibit rather than promote social advancement. The Classic development of important centers like Teotihuacán (Millon 1973) has been partially attributed to precisely such strategic control of communication exchange routes. Given the precocious developments in Chiapas, why did not these early vigorous societies develop a critical monopoly over trade routes rather than succumbing to foreign control? In a much later period the Putun Maya evidently maintained such a monopoly over the northern isthmian area in the face of pressure from the Mexica, the most powerful and predatory empire in Mesoamerica. This area, like the southern area, constituted a major communication artery between western and eastern Mesoamerica. Lowe argues that the environment of interior Chiapas may have been intrinsically less productive agriculturally than the lowlands and consequently suffered some overexploitation in early periods. This reasoning cannot be generalized to other parts of Chiapas or to the rest of the highlands.

Finally, Lowe notes that the highland region is more subject to natural catastrophe in the form of droughts, floods, hurricanes, vulcanism, and earthquakes than are the lowlands. It is doubtful that the lowlands are free of the first three kinds of disaster. Certainly flooding and hurricanes are germane to the coastal areas. Nonetheless, there is increasing evidence that the coasts and riverine basins in the lowlands participated vigorously in early Maya civilization (Freidel 1978; 1979). Drought does not spare the lowlands if modern and historical records are any guide. Moreover, the lowlands suffer unique chronic problems such as an adequate supply of potable water that should have inhibited the development of complex communities there. It cannot be denied that vulcanism and earthquakes have had a lethal impact on some parts of the highlands (Sharer 1974, 1978; Sheets 1979). At least one major center, Chalchuapa, evidently succumbed to volcanic disaster in the Late Preclassic period (Sharer 1978). Other highland centers, however, such as Kaminaljuyú and Izapa, do not seem to have shared this fate directly. Despite these problems, Lowe's (1977:237) notion that these disasters may have had as great an impact on the integrative religious systems as they did upon the lives and physical welfare of the highlanders is intriguing.

Cultural approaches to the problem

In a key statement, Lowe articulates a critical distinction to be made between highland and lowland society in the Late Preclassic period, "Fully shared, deeply ingrained social values seem to have defined a different, superior, more orderly world for the early lowland Maya, as compared to their Zoquean and other neighbors" (Lowe 1977:247).

The "Zoque" refers to the Preclassic peoples of Chiapas, whereas "the other neighbors" refers to the Maya-speaking societies in the highlands of Guatemala. Although the Maya lowlands may have been populated from a number of bordering regions during the Middle Preclassic, including the Olmec heartland of Tabasco-Veracruz, the Isthmian area and the highlands further east, Lowe argues that by the Late Preclassic period there were three major ethnic areas, the Mixe-Zoque in Chiapas, the highland Maya, and the lowland Maya. Identifying groups by language is a tricky business in the pre-Columbian era, but Lowe seems to be successful by using significantly distinctive distributions of material culture styles like those found in ceramics. In addition to Lowe's ethnic diversity, it can be argued that the Late Preclassic ceramics of these three regions also signify the operation of distinctive internal dynamics among their producers:

> Unlike the stylistically integrated Late Preclassic Lowland Maya, the Zoquean population which apparently remained relatively intact in the western and coastal regions of Southern Chiapas allowed itself to become increasingly divided during the Late Preclassic and Protoclassic periods ... Izapa, of course, within its moist Soconusco piedmont habitat, did create or participate in a great art and religious tradition ... but this scarcely made itself felt in the central depression and did not survive into the Classic period (Lowe 1977:230–1).

Unfortunately, Lowe does not directly discuss the ceramic patterns occurring in the Maya highland region during the Late Preclassic. The available literature (Rands and Smith 1965; Wetherington 1978; Sharer 1978; L. Parsons 1967) indicates that the situation lies somewhere between the "fragmented" diversity found in Chiapas and the relatively homogeneous Chicanel ceramic sphere in the Maya lowlands. In their synthesis Rands and Smith (1965:121) note what appears to be a significant diversity in surface treatment and some modes when the highlands are viewed as a whole. On the other hand, L. Parsons (1967) observes important ties between Bilbao and Kaminaljuyú. In his discussion of the Late Preclassic ceramics at the important center of Chalchuapa in El Salvador, Sharer states, "In many ways the Chul complex is a near duplicate of the Miraflores Phase at Kaminaljuyu. There are regional/local/variations, and the internal Chalchuapa pottery traditions remain viable, but there are undeniably strong ceramic ties to Kaminaljuyu" (Sharer 1978:126). Later on, Sharer notes that the ceramic ties are even stronger in the succeeding Caynac complex (200 B.C.–A.D. 0). Despite the documentation of such ties, no one to my knowledge has ever described an overall ceramic homogeneity in the Late Preclassic highlands comparable to that which is seemingly characteristic of the Maya lowlands in this period. This pattern may simply reflect the absence of a comprehensive synthetic treatment. Alternatively, it may indicate strong ceramic ties between important centers in a region otherwise characterized by a moderately high degree of diversity at the local level. The latter situation resembles the balkanized polities of the Late Classic period in the lowlands (Willey and Shimkin 1973).

If these distinctions found in the ceramic inventories of highland Chiapas, highland Guatemala – El Salvador, and the lowlands are reasonable reflections of the data found in these regions, then they serve to underscore the processes of fragmentation, balkanization, and unification, respectively, that can be monitored in other materials, particularly symbolic imagery. In establishing a model for these processes in the Late Preclassic period, Lowe emphasizes the patterns seen in public art, in particular carved stone megaliths or stelae. He focuses on two interesting problems. In the first place, there are a large number of carved stone monuments dating to the Late Preclassic period in the highlands. A substantial number of these are battered, broken, moved, or buried, whereas those at Izapa are intact and apparently in situ. Secondly, the earliest evidence for hieroglyphic texts in a lowland Maya-related style occurs in the highlands. Yet it is in the lowlands that writing reaches its apogee during the Classic era. According to Lowe, these problems are related. The monuments at Izapa, unadorned with Maya-style hieroglyphics, register the old Zoquean–Olmec inspired religious practices that pervaded the highlands. The innovation and use of hieroglyphic writing, in contrast, registered the advent of radical, elitist cult practices. The vulcanism that occurred near the end of the Preclassic era in some parts of the highlands triggered a violent reaction on the part of conservative factions against the radical factions. This reaction resulted in the destruction of the hieroglyphic monuments and in the preservation of the nonglyphic monuments at Izapa. The practice of carving stelae and using hieroglyphic writing flourished in the lowlands during the Classic period because either the radical cult practices originated there in Preclassic times and were obscured by overburden and recarving or the practices originated in the highlands. In the latter case the followers of the radical cult were forced to leave the highlands in the face of conservative reaction and reestablished the cult among the less developed communities of the lowlands.

In correlating this historical scenario with the processes of fragmentation and unity characterizing highland Chiapas and the lowlands, respectively, Lowe observes:

> the glyph system was an all-important tool, one that made concrete the Maya millennial philosophy of cosmic order, divine preordination, ancestral ritual requirements, and, no doubt, a strong concept to the ethnic superiority of the lowland Maya elite with its fixed social classes, warfare, and slave categories . . . We do not see this pattern in the looser small-center Classic civilizations of Chiapas which abstained from carved inscriptions (Lowe, 1977:240).

The use of a standardized complex symbol system like hieroglyphics is undoubtedly a critical factor in the cultural unity displayed in Classic civilization in the lowlands. Whatever strife there may have been within and between lowland Maya communities, the widespread use of hieroglyphic writing reflects a potential for the precise coordination of political, economic, and social institutions, as well as for a state religion that is not seen in the neighboring societies of the Classic period. Lowe suggests that hieroglyphics of the Maya style

> do not communicate news of events, thoughts, and instructions, or record transactions, except insofar as these categories concerned a narrow range of ritual . . . The recently acclaimed Maya practice of including bare dynastic evidence in this system seems to me to fortify, rather than weaken the idea that Maya hieroglyphics were only cultic tools (Lowe 1977:240).

Leaving aside the matter of preservation of perishable mediums, the close association of hieroglyphics with public art, religious symbolism, astrology, and political dynasties indicates that we are dealing with the kind of manifold symbol system earlier suggested to be a reflection of the reality of government. Such symbols simultaneously express the overarching, integrating concepts and values that dictate the acceptable parameters of policy (public religion) and define the positions of power relative to one another (Marcus 1976). The hieroglyphics indicate more than a shared cult. There had to be a structure shared among the central administrative institutions of the Classic lowland polities. Government is predicated upon management of the economy, and no matter how ephemeral such management might be, political and economic institutions must be articulated. Maya hieroglyphic writing, with its wide geographical spread and endurance, makes little sense if it is considered epiphenomenal to Maya evolution. If a standardized central symbol system of this kind has adaptive value, it lies in the coordination of policy and economic activity between participating communities.

Hieroglyphic writing, however, is a feature of Classic rather than of Preclassic Maya civilization in the lowlands. Both Lowe (1977) and Graham (1971) believe that hieroglyphic writing was probably being used during the Late Preclassic in the lowlands but that the evidence has been obscured. Although portable small objects have been found in the lowlands with primitive texts (M. Coe 1976), monumental public art has yielded only isolated glyphs (W. Coe 1965a). Although the corpus of monumental art from Preclassic contexts is steadily expanding, primarily in the form of architectural decoration (Freidel 1978, 1979), no texts have been forthcoming. Continuing excavations at Cerros, a Late Preclassic center in Belize, have yielded symbolically rich decoration on three pyramids, but, as at Tikal, glyphs occur as isolates integrated into larger compositions. It can be argued that we are dealing not with negative evidence but with a genuine absence of hieroglyphic texts in the public art of the Late Preclassic lowlands. Not only are texts absent but the carved megaliths that are the primary public medium for their expression in the highlands are poorly represented when compared to other mediums such as architecture. This absence cannot be simply attributed to greater Classic overburden in the lowlands. Major excavations in highland pyramids have yielded many broken and buried stone monuments, whereas comparable excavations in Late Preclassic architecture in the lowlands (W. Coe 1965a; Ricketson and Ricketson 1937; Freidel 1978, 1979) have produced only a handful of problematic fragments. These fragments are restricted to Tikal and possibly Mirador (I. Graham 1967). Thus the current evidence seems to support the prospect that the art of hieroglyphic writing and stela carving was adopted by lowland communities from the highlands at the end of the Preclassic era and subsequently developed there with revolutionary rapidity.

Returning to the problems addressed by Lowe, two questions arise: (1) Why does hieroglyphic writing and stone monument carving undergo a precipitous decline in the highlands at the end of the Preclassic. (2) Why do these same features undergo such rapid development and dissemination in the lowlands at the same time? Lowe must be

partially correct in suggesting that large-scale vulcanism contributed
to these events. However, if we examine the primary function of
hieroglyphic writing, we can move beyond its characterization as being "radical" religiously. In a detailed discussion of early writing systems in southeastern Mesoamerica, Prem (1971:122) states, "The
most striking characteristic of this Intermediate group is the presence
of the Long Count. All these inscriptions have in common the employment of bar and dot numerals (dots positioned above), without
period signs and are arranged in columns." Later, he also notes that
there is an unbroken linkage of the Long Count with the *Tonalpohualli*
or *Tzolkin*, the sacred 260-day astrological cycle. From the Late Postclassic native Maya documents, such as the *Chilam Balam of Chumayel*
(Roys 1967), it is clear that the correlation of events occurring in
sacred, cyclical time with accumulative linear and historical time provided the key to Maya prognostication. Routine cyclical events, such
as the flow of the seasons relative to agriculture, played a minor role
in such prognostication. Of primary interest were disasters, both natural and man-made, and great events in the history of society. Wars,
conquest, plague, drought, the advent of great leadership, economic
depression, and prosperity are the kinds of events that figured promi-
nently in public foretelling. Moreover, such prognostication was a
matter of central concern to Maya governments. Beyond the functions of historical record keeping and the transmission of information, hieroglyphic writing as used by the highland Maya and
subsequently by the lowland Maya was the central instrument of a
predictive science of astrology. It was a source of legal and historical precedent and a guide to the future. Government by historical
precedent that is accumulated, recorded, and codified is government by law. Such government is one of the key ingredients in the
establishment of state society.

If the prediction of disaster was as important to Preclassic astrolo-
gers as it was to their Postclassic counterparts, then the occurrence of
a set of unique and profound catastrophes like the explosion of Ilo-
pongo (Sharer 1974, 1978) may have been sufficient to severely undermine the credibility of what was evidently a radical science still in
its infancy (Prem 1971:123). Such disaster might not indicate the
anger of supernatural forces, as posited by Lowe, as much as the
simple failure of religious specialists to understand them. This failure
would constitute a failure of the axiom upon which their science was
founded, namely, the past is a comprehensive guide to the future.

If we are searching for an evolutionary explanation, then the effects of great events, like great people, must be understood in terms
of the conditions under which they occur. It can be argued that the
ideological conditions in the highlands and lowlands during the Late
Preclassic period determined the precipitous rejection of a "stela

cult" in the former region and its revolutionary acceptance in the latter. An examination of the material symbol systems operating in the highlands and lowlands during the Late Preclassic period registers the critical differences that led to cultural and political fragmentation on the one hand and to unity on the other.

Public art and cultural dynamics: the highlands

> It is difficult to conceive the rich variety of sculpture found at Kaminaljuyu as the product of a single developing style. Apparently sculptors from many localities resided and worked in this cosmopolitan center (Proskouriakoff 1971:150).

The Late Preclassic public art of the highlands has been glossed by the general term Izapan-style after the famous site of Izapa in Chiapas where a large sample of carved stone monuments dating to this period have been found and studied (Norman 1973, 1976; Quirarte 1973, 1976, 1977). Beginning with a shared medium in the form of carved stone, one can have no doubt that the schools of art found in the highlands are related to one another in a fashion that suggests significant interaction between polities. Quirarte (1973, 1976) has carefully documented the shared elements, such as "U" glyphs and "crossed bands" as well as the shared compositions, such as double-headed compound dragons, god impersonators, downward gazing figures in the upper register, and profile grotesque "dragon" or deity masks that pervade the sample of highland monuments. In summarizing a formal analysis of the Izapan-style, Quirarte (1977: 282) observes, "Although Izapan-style images appear overly complicated at first glance, the fact is that the repertoire of elements, motifs, and themes is not that extensive. Neither is their presentation." Even so, there are grounds for Proskouriakoff's statement. Earlier Quirarte (1977:281) states:

> The Izapan-style artists rely alternately on figuration and abstraction in the creation of images. Both approaches can be used simultaneously within the same image. Figurative solutions can range from a stylized representation of a compound creature . . . to realistic portrayals of animals . . . all on the same stela . . . The arrangement of figures within primarily vertical formats in Izapan-style art follows a similar unpredictable alternation between symmetry and asymmetry (Quirarte 1977:281).

In contrast, lowland art of the Classic period is described as:

> The arrangement and placement of figures as well as their poses and postures are simple, predictable and

straightforward . . . the Maya artist does not have to contend with all of the constantly opposing tendencies and tensions presented by elements, motifs and themes, as in Izapan-style art. All aspects of the image-making process are firmly under control (Quirarte 1977:232–3).

Thus, although the Late Preclassic public art of the highlands can be glossed as a style, it is a style singularly lacking in standardized imagery and composition of the kind that characterizes lowland Classic art. Even within the large assemblage of monuments at Izapa, considered by Proskouriakoff (1971:150) to be more uniform stylistically than the Kaminaljuyú materials, there is a wide variety of compositions. Norman (1976:327) argues that stelae at Izapa are thematically related fragments of mythological and cosmological concepts. This seems to be a reasonable supposition. Attempts to convey a central theme on one monument evidently resulted in the extremely complicated imagery found on Stela 5 at Izapa (Norman 1976:165). The monuments at Izapa suggest that highland art, in addition to being nonstandardized, is lacking in a central concept and visual focus because cosmic themes require complex combinations of images in order to be adequately conveyed. Central, standard images are passed over in favor of pervasive images embedded in larger compositions such as the grotesque feline-saurian dragon masks that appear in a wide variety of contexts.

Under the circumstances there are grounds for arguing that the Late Preclassic monumental art of the highlands does not register a single style but, rather, represents a set of related styles. This impression is strengthened when the full range of carved stone art is considered:

> Many of the sculptured types . . . are limited in distribution not only to the general area under discussion (highlands) but quite a number are found only within a very restricted zone within that area. For example, silhouette sculptures have been surely documented only at the Kaminaljuyu site and immediate surroundings. The small bench figures, some showing Olmecoid features, are reportedly found exclusively in a restricted Highland plateau region . . . although fragments of such figures have been recovered from mound fill . . . at Kaminaljuyu (Shook 1971:74).

The shared elements, motifs, and themes that crosscut these styles can be partially attributed to the intensive interaction among the various polities of the highlands that fostered schools of art during the Late Preclassic. An equally potent source of similarity, however, is a common Olmec heritage.

As Norman (1976:311) observes, one of the ways to approach the difficult problem of factoring out common heritage from concurrent innovation in the Late Preclassic art styles of the highlands is to examine pervasive images such as the profile grotesques. Norman suggests that although a blunt-snouted or straight alveolar bar mask form is directly inspired by the Olmec "were-jaguar" image, a down or upcurving long-lipped dragon image is an innovation of the Late Preclassic peoples. If this position could be argued convincingly, then it could be asserted that a major pervasive image in Late Preclassic highland art resulted from direct contact and interaction among communities during that period.

A case can be made, however, for the derivation from late Olmec iconographic conventions of both the blunt-snouted and long-lipped variants of the profile grotesque, as well as for their often dichotomous juxtaposition. In a lengthy treatise on Olmec iconography, Joralemon (1976) shows that even though the predominant "dragon" image is "pug-nosed," long-lipped, and down-curving, beaked images occur with some frequency in Olmec art. Although Joralemon (1976:37) does not specifically pursue the formal problem at hand, he does argue persuasively that his "God I" is basically "a reptilian being." Moreover, on the famous Las Limas figurine the four primary profiles engraved on the knees and shoulders of the figure not only exhibit both the long-lipped and blunt-snouted variants but their dichotomy as well. The two shoulder profiles (M. Coe 1973:Fig.2) are both long lipped, whereas the two lower profiles are short lipped. Joralemon (1976:33) has considered the Las Limas figurine to be the "key to Olmec iconography." The presence of both long- and short-lipped variants of the profile grotesque in dichotomous relationship on this piece suggests that these forms were already important during the height of Olmec civilization.

Direct, formal connections between the Middle Preclassic iconography of the Olmec civilization and the iconography of highland peoples under Olmec influence are still rare. The discovery of two carved stone slabs flanking an outset stairway on a Middle Preclassic platform at the site of Tzutzuculi, Chiapas (McDonald 1977), registers not only the earliest documented use of architectural decoration but also the persistence of the long-lipped, blunt-snouted imagery as a principle dichotomy during the Epi–Olmec phase in southeastern Mesoamerica. McDonald (1977:565) suggests that the blunt-snouted image, presented here in full face, reflects the old were-jaguar concept, whereas the long-lipped image, presented in profile, represents the reptilian "dragon" concept. Attaching natural referents to grotesques is notoriously difficult in Mesoamerican iconography. Nonetheless, there is support for McDonald's notion in the Late Preclassic materials.

Although the Tzutzuculi monuments are unique in their architectural context, they are not peculiar in their iconography as McDonald ably demonstrates. Drawing on discussions by Navarrete (1971 and 1974), McDonald shows that the full-faced, blunt-snouted image in juxtaposition with a long-lipped profile image is a standard and well-distributed Olmec convention. This combination occurs on several Classic Olmec carved stone "scepters" that are iconographically close enough to be considered replications of the same form and concept. That these objects truly functioned as power objects or scepters is demonstrated by Navarrete's (1974:Fig.18) illustration of a typical Olmec figurine holding in one hand what is undoubtedly one of these objects. Given the dynamics of the interaction of the Olmec with the developing societies on their borderlands posited by Flannery (1968) in Oaxaca, such portable power objects would seem an ideal means of transmitting both an important image and an important concept.

The pervasive nature of the blunt-snouted "feline" and long-lipped "reptilian" images in highland Late Preclassic art styles is well documented (Quirarte 1976, 1977). Quirarte (1976) also shows a significant dichotomy between these images in a careful discussion of double-headed compound images. It has been argued that there is some reason to believe that both the images and their relationship can be traced to Olmec antecedents. In contrast to the Olmec examples, the double-headed figures of the Late Preclassic highlands are not standardized in their associated elements or as a compositional strategy (Quirarte 1976:82–3). Indeed, double-headed compound images comprise only one of many themes displayed in highland Late Preclassic art. Other themes, elements, and motifs that can be traced to Olmec antecedents (Norman 1976; Quirarte 1976) likewise show a lack of standard presentation in the Late Preclassic highlands. It seems reasonable to suggest that the basic commonality indicates a shared Olmec heritage and that the lack of standardization indicates a lack of coordination and a limited mechanism for the transmission of iconographic innovation among the localized schools of art during the Late Preclassic period. Even at "cosmopolitan" Kaminaljuyú, images such as Stela 11 (Norman 1976:Fig. 6.2), which exhibit strong iconographic ties with Izapa, are contemporaneous with images such as Stela 10 (Norman 1976:Fig. 6.6), which are unique in composition and style. No real synthesis of style is forthcoming in the highlands during the Late Preclassic or in subsequent periods (discounting, of course, the highland Mexican influence).

A situation wherein the artisans of local schools are not forced to conform to particular regional conventions of composition in order to bolster ideological relationships between polities but, rather, are encouraged to create distinctive variations on shared themes can be described as balkanized. The variability in the central imagery of public art in the Late Preclassic highland polities supports such a description. Apparently, even though certain fundamental concepts were undoubtedly shared on a regional basis and religiously sanctioned economic and political interaction between polities occurred (Parsons and Price 1971; Kubler 1971; Brown 1977:308), there was no overarching, shared ideology and religion integrating governments into a regional institution that coordinated interpolity affairs. The maintenance to each polity was based upon a related but separate and equal status.

Regional integration in the highlands: attempt and failure

The incipient development of a regional elite identifying itself as a distinct social entity may be seen in the pervasive god-impersonator composition and its correlation with the new and developing hieroglyphic writing system. The fates of rulers and their realms are closely related in the Classic and Postclassic lowlands (J. E. S. Thompson 1973; Proskouriakoff 1960; Roys 1967), and both are clearly tied to prognostication. The shift from god-impersonator to the mouthpiece of a god through astrology may be taking place in the Late Preclassic highlands. Although a shift from this stage to one in which prognostication provides the basis for contemplating the fate of a group of polities should not be a difficult one, it is evidently the step that the highland polities did not, and perhaps could not, take.

Aside from the disastrous effects of vulcanism, there is reason to believe that the ideologies and public imagery of the highland polities inhibited further consolidation of a voluntary nature during the Late Preclassic period. Generally, there was a prevailing concern for minutae and detail in the Late Preclassic highland styles. Complex concepts were expressed with complex imagery. In terms of ideology this suggests that the artisans operating in the ·highlands were pursuing the theological ramifications of primary concepts. The prevailing monumental images are of particular mythological occurrences and particular rituals. Such a concern for detail would inevitably mitigate against the consolidation of all the various ideologies into a single, universal one. At the same time, religious symbolism penetrated the mediums and objects that were widely disseminated in the populations that supported these polities (Borhegyi 1965). This penetration suggests that the ideological integration within polities was replicating ritual in the public and private domains rather than bringing the populace together in order to witness all important ritual activity. This process would inevitably build up popular support for localized religious concepts and practices. It would also mitigate against revolutionary change imposed from above by governments interested in consolidating policy around interpolity religious concepts and practices. The particular direction taken by highland religious institutions during the Late Preclassic period resulted in precisely the sort of conservative bulwark hypothesized by Lowe (1977). Notwithstanding the rapid development and dissemination of hieroglyphic writing, the potential for a coordinated elitist cult in the highlands to become a broader confederacy of politically and economically integrated societies was severely limited by prior cultural developments.

Public art and ideological unification: the lowlands

The Middle Preclassic
During the Middle Preclassic period (1000–300 B.C.) while highlands societies were advancing toward complex organization, the Maya lowlands were being populated by pioneers from the highlands as well as from the adjacent lowlands of Tabasco–Veracruz (Willey 1977b: 400–1). Although there is some reason to believe that pioneers bringing advanced ceramic technology and architecture were already established in northern Belize by Early Preclassic times (2000–1000 B.C.) (Hammond et al. 1979), the relationship of the Swasey complex to other early developments in the lowlands remains problematic. The weight of evidence currently favors rapid pioneering of the lowlands during the early part of the Middle Preclassic period. As Willey (1977b:401) has observed in discussing these pioneers, "the Xe and Eb communities were small and their cultural repertory modest. There are no public structures, no sumptuary goods. The social profile is an egalitarian one." In the course of the Middle Preclassic period, however, modest public architecture appears at widely distributed locations (Rice 1976; Hammond et al. 1979). This development and its distribution suggests the presence of conditions encouraging local centralization of communities. The presence of extralocal materials such as jade and obsidian indicates continued contact between these pioneers and the more advanced societies on their periphery (Willey 1977b:401).

Concepts of community organization may well have been brought into the lowlands by pioneers. These concepts would have been reinforced through continued contact with the parent communities in the peripheral areas. In sharp contrast to the highland and Pacific Coast areas, however, the evidence of direct Olmec contact is extremely scanty in the lowlands during this period. A single fragmentary jade bloodletter from Seibal (Willey 1977a:138) is the only evidence for contemporaneous Olmec–lowland Maya contact during the Middle Preclassic period. Other Olmec objects occur in the lowlands in later or equivocal contexts. Although there is reason to believe that the Olmec were aware of their lowland neighbors, it seems that they were not particularly interested in cultivating enduring relationships with them. If the Olmec were interested in establishing trade relationships, it may well be that the early lowland pioneers lacked the desired exotic resources and/or the organization to produce commodities for export on a large scale.

Under the circumstances it would seem that the lowland Maya were left to their own devices in matters of religion and ideology. Their external contacts, seen in ceramic styles and ritual objects like figurines, seem to be primarily with the southern highland regions. An overall trend toward ceramic uniformity occurring near the end of the Middle Preclassic and the beginning of the Late Preclassic indicates that the most important interaction may have been between lowland communities rather than with other areas (Willey 1977:387). Lacking strong acculturative pressure from more advanced societies and sharing a common dislocation from tradition-bound home communities, the lowland pioneers were in a position to establish new social and cultural identities as "lowlanders." At this point they could have reestablished highly localized, balkanized traditions. The fact that they did not might be attributed to the fact that the pioneers came into the lowlands with certain values or "cultural baggage" (Lowe 1977) and to a desire for the commodities, like jade and obsidian, which expressed these values. Such goods occur in Middle Preclassic contexts and generally increase in frequency throughout that period. These goods could only be obtained through trade and the maintenance of open lines of communication between lowland communities.

The Late Preclassic
In the transition between the Middle Preclassic and Late Preclassic periods in the lowlands, the widespread initiation of public architecture was accompanied by a marked decline in the production and use of figurines. Perhaps this is only coincidence, but the pattern persists into the Late Preclassic when ritually significant objects and decoration were strongly confined to public contexts. This demise of figurine manufacture in the lowlands is contemporaneous with the occurrence of figurines, censers, and a wide profusion of locally consumed ritual items in the southern highlands. It seems that lowland communities centralized ritual in public places and established social integration, not through the replication of ritual in public and private but through community participation. This correlation takes on greater significance because it is a regional phenomenon and consequently is not confined to any local area within the lowlands.

At the beginning of the Late Preclassic period (ca. 300 B.C.) a distinctive medium for the display of public art was already present in the lowland region – architecture. Not only were the techniques of building with limestone and lime plaster present but characteristic design elements like apron moldings occurred at Tikal (W. Coe 1965a) and at Cerros (structure 2A-sub 4-1st). These elements remained standard features of later lowland architecture. Although it is quite possible that the use of architecture as an artistic medium will ultimately be traced to Middle Preclassic, Epi–Olmec antecedents like the monuments at Tzutzuculi (McDonald 1977), the fact remains that this medium was of minor importance to the Late Preclassic highland peoples, whereas it was of primary importance to the contemporary societies of the lowlands. This pattern is in keeping with the argument that the communities of the lowlands developed central, communitywide public ritual as a means of social integration. Whereas stelae and carved stone monuments represent the "large" end of a continuum of symbolically significant objects in the highland repertoire, decorated pyramids represent not only art objects but *places* as well. Such places required the joint efforts of the entire community to construct.

The beginnings of architectural decoration beyond design elements like the apron molding remain obscure. Nevertheless, there is now a large enough sample of Late Preclassic architectural decoration in lowland contexts to suggest with confidence that this is the primary symbolic medium of the period. Three lowland centers have produced information on the elements, themes, and compositions depicted with such decoration: Uaxactun (Ricketson and Ricketson 1937), Tikal (W. Coe 1965a, b) and Cerros (Figures 2 and 3) in northern Belize (Freidel 1978, 1979). Because the architectural decoration at Cerros has only been briefly described (Freidel 1979), a fairly detailed description is in order.

Cerros has produced the remains of architectural decoration in the form of molded and painted stucco elements on four out of five Late Preclassic pyramids at the site (Figure 4). The fifth pyramid has not been tested. Structure 5C-2nd, is beautifully preserved (Figure 4). In each case the primary motif is a monumental, full face grotesque mask.

Structure 5C-2nd consists of a broad, low substructure surmounted by a tall building platform that in turn supports a multi-roomed masonry superstructure (Figure 6). The design involves a single main axis oriented north-south and a single outset stairway opening to the south and extending from the doorway of the superstructure to the plaza below. There is a single broad step slightly above the level of the lower terrace. The sides of both the lower terrace (or substructure) and the building platform are decorated

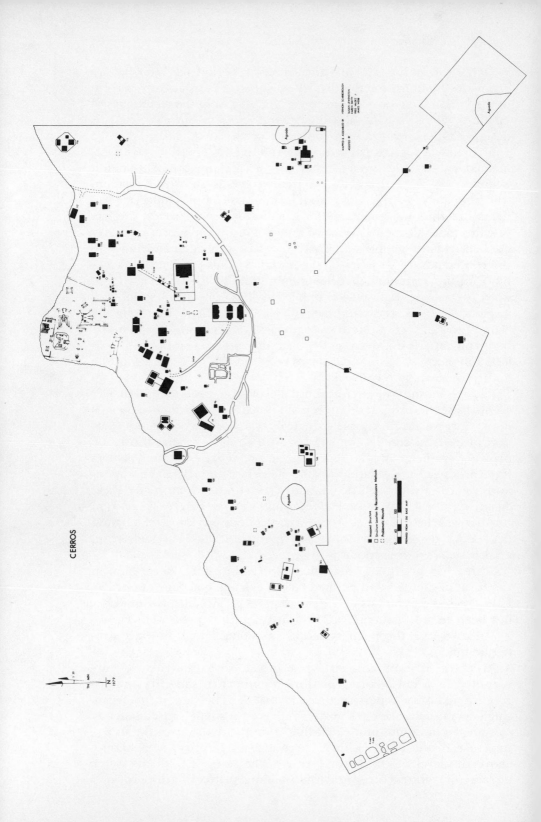

CERROS

■ Mapped Structure
□ Structure Location by Reconnaissance Methods
▢ Prehistoric Mounds

PREPARED FROM 1:100 BASE MAP

MAPPED & ASSEMBLED BY   VERNON SCARBOROUGH

ASSISTED BY   SUSAN CONNINGTON
              KAREN SMITH
              FRED VALDEZ Jr
              JAMES WEBB

Aguada

Aguada

Aguada

N
1979

TM MN
5 30

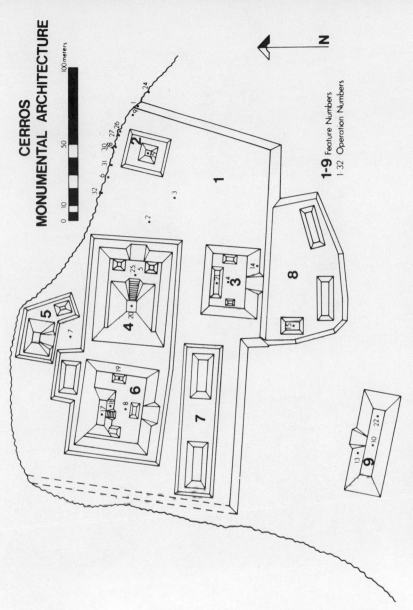

Figure 3. Planimetric map of central architecture at Cerros

Figure 4. Structure 5C-2nd viewed from the southeast

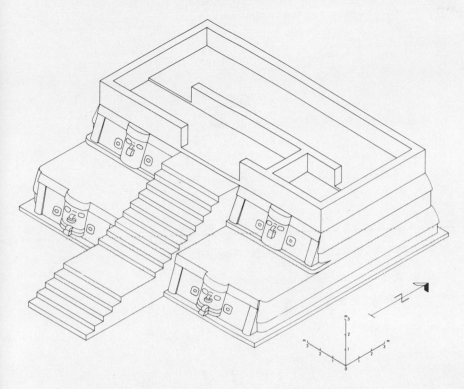

Figure 5. Isometric drawing of structure 5C-2nd

with apron moldings. The southern faces of the substructure and the building platform are decorated with four elaborate façades rendered in stucco and paint over crude masonry armatures. The central focus of each façade is a monumental grotesque mask approximately 2 meters wide and 2.5 meters high. The two lower masks located on the substructure are compound figures. Each consists of a blunt-snouted entity emerging from the head of a long-lipped entity (Figures 7 and 8). The two upper masks located on the building platform are both long-lipped entities (Figures 9 and 10). Earplug assemblages flank all four main masks. Each consists of a flare, upper and lower knots, curved binding elements, dependent lower trilobed element, and surmounting feather and scroll elements. Profile long-lipped grotesques flank these earplug assemblages. These grotesques lack lower jaws and have great scrolls emanating from the upper mouth region. Elongated down-facing profile grotesques form the side panels of each façade, whereas the upper registers are decorated with "j" or "breath" scrolls and brackets, representing abbreviations of open dragon mouths (Norman 1976; Quirarte 1976).

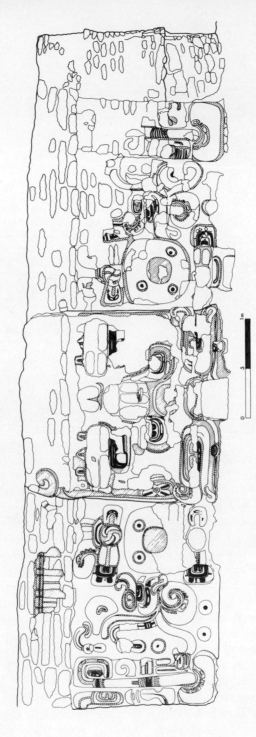

Figure 6. The lower east façade of structure 5C-2nd

Figure 7. The lower west façade of structure 5C-2nd

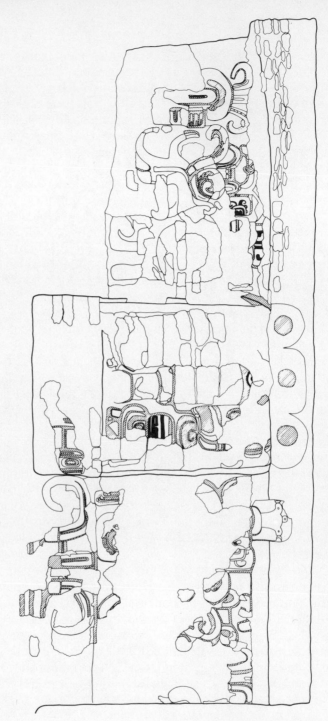

Figure 8. The upper east façade of structure 5C-2nd

Figure 9. The upper west façade of structure 5C-2nd

215

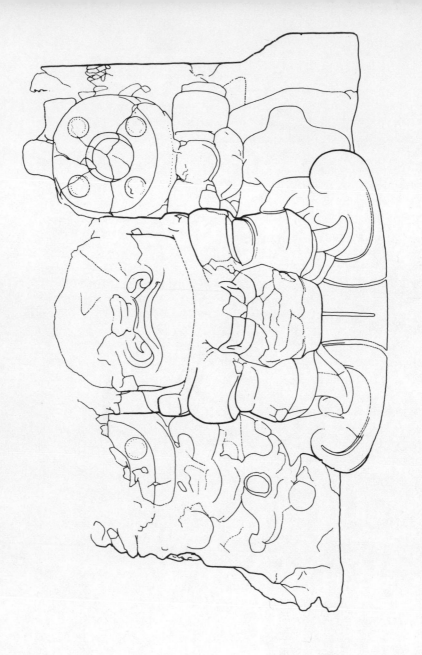

Figure 10. The northern façade of the central platform on structure 29B

In terms of general formal presentation, these façades are clearly within lowland Maya artistic conventions. The primary imagery is symmetrical. Asymmetry is rendered in details only. Each element and motif has a definite place and, aside from the details, each upper and lower façade mirrors the other. Naturalistic imagery is entirely lacking, and the primary imagery focuses exclusively on variations of the long-lipped and blunt-snouted grotesque "dragons." At the same time, elements, themes and motifs can be matched virtually on a one-to-one basis with examples from carved stone monuments in the highlands. In general, this structure and other early lowland sculptured pyramids are distinctive because of the overwhelming representation of the "dragon" grotesque in its long-lipped and blunt-snouted modes. Although a grotesque monumental head in carved stone has been reported from Monte Alto (Bernal 1969:plate 88), it can be viewed as the exception that proves the rule. There is every reason to believe that the artisans who built 5C-2nd were fully cognizant of the Late Preclassic highland repertoire of symbols and images, but, in the transition from the highlands to the lowlands, the imagery had been standardized, ordered, and focused on the primary form of the dragon mask. Moreover the imagery of structure 5C-2nd depicts neither mythical scenes nor ritual activities. It is entirely in a cosmic mode, depicting timeless (or timely) entities. The dichotomy of the blunt-snouted and long-lipped grotesques is not crowded onto the belts or helmets of god impersonators, but stands out focused and dominant.

What is the meaning of this composition when it is taken as a whole? Correlation of form and meaning is difficult when dealing with Preclassic images, given the potential for disjunction (Kubler 1973). Nevertheless, it seems that the pyramid does represent a composition, the theme of which is cosmic. Despite the monumental scale, this pyramid may depict a "miniature" model of the world.

Long-lipped images in highland Late Preclassic art have both terrestrial and celestial connotations (Quirarte 1976, and Norman 1976). Blunt-snouted images are more difficult to place, but there are examples of the juxtaposition of blunt-snouted and long-lipped entities at Izapa and elsewhere in the highlands. Stela 11 at Izapa (Norman 1973: plate 22), for example, depicts a blunt-snouted individual emerging from the jaws of a long-lipped squatting entity. A double-headed serpent with blunt-snouted masks flanks the base of the scene. Here the principle of a blunt-snouted entity emerging from a long-lipped entity seems replicated. A closer resemblance is found on Stela 3 at Izapa (Norman 1973:plate 6). There a long-lipped entity straddles another long-lipped entity with a snake body. The latter grotesque either is bearing a blunt-snouted mask on its head, or a blunt-snouted mask is emerging from its head. As on

5C-2nd, the blunt-snouted entity seems to be sandwiched in between long-lipped entities.

Perhaps the key to the composition can be found on 5C-2nd itself. The cheeks of the lower blunt-snouted masks bear distinctive tattoos in the form of cartouched glyphs. In one case (Figure 8), the glyph is the *Kin* glyph of later Classic and Postclassic lowland art. Enough remains of the others (Figure 9) to indicate that they too are *Kin* glyphs. If this glyph had the same connotations in Late Preclassic times as it did in later periods, then it represents the sun. If the blunt-snouted masks represent the sun, then their position in the composition becomes clear. The totality would then represent the sun emerging from the long-lipped double-headed earth dragon in the east, merging with the long-lipped double-headed sky dragon, and descending back into the earth in the west. The notion that the blunt-snouted entity is ascending and merging into the long-lipped entity of the upper eastern façade and then being regurgitated in the west finds some iconographic support in the helmet designs of the lower blunt-snouted masks. These helmets depict upcurling scrolls flanking a central panel. Although these scrolls strongly resemble horns, they probably represent the split image of an upturned long-lipped mouth. Support for this identification is found in the central panel of the preserved western helmet. Here at the center of the panel is a distinctive double-loop droplet motif that is identical to droplets extending from the tooth ridges of profile grotesques flanking the earplug assemblages. It should also be noted that there are several indications of significant east–west dichotomies. For example, the tassels of the knots on the eastern earplug assemblages terminate in cartouched glyphs. The same tassels on the west lack glyphs and end in bifurcated scrolled tips. The profile grotesques all have flame brows, but those on the east contain cartouched "u" glyphs, whereas those on the west have distinctive upcurling scroll ends on the front rather than glyphs. Finally, in addition to such east–west distinctions, the three preserved outward-facing, profile grotesques flanking the earplug assemblages have the upper lip or snout detached from the tooth ridge in an open "snarl," whereas the three preserved inward-facing grotesques have the snout and tooth ridge attached in a closed "snarl."

Whether or not the meaning attached to the composition on structure 5C-2nd bears up under scrutiny, the image itself is elementary and is fundamental to later lowland iconography. Moreover, it is significant that the same basic composition is found on the famous E-VII-sub pyramid at Uaxactun. On E-VII-sub, the lower register of masks represents reptilian grotesques (Ricketson and Ricketson 1937). If the sides of these images are examined (Ricketson and Ricketson 1937:Figures 39, 41), it can be argued that the entity has an upcurling long lip. The front "horns" or "nostrils" seem to represent the artisan's attempt to depict a split image of the upcurling long lip in a flattened, virtually two-dimensional, field. The central set of masks on E-VII-sub are all blunt snouted as on 5C-2nd. Four of the six masks clearly have "Tau"-shaped elements in the central mouth area. Tau-shaped teeth are diagnostic of Kinich Ahau, the Maya sun god, in Classic and Postclassic imagery. The upper register has two masks on E-VII-sub. Both masks depict long-lipped entities with downcurling lips. Despite the differences in the design of the buildings in question, and their differences in style, repertoire, and medium (E-VII-sub lacks polychrome paint), both buildings portray the same formal composition and the same dominance of grotesque "dragon" entities over other imagery.

The dichotomy between the blunt-snouted and long-lipped entities is also illustrated on structure 29B at Cerros. This structure is somewhat later than 5C-2nd and was evidently in use right up to the abandonment of Cerros, just prior to the introduction of Protoclassic Floral Park ceramics in the region. Structure 29 is a two-stepped substructure supporting three building platforms at the summit. The central building platform faces west, which is also the primary orientation of the overall structure. The flanking building platforms face inward toward the central one. All three have outset stairways flanked by compound masks consisting of large grotesque heads with smaller, anthropomorphic masks emerging from them. Each mask is flanked by earplug assemblages. Three of the six masks are well preserved. The other three have preserved armatures or fragments. The northern mask on the central platform is clearly a feline image (Figure 10). It bears flame brows, a "J" scrolled tongue with central bracket, and other elements indicating that it is the blunt-snouted variant of the primary grotesque image. Remains of the southern mask on the central platform show that the same image was portrayed there. Both of the flanking masks on the northern platform are the long-lipped grotesque with downcurling lip (Figures 11 and 12). Commensurate with the interpretation offered for structure 5C-2nd, it seems that the flanking masks on the northern and southern platforms depict the rising and setting sun emerging and returning into the long-lipped terrestrial dragon. In this case the awkward placement of the stairways on the flanking platforms oriented to the north and south suggests that these were used for the celebration of the equinoxes when the sun at zenith was either to the north or south of the platform. The central jaguar images suggest the primary dichotomy of the sun as earth and sky deity; the upper masks represent the sky aspect. The preserved portions of these upper masks indicate that they depicted blunt-snouted, snarling mouthed entities; they were clearly more "human" than the

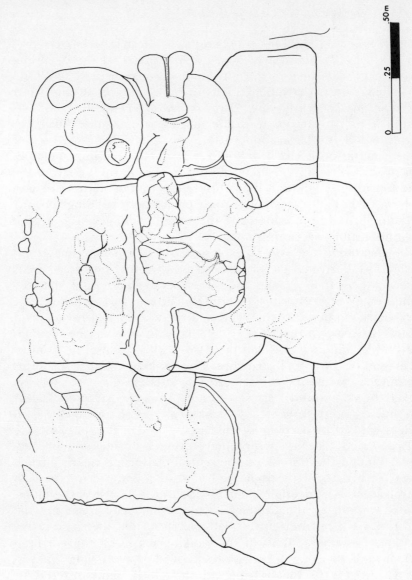

Figure 11. The west façade of the northern platform on structure 29B

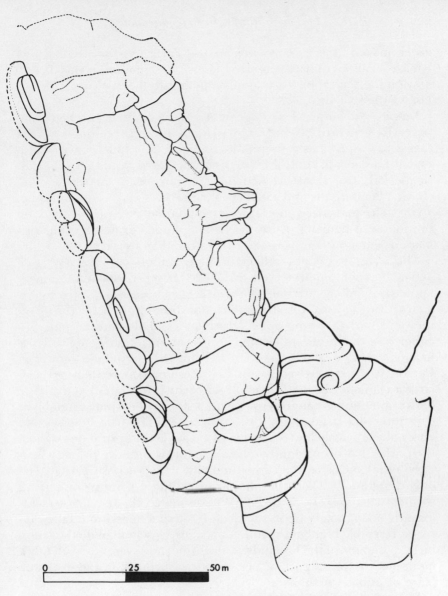

0   .25   .50 m

Figure 12. The eastern façade of the northern platform on structure 29B, profile view looking east

lower masks. It is notable that in the Early Classic the image of Kinich Ahau is primarily human. The representation of this dichotomy on the central platform is in keeping with the east–west orientation of the structure.

Despite the unusual arrangement of structure 29B when compared to structure 5C-2nd or E-VII-sub, there is reason to believe that it too represents a standard composition. A much larger pyramid at Lamanai in central Belize, recently dated to the Late Preclassic period, has a virtually identical arrangement at the summit (David Pendergast and Stanley Loten, personal communication 1978). The masks are poorly preserved, but at least one of them on the southern flanking platform is a long-lipped grotesque. The primary orientation here is to the east rather than to the west.

The Late Preclassic architectural decoration at Tikal (W. Coe 1965a, b) is not well preserved. Structure 5D-sub-1-1st has monumental masks flanking the stairway, which have been interpreted as "jaguars." In the unrestored isometric illustration (W. Coe 1965a:15) they look more like long-lipped grotesques with flanking earplugs. In either case this structure would conform to the other Late Preclassic imagery previously discussed. In light of the compound figures at Cerros, it is perhaps significant that these masks are depicted with large cartouches in the fontanel area. Structure 5D-sub-3-3rd has a flanking monumental grotesque with a standard earplug assemblage consisting of a large plug with four symmetrically placed bosses and knots above and below. In terms of major architectural decoration, then, what has been found at Tikal conforms with the primary imagery found at Cerros and Uaxactun in the Late Preclassic period. The only deviation at Tikal is in the exquisite mural painting on a small shrine, structure 5D-sub-10-1st. (W. Coe 1965a: 18–19). These paintings, depicting many figures wearing grotesque masks and fancy apparel, resemble highland monuments more closely than do the sculptured pyramids of the lowlands. This shrine, however, was evidently a monument to an important person buried beneath it, rather than a place of public worship.

The weight of available evidence suggests that the structure of lowland Maya iconography and ideology was already well established in the Late Preclassic period prior to the advent of the stelae and hieroglyphic writing characteristic of the Classic period. In contrast to contemporary highland society, the lowlanders focused attention in their public art upon a select number of primary images that are broadly shared and replicated in the known instances. It has been suggested that the primary images are the blunt-snouted feline entity, representative of the sun, and the long-lipped reptilian entity, representative of the earth and the sky.

Regardless of whether or not this interpretation is found to be acceptable in the long run, the formal qualities of lowland public art in the Late Preclassic period are clear. The lowland Maya emphasized symbolically decorated places over objects and focused upon primary images that were broadly shared and depicted in symmetrical arrangements that are parts of overall compositions. These features, coupled with a strong centralization of ritual in public places, suggest that the Late Preclassic lowlands witnessed the development of a shared reality of government in the context of an iconographically simplified and conceptually centralized religion. The iconographic ties between the highlands and lowlands during the Late Preclassic period indicate that the highlands are the probable Middle Preclassic source of the earliest lowland symbols and a continued source of novel imagery thereafter. It is equally probable that the lowland Maya adhered to their distinctive medium, the sculptured pyramid, their centralization of ritual, and their focus on central cosmic themes in the face of continual interaction with the old highland centers.

The lowland Maya: civilization as a state of mind

The identification of a regional universalizing religion in the Late Preclassic lowlands has significant ramifications for social, economic, and political organization at the beginning of Maya civilization. If religious and ideological integration are considered as aspects of an evolutionary development, then they must have been selected for. They must have adaptive value. The environmental deterministic model for the evolution of complex society in Mesoamerica offered by Sanders and Webster (1978) provides a useful context for consideration of this issue. Their model is multilinear in the sense that the authors envision two distinct initial forms for complex society, either stratified or ranked (chiefdom). The former leads inevitably to the true state in which its legally constituted class structure is based upon economic inequality backed by force. The latter rarely transcends the fundamentally reciprocal obligations of kinship sanctions.

According to Sanders and Webster,

> stratified societies are those in which there is differential economic access to basic subsistence resources – that is, capital, productive resources such as land, and water. Such differential access implies accretion of wealth, and all of the internal social stresses related to it . . . wealth becomes a political tool in a more fundamental sense than the manipulation of noncapital resources previously allowed (Sanders and Webster 1978:272).

Sanders and Webster suggest that stratified society in Mesoamerica arose in regions such as the central plateau of Mexico and Oaxaca valley, which are characterized by agricultural risk in the form of fluctuations in rainfall and temperature. In contrast, regions of low risk, such as the Maya highlands and lowlands, gave rise to a ranked or chiefdom society. In these authors' opinion the lowland Maya state of the Late Classic period (A.D. 600–900) constitutes one of the rare cases of a chiefdom that evolves to a higher evolutionary stage. In this case the unusual condition is unimpeded population growth, resulting in unequal access to productive land.

Sanders and Webster do not directly address the adaptive value of stratified versus ranked society, but the implications are clear. Stratified society evolves in response to stress in the natural environment. Ranked society, on the other hand, evolves in response to stress in the social environment. In ranked society social conflict is generated by the increasing potential for face-to-face interaction between people who are not kin, which accompanies even modest population growth in sedentary society. In the sense that kin sanctions do not apply, such people can be, quite literally, outlaws relative to one another. There are several ways to deal with this situation. One alternative lies in the elimination of individual conflict through severely curtailing contact by means of a chronic, highly ritualized state of intercommunity conflict. Another possibility is establishing specialists in intercommunity relations, such as trading partners, "big men" or chiefs (Harding 1970:103).

Grant, for the sake of argument, that the lowlands witnessed the initial development of a ranked society during the Preclassic era in the context of a growing sedentary population. Prior to the Late Preclassic florescence, the lowland Maya could have stabilized into a mosaic of petty chiefdoms. Instead, they standardized and shared a structure of power based upon a cosmic rather than a kinship ideology. The social concomitant of this development may be stratification. This position can be argued as follows. Although it is unclear in Sanders and Webster's model how the classes made up of the "owners" of productive resources actually consolidate into a social stratum, presumably it occurs because such people recognize a common interest distinct from that of the "nonowners" and coordinate accordingly. But if a common interest is vital to stratification, is such an interest inherently lacking in ranked society? In ranked society, Sanders and Webster declare:

> Everyone . . . is related to the chief, and everyone also occupies a unique position of rank that is determined by calculation of the exact degree of closeness (or distance) to the chief. A theoretical result is that true stratification into classes is absent, as there are not large groups made up of people of equivalent rank (Sanders and Webster 1978: 270).

If, however, one considers not a single chiefdom but, rather, a network of chiefdoms between which sumptuary "noncapital" goods are circulating, then large groups of equivalent noble rank are present. It is quite clear in the ethnographic literature (e.g., Harding 1970; Smith 1976) that a common interest is present between the sociopolitical elites of ranked and big man societies in the context of such extensive exchange networks. Extensive trade networks, however, rarely give rise to regional elites because: (1) each society on the network can incorporate the goods into its political system in a distinctive fashion; (2) different sets of goods are selected out as prestigious by different societies; and (3) without an effective institutional coordination among participants in the trade network, it is impossible to limit access to the trade networks to one segment of society at the regional level (Harding 1970).

The key problem in the evolutionary transition between ranked and stratified society is not found in the absence of a common interest or a common economic basis (control of distribution, cf. Smith 1976) but, rather, in the difficulty of setting up a coordinated institutional basis between chiefdoms that establishes monopolized, unequal access to scarce and desirable goods (or "political currency" in Harding's [1970] happy phrase). This is the problem that the highland Maya failed to overcome and that the lowland Maya succeeded in solving. The lowland Maya solved this problem by promoting the ritual that is a key feature of trade encounters in regional networks into a centralized religious institution; moreover, they standardized that institution at the regional level and limited access to its offices and their concomitant economic perogatives (Freidel 1979). The result was a regional social stratum of chiefly nobles and merchant priests whose joint control of the mode of distribution provided a solid economic alternative to kinship sanction as a source of permanent power.

The practical benefits of control over sumptuary goods are well established (Harding 1970; Smith 1976). Such political currency does not circulate without the existence of trade in the more mundane necessities. More importantly, there is usually a system of equivalencies between wealth objects and other goods. Such equivalencies are clearly manifest among the lowland Maya of the contact period (Tozzer 1941). Given the continuities in form and material of the basic wealth objects, such as jade and shell ornaments, throughout Maya culture history, there is reason to believe that such equivalencies existed at the beginning of Maya civilization as well. Sumptuary goods are "noncapital" goods only if they cannot realize a profit. In the generally uncoordinated trade that occurs in ethnographically known exchange systems, profit is marginal and uncertain (Harding

1970). In a coordinated exchange system such as that envisioned here for the lowland Maya, the potential for profit is contingent only upon a sustained demand in the face of monopolized supply. Empirically, the distribution of wealth objects, such as shell, jade, and obsidian, penetrated all the way down to the lower levels of Maya society throughout its history. Hence although the supply was always limited and the upper stratum of Maya society always enjoyed unequal access to such goods, it can be argued that the demand for political currency was not only sustained but was also throughout society.

From this perspective, the Late Classic Maya state organization was not primarily an adaptive response to population pressure. Instead, it was produced by the ramification of social stratification already established by Late Preclassic times. The Early Classic period (A.D. 300–600) witnessed the exuberant development of an economically integrated regional society. Through the stela cult and hieroglyphic writing, access to political power became codified into law. At the same time, a burgeoning bureaucracy administering the pilgrimage fairs at centers opened its ranks to commoners. Thus it created a "middle class" that was supportive of the elite (Rathje 1971a). Concomitant with these developments, there was an explosive demand for more, and more varied, production of wealth objects. That this demand far outstripped the uncertain supply of nonlocal exotic resources is documented in the widespread innovation of wealth objects made from local materials like elaborate painted pottery, eccentric flints, worked bone, textiles, and wood and feather ornaments. Such a rapid development of crafts no doubt resulted in additional social distinctions.

The class structure of the Late Classic period can be viewed as the product of two processes: (1) the downward penetration of codified astrological law, which transformed the social destiny of any individual or group into a castelike social fate and (2) the concomitant tendency to maintain desirable social status by making it hereditary. The first process could work to close off upward mobility, whereas the second would reinforce class identification in the upper strata. But a legally sanctioned class structure would inevitably weaken a political economy predicated upon societywide participation in a complex distribution network of political currency and "essentials" as access to desirable goods became a matter of hereditary prerogative rather than of ambition and talent. The adaptive response to such social stress is clear: involuntary exploitation of the lower classes through a variety of means. These would include taxation, outright ownership of the productive resources such as land and people, and legally sanctioned coercion.

As Sanders and Webster propose, social stratification, once established, inevitably leads to state formation. However, in the last analysis, social stratification is a cultural invention. The "natural selection" of culturally informed inequality and its adaptive superiority need not be grounded in the practical problems of physical human survival. The human imperative is survival of the social group and the reality it shares. In this light, the selective advantage of hierarchically structured, culturally heterogeneous societies is size. Drawing on biological ecology, we see that the adaptation of juxtaposed societies in a contiguous geographic region is a dynamic interdependent process. Some regions in antiquity, such as Mesoamerica, were characterized by the precocious development of an encompassing social ecosystem in which the participant societies were conscious of, and responded to, the existence and behavior of each other. Such regions gave rise to a variety of adaptive relationships between constituent societies that ranged from mutually beneficial to predatory (cf. Blanton 1976b). Finally, the social ecosystems of such areas were highly unstable and were characterized by severe competition for sociocultural survival.

Within this kind of social ecosystem, adaptive pressure on cultural realities is acute, producing a wide variety of sociocultural forms. The most enduring forms are the largest and most complex – the civilizations. Although most civilizations result from the predatory expansion of societies in which the cultural realities are marked by conceptions considered inherently superior and universally applicable, this is not the only route to great size. The lowland Maya evidently achieved great social size through consolidation around universal conceptions rather than by expansion. In the short run, the adaptive strategy of the Maya was highly successful and resulted in the largest and most enduring civilization in ancient Mesoamerica. In the long run, however, predatory civilization is the more adaptive form, because the predatory absorption of alien societies is the critical way of transmitting and perpetuating sociocultural innovations that evolve in the context of civilization (Service 1975).

No doubt there are critical, "necessary" material conditions to be found in the regions supporting unstable social ecosystems. It remains to be demonstrated, however, that the same set of conditions occurred in all the regions of the world that gave rise to civilization and the state and that these conditions occur exclusively in those regions. Even if this is demonstrated, the evolution of unstable social ecosystems will remain obscure until the dynamics of the cultural realities involved are understood. For it is the capacity of cultural realities to undergo change in structure and content that ultimately allows new social forms to evolve.

Works cited

Adams, Richard E. W. 1977. *Prehistoric Mesoamerica*. Little, Brown, Boston.
Adams, Richard E. W. and T. Patrick Culbert. 1977. The Origins of Civilization in the Maya Lowlands. In *The Origins of Maya Civilization*, ed. Richard E. W. Adams, pp. 3–24. University of New Mexico Press, Albuquerque.
Adams, Richard N. 1975. *Energy and Structure: A Theory of Social Power*. University of Texas Press, Austin.
Adams, Robert McC. 1966. *The Evolution of Urban Society: Early Mesopotamia and Prehistoric Mexico*. Aldine, Chicago.
Althabe, G. 1965. Changements sociaux chez les Pygmées Baka de l'Est Cameroun. *Cahiers d'Etudes Africaines* 5(4):561–92.
Attenborough, F. L. 1963. *The Laws of the Earliest English Kings*. Russell & Russell, New York.
Aveleyra Arroyo de Anda, Luis. 1964. The Primitive Hunters. In *Handbook of Middle American Indians*, ed. Robert Wauchope, Vol. 1, pp. 384–412. University of Texas Press, Austin.
Ball, Joseph W. 1977. The Rise of the Northern Chiefdoms: A Sociopolitical Analysis. In *The Origins of Maya Civilization*, ed. R. E. W. Adams, pp. 101–32. University of New Mexico Press, Albuquerque.
Bawden, Garth. 1977. *Galindo and the Nature of the Middle Horizon in Northern Coastal Peru*. Unpublished Ph.D. dissertation, Harvard University.
Beaglehole, Ernest and Pearl Beaglehole. 1938. Ethnology of Pukapuka. *Bernice P. Bishop Museum, Bulletin* 150.
Bean, L. J. and T. F. King. 1974. ANTAP: California Indian Political and Economic Organization. *Ballena Press Anthropological Papers* 2. Ramona, California.
Beckner, M. 1959. *The Biological Way of Thought*. Columbia University Press, New York.
Bennett, Wendell C. 1950. The Gallinazo Group; Viru Valley, Peru. *Yale University Publications in Anthropology* 12.
Bennett, Wendell C. and Junius B. Bird. 1949. Andean Culture History. *American Museum of Natural History, Handbook* 15. American Museum of Natural History, New York.
Benson, Elizabeth. 1972. *The Mochica, a Culture of Peru*. Praeger, New York.
Bernal, Ignacio. 1969. *The Olmec World*, transl. N. Heyden and F. Horcasitus. University of California Press, Berkeley, Los Angeles.
Bierstedt, Robert. 1950. An Analysis of Social Power. *American Sociological Review* 15:730–8.

Binford, Lewis R. 1962. Archaeology as Anthropology. *American Antiquity* 28(2):217–25.

Blanton, Richard E.
1972. Prehistoric Settlement Patterns of the Ixtapalapa Peninsula Region, Mexico. *Pennsylvania State University, Department of Anthropology, Occasional Paper* 6.
1976a. The Origins of Monte Alban. In *Cultural Change and Continuity*, ed. Charles E. Cleland; pp. 223–32. Academic Press, New York.
1976b. The Role of Symbiosis in Adaptation and Socio-cultural Change in the Valley of Mexico. In *The Valley of Mexico: Studies in Pre-Hispanic Ecology and Society*, ed. Eric R. Wolf, pp. 179–80. University of New Mexico Press, Albuquerque.

Blanton, Richard E., Jill Appel, Laura Finsten, Steve Kowalewski, Gary Feinman, and Eva Fisch. 1979. Regional Evolution in the Valley of Oaxaca, Mexico. *Journal of Field Archaeology* 6:369–90.

Borhegyi, Stephan F. de. 1965. Archaeological Synthesis of the Guatemalan Highlands. In *Handbook of Middle American Indians*, ed. Robert Wauchope, Vol. 2, Part 1 pp. 3–58. University of Texas Press, Austin.

Boserup, Ester. 1965. *The Conditions of Agricultural Growth*. Aldine, Chicago.

Brown, Kenneth L. 1977. Toward a Systematic Explanation of Culture Within the Middle Classic Period of the Valley of Guatemala. In *Teotihuacán and Kaminaljuyu: A Study in Prehistoric Culture Contact*, ed. William T. Sanders and J. W. Michels, pp. 411–40. Pennsylvania State University Press, University Park.

Brush, Charles F. 1965. Pox Pottery, Earliest Identified Mexican Ceramic. *Science* 140:195.

Burger, Richard L.
1975. New Discoveries in the Trace Element Analysis of Andean Obsidian. Paper presented at the Annual Meeting of the Institute of American Studies, Berkeley, California.
1978. *The Occupation of Chavín, Ancash, in the Initial Period and Early Horizon*. Unpublished Ph.D. dissertation, University of California, Berkeley.

Caetani, Leone. 1905. *Annali dell' Islam*, Vol. 1. Hoepli, Milan.

Campbell, Donald T. 1965. Variation and Selective Retention in Sociocultural Evolution. In *Social Change in Developing Areas*, ed. Herbert R. Barringer, George I. Blanksten, and Raymond W. Mack, pp. 19–49. Schenkman, Cambridge, Mass.

Carneiro, Robert L.
1961. Slash-and-Burn Cultivation Among the Kuikuru and its Implication for Cultural Development in the Amazon Basin. In *The Evolution of Horticultural Systems in Native South America, Causes and Consequences*, ed. Johannes Wilbert. *Antropologica, Supplement Publication* 2:47–67: Sociedad Ciencias Naturales La Salle, Caracas.
1970. A Theory of the Origin of the State. *Science* 169:733–8.
1972. From Autonomous Villages to the State, A Numerical Estimation. In *Population Growth: Anthropological Implications*, ed. Brian Spooner, pp. 64–77. MIT Press, Cambridge, Mass.
1974. A Reappraisal of the Roles of Technology and Organization in the Origin of Civilization. *American Antiquity* 39:179–86.
1978. Political Expansion as an Expression of the Principle of Competitive Exclusion. In *Origins of the State: The Anthropology of Political Evolution*, ed. Ronald Cohen and Elman R. Service, pp. 205–44. Institute for the Study of Human Issues, Philadelphia.

Carneiro, Robert L. and Daisy F. Hilse. 1966. On Determining the Probable Rate of Population Growth During the Neolithic. *American Anthropologist* 68:177–81.

Carrasco, Pedro and J. Broda. 1978. *Economía, política e ideologia en el Mexico prehispanico*. Centro de Investigaciones Superiores del Instituto Nacional de Antropología e Historia, México, D. F.

Carrion Cachot, Rebecca. 1948. La cultura Chavín; dos nuevos colonías; Kuntur Wasi y Ancón. *Revista del Museo Nacional de Antropología y Arqueología* 2(1):99–172.

Chagnon, Napoleon. 1970. Ecological and Adaptive Aspects of California Shell Money. In *Department of Anthropology, University of California, Los Angeles, Archaeological Survey, Annual Report* 12, ed. N. Nelson Leonard, III, Judith A. Rasson, and Dean A. Decker, pp. 1–25.

Chang, Kwang-chih. 1963. *The Archaeology of Ancient China*. Yale University Press, New Haven.

Childe, V. Gordon. 1951. *Man Makes Himself*. Watts, London.

Cieza de León, Pedro de. 1959. *The Incas of Pedro de Cieza de León*, transl. Harriet de Onis; ed. V. W. Von Hagen. University of Oklahoma Press, Norman.

Claessen, Henri J. M. and Peter M. Skalnik (ed.). 1978. *The Early State*. Mouton, The Hague.

Coe, Michael D.
   1966. *The Maya*. Praeger, New York.
   1968a. *America's First Civilization*. American Heritage, New York; Van Nostrand, Princeton, N.J.
   1968b. San Lorenzo and the Olmec Civilization. In *Dumbarton Oaks Conference on the Olmec*, ed. Elizabeth P. Benson, pp. 41–71. Dumbarton Oaks, Washington, D.C.
   1976. The Iconology of Olmec Art. In *The Iconography of Middle American Sculpture*, pp. 1–12. Metropolitan Museum of Art, New York.

Coe, William R.
   1965a. Tikal, Guatemala, and Emergent Maya Civilization. *Science* 147: 1401–23.
   1965b. Tikal: Ten Years of Study of a Maya Ruin in the Lowlands of Guatemala. *Expedition* 8(1):5–56.
   1967. *Tikal: A Handbook of the Ancient Maya Ruins*. University of Pennsylvania, Philadelphia.

Cohen, Mark N.
   1977. *The Food Crisis in Prehistory*. Yale University Press, New Haven.
   1978. General and Local Models of Prehistoric Change: Their Applicability to Different Periods of Prehistory. Paper presented at the Annual Meeting of the Society for American Archaeology, Tucson.
   1980. Speculations on the Evolution of Density Measurement and Population Regulation in Homo sapiens. In *Biosocial Mechanisms of Population Regulation*, ed. Mark N. Cohen, Roy Malpass, and Harold Klein, pp. 275–304. Yale University Press, New Haven.

Cohen, Ronald.
   1978a. Introduction. In *Origins of the State: The Anthropology of Political Evolution*, ed. Ronald Cohen and Elman R. Service, pp. 1–20. Institute for the Study of Human Issues, Philadelphia.
   1978b. State Origins: A Reappraisal. In *The Early State*, ed. Henri J. M. Claessen and Peter M. Skalnik, pp. 31–76. Mouton, The Hague.

Collier, Donald. 1962. Archaeological Investigations in the Casma Valley,

Peru. *Akten des 34. Internationalen Amerikanistenkongresses, Wien, July,* 1960, pp. 411–17. Vienna.

Conklin, William J. 1978. The Revolutionary Weaving Inventions of the Early Horizon. *Nawpa Pacha* 16:1–12.

Covarrubias, Miguel. 1957. *Indian Art of Mexico and Central America.* Knopf, New York.

Dahl, Robert A. 1969. The Concept of Power. In *Political Power: a Reader in Theory and Research,* ed. Roderick Bell, David V. Edwards, and R. Harrison Wagner, pp. 79–93. Free Press, New York. (Originally published 1957.)

Dalton, George. 1977. Aboriginal Economies in Stateless Societies. In *Exchange Systems in Prehistory,* ed. Timothy Earle and J. E. Erickson, pp. 191–212. Academic Press, New York.

Day, Kent C. 1976. Storage and Labor service, Two Aspects of Ancient Peruvian Socio-Economic Organization. Paper presented at seminar on Chan Chan: City and Hinterland, School of American Research, Santa Fe, New Mexico.

Deetz, James F. and Edwin S. Dethlefsen. 1967. Death's Head, Cherub, Urn and Willow. *Natural History* 76(3):29–37.

Diakanov, I. M. (ed.). 1968. *Ancient Mesopotamia.* Nauka Press, Moscow.

Donald, Leland. 1979. Was Nootka Society Based on Slave Labour? *Proceedings of the 1979 Annual Meeting of the American Ethnological Society,* in press.

Donnan, Christopher B. 1978. *Moche Art of Peru.* Museum of Cultural History, University of California, Los Angeles.

Downs, Anthony. 1967. *Inside Bureaucracy.* Little, Brown, Boston.

Drennan, Robert D.
  1976a. Fábrica San José and Middle Formative Society in the Valley of Oaxaca. *Memoirs of the Museum of Anthropology, University of Michigan* 8.
  1976b. Religion and Social Evolution in Formative Mesoamerica. In *The Early Mesoamerican Village,* ed. Kent V. Flannery, pp. 345–68. Academic Press, New York.

Drucker, Philip, Robert F. Heizer, and R. J. Squier. 1959. Excavations at La Venta, Tabasco, 1955. *Bureau of American Ethnology, Bulletin* 170.

Durkheim, Emile. 1915. *The Elementary Forms of the Religious Life.* Allen & Unwin, London.

Earle, Timothy K.
  1973. *Control Hierarchies in the Traditional Irrigation Economy of Halelea District of Kauai, Hawaii.* Unpublished Ph.D. dissertation, University of Michigan.
  1977. A Reappraisal of Redistribution: Complex Hawaiian Chiefdoms. In *Exchange Systems in Prehistory,* ed. Timothy K. Earle and Jonathon E. Ericson, pp. 213–29. Academic Press, New York.
  1978. Economic and Social Organization of a Complex Chiefdom: The Halelea District, Kaua'i, Hawaii. *University of Michigan, Museum of Anthropology, Anthropological Papers* 63.

Earle, Timothy and T. N. D'Altroy. 1979. The Function of Storage in Traditional Economies. Paper presented at the Annual Meeting of the Society for American Archaeology, Vancouver.

Engel, Frederick A.
  1957. Sites et establissements sans céramique de la côte Péruvienne. *Journal de la Société des Américanistes* 46:67–155.
  1967. Le complexe précéramique d'El Paraiso (Pérou). *Journal de la Société des Américanistes* 55:43–95.

1970. *Las lomas de Iguanil y el complejo de Haldas.* Universidad Nacional Agraria La Molina, Lima.

Engels, Frederich. 1972. *The Origin of the Family, Private Property and the State,* ed. Eleanor Burke Leacock. International Publishers, New York. (Originally published 1891.)

Estete, Miguel. 1872. Report of Miguel de Astete on the Expedition to Pachacamac. In *Reports on the Discovery of Peru,* transl. Clements R. Markham, Pp. 74–109. Burt Franklin, New York.

Farb, Peter. 1978. *Man's Rise to Civilization: The Cultural Ascent of the Indians of North America.* 2d ed. Bantam Books, New York.

Feldman, Robert A.
1977a. Life in Ancient Peru. *Field Museum of Natural History, Bulletin* 48(6):12–17.
1977b. Preceramic Corporate Architecture from Aspero: Evidence for the organization of the Andean State. Paper presented at the Annual Meeting of the American Anthropological Association, Houston, Texas.

Flannery, Kent V.
1968. The Olmec and the Valley of Oaxaca: A Model for Interregional Interaction in Formative Times. In *Dumbarton Oaks Conference on the Olmec,* ed. Elizabeth P. Benson, pp. 79–110. Dumbarton Oaks, Washington, D.C.
1970. *Preliminary Archaeological Investigations in the Valley of Oaxaca, Mexico, 1966–1969.* University of Michigan, Ann Arbor.
1972. The Cultural Evolution of Civilizations. *Annual Review of Ecology and Systematics* 3:399–426.

Flannery, Kent V. and Joyce Marcus.
1976a. Evolution of Public Building in Formative Oaxaca. In *Cultural Change and Continuity,* ed. Charles E. Cleland, pp. 205–22. Academic Press, New York.
1976b. Formative Oaxaca and the Zapotec Cosmos. *American Scientist* 64:374–83.

Freidel, David A.
1978. Maritime Adaptations and the Rise of Maya Civilization: The View from Cerros, Belize. In *Prehistoric Coastal Adaptations: The Economy and Ecology of Maritime Middle America,* ed. B. Stark and B. Voorhies, pp. 232–62. Academic Press, New York.
1979. Culture Areas and Interaction spheres: Contrasting Approaches to the Emergence of Civilization in the Maya Lowlands. *American Antiquity* 44(1):36–54.

Fried, Morton H.
1960. On the Evolution of Social Stratification and the State. In *Culture in History, Essays in Honor of Paul Radin,* ed. Stanley Diamond, pp. 713–31. Columbia University Press, New York.
1967. *The Evolution of Political Society: An Essay in Political Anthropology.* Random House, New York.
1968. State: The Institution. *International Encyclopedia of the Social Sciences,* Vol. 15, pp. 143–50. Macmillan and Free Press, New York.
1976. Energy and the Evolution of Leslie A. White. *Reviews in Anthropology* 3:592–600.
1978. The State, the Chicken, and the Egg, or What Came First. In *Origins of the State: The Anthropology of Political Evolution,* ed. Ronald Cohen and Elman R. Service, pp. 35–48. Institute for the Study of Human Issues, Philadelphia.

Friedman, J. and M. J. Rowlands. 1978. Notes Towards an Epigenetic Model of the Evolution of "Civilisation." In *The Evolution of Social Systems*, ed. J. Friedman and M. J. Rowlands, pp. 201–76. University of Pittsburgh Press, Pittsburgh.

Fritz, John M. 1978. Paleopsychology Today: Ideational Systems and Human Adaptation in Prehistory. In *Social Archaeology: Beyond Subsistence and Dating*, ed. Charles Redman, Mary Jane Berman, Edward Curtin, William Langhorne, Jr., Nina Versaggi, and Jeffrey Wanser, pp. 37–59. Academic Press, New York.

Fung Pineda, Rosa.
1969a. Las Aldeas: *Su ubicación dentro del proceso histórico del Perú antiguo.* (Dédalo 5[9–10]) Museu de Arte e Arqueología Universidade de São Paulo, São Paulo.
1969b. Los anzuelos de concha de Las Aldeas: un análisis comparativo. *Boletín del Seminario de Arqueología* 4:29–47. Instituto Riva-Aguero, Lima.
1972. Nuevos datos para el Periodo de Cerámica Inicial en el Valle de Casma. *Arqueología y Sociedad* 7–8:1–12. Museo de Arqueología y Etnología de la Universidad Nacional de San Marcos, Lima.
1975. Excavaciones en Pacopampa, Cajamarca. *Revista del Museo Nacional* 51:129–207.

Gall, Patricia and Arthur Saxe. 1977. The Ecological Evolution of Culture: The State as Predator in Succession Theory. In *Exchange Systems in Prehistory*, ed. Timothy Earle and J. E. Erickson, pp. 255–68. Academic Press, New York.

García Moll, R. 1977. *Analysis de los Materiales, Arqueologicos de la Cueva del Texcal Puebla.* Collección Cientifica, Departamento de Prehistoria. Vol. 56. Mexico, D. F.

Gay, C. T. E. 1967. The Oldest Paintings in the World. *Natural History* 76(4):28–35.

Gearing, Fred. 1962. Priests and Warriors: Social Structures for Cherokee Politics in the 18th Century. *American Anthropological Association, Memoir* 93.

Gluckman, Max.
1940. The Kingdom of Zulu of South Africa. In *African Political Systems*, ed. Meyer Fortes and E. E. Evans-Prichard, pp. 25–55. Oxford University Press, New York.
1955. *Custom and Conflict in Africa.* Blackwell, Oxford.

Godelier, Maurice.
1978a. Economy and Religion: An Evolutionary Optical Illusion. In *The Evolution of Social Systems*, ed. J. Friedman and M. J. Rowlands, pp. 3–11. University of Pittsburgh Press, Pittsburgh.
1978b. Politics as "Infrastructure": An Anthropologist's Thoughts on the Example of Classical Greece and the Notions of Relations of Production and Economic Determination. In *The Evolution of Social Systems*, ed. J. Friedman and M. J. Rowlands, pp. 13–28. University of Pittsburgh Press, Pittsburgh.

Goggin, John M. and William C. Sturtevant.
1964. The Calusa: A Stratified, Nonagricultural Society (With Notes on Sibling Marrage. In *Explorations in Cultural Anthropology: Essays in Honor of George Peter Murdock*, ed. Ward H. Goodenough, pp. 179–219. McGraw-Hill, New York.

Graham, Ian. 1967. Archaeological Explorations in El Petén, Guatemala. *Tulane University, Middle American Research Institute, Publication* 33.

Graham, John A. 1971. Commentary on: Calendrics and Writing in Mesoamerica. In Observations on the Emergence of Civilization in Mesoamerica, ed. Robert F. Heizer and John A. Graham. *Contributions of The University of California Archaeological Research Facility* 11:133–40. Berkeley.

Grieder, Terence. 1975. A Dated Sequence of Building and Pottery at Las Haldas. *Nawpa Pacha* 13:99–112.

Gross, Daniel R. 1973. Introduction to Types of Social Structure Among the Lowland Tribes of South and Central America. In *Peoples and Cultures of Native South America*, ed. Daniel R. Gross, pp. 185–8. Doubleday/Natural History Press, Garden City, N.Y.

Haas, Jonathan.
　1976. Huaca Excavations at Pampa Grande, Lambayeque. Paper presented at the 41st Annual Meeting of the Society for American Archaeology, St. Louis.
　1979. *The Evolution of the Prehistoric State: Toward an Archeological Analysis of Political Organization*. Unpublished Ph.D. dissertation, Columbia University.
　n.d. Excavations on Huaca Grande: An Initial View of the Elite at Pampa Grande, Peru. Unpublished manuscript, Columbia University.

Hammond, Norman, and D. Pring, L. Wilk, S. Donaghey, F. P. Saul, E. S. Wing, A. V. Miller, and L. H. Feldman. 1979. The Earliest Lowland Maya: Definition of the Swasey Phase. *American Antiquity* 44(1):92–110.

Hardesty, Donald.
　1978. Human Evolutionary Ecology. In *Human Evolution*, ed. Noel Korn, pp. 234–244. Holt, Rinehart and Winston, New York.
　1979. Niche Theory and Economic Diversity. Paper presented at the Annual Meeting of the Society for American Archaeology, Vancouver.

Harding, Thomas G. 1970. Trading in Northeast New Guinea. In *Cultures of the Pacific: Selected Readings*, ed. T. G. Harding and B. J. Wallace, pp. 94–111. Free Press, New York.

Harner, Michael. 1977. The Ecological Basis for Aztec Sacrifice. *American Ethnologist* 4:117–35.

Harris, David. 1977. Alternative Pathways Toward Agriculture. In *The Origins of Agriculture*, ed. Charles Reed, pp. 179–244. Mouton, The Hague.

Harris, Marvin.
　1968. *The Rise of Anthropological Theory*. Crowell, New York.
　1971. *Culture, Man and Nature*. Crowell, New York.
　1979. *Cultural Materialism*. Random House, New York.

Hassan, Fekri. 1980. The Growth and Regulation of Human Populations in Prehistoric Times. In *Biosocial Mechanisms of Population Regulation*, ed. Mark N. Cohen, Roy Malpass, and Harold Klein, pp. 305–20. Yale University Press, New Haven.

Haviland, William A.
　1967. Stature at Tikal, Guatemala: Implications for Ancient Maya Demography and Social Organization. *American Antiquity* 36: 316–25.
　1970. Tikal Guatemala and Mesoamerican Urbanism. *World Archaeology* 2:186–98.

Heizer, Robert F. 1960. Agriculture and the Theocratic State in Lowland Southeastern Mexico. *American Antiquity* 26:215–22.

Helms, Mary W. 1979. *Ancient Panama: Chiefs in Search of Power*. University of Texas Press, Austin.

Heyden, Doris. 1975. An Interpretation of the Cave Underneath the Pyramid of the Sun in Teotihuacán, Mexico. *American Antiquity* 40(2): 131–47.

Hill, James N. (ed.). 1977. Discussion. In *Explanation of Prehistoric Change,* ed. James N. Hill, pp. 271–318. University of New Mexico Press, Albuquerque.

Hockett, Charles F. and Robert Ascher. 1964. The Human Revolution. *Current Anthropology* 5:135–68.

Hoebel, E. Adamson. 1949. *Man in the Primitive World.* McGraw-Hill, New York.

Hume, David. 1953. *David Hume's Political Essays,* ed. C. W. Hendel. Liberal Arts Press, New York.

Irwin-Williams, Cynthia. 1967. Associations of Early Man with Horse, Camel, and Mastadon at Hueyatlaco, Valsequillo (Pueblo, Mexico). In *Pleistocene Extinctions: Search for a Cause,* ed. Paul S. Martin and Herbert E. Wright, Jr., pp. 337–50. Yale University Press, New Haven.

Isaac, Barry L. 1975. Resource Scarcity, Competition, and Cooperation in Cultural Evolution. In *A Reader in Culture Change, Vol. 1, Theories,* ed. Ivan A. Brady and Barry L. Isaac, pp. 125–43. Schenkman, Cambridge, Mass.

Isaac, Glyn. 1972. Early Phases of Human Behavior: Models in Lower Paleolithic Archaeology. In *Models in Archaeology,* ed. David Clarke, pp. 167–99. Methuen, London.

Isbell, William H. 1978. Environmental Perturbations and the Origin of the Andean State. In *Social Archaeology: Beyond Subsistence and Dating,* ed. Charles Redman, Mary Jane Berman, Edward Curtin, William Langhorne, Jr., Nina Versaggi, and Jeffrey Wanser, pp. 303–13. Academic Press, New York.

Izumi, Seiichi. 1971. Development of the Formative Culture in the Caja de Montaña of the Central Andes. In *Dumbarton Oaks Conference on Chavin,* ed. Elizabeth P. Benson, pp. 49–72. Dumbarton Oaks, Washington, D.C.

Izumi, Seiichi and T. Sono. 1963. *Andes 2: Excavations at Kotosh, Peru, 1960.* University of Tokyo, Scientific Expedition to the Andes. Kodokawa Publishing, Tokyo.

Izumi, Seiichi and Kazuo Terada. 1972. *Andes 4: Excavations at Kotosh, Peru, 1963 and 1966.* University of Tokyo Press, Tokyo.

Janssen, J. J. 1978. The Early State in Ancient Egypt. In *The Early State,* ed. Henri J. M. Claessen and Peter Skalnik, pp. 213–34.

Jevons, W. S. 1877. *The Principles of Science: a Treatise on Logic and Scientific Method.* 2nd ed. Macmillan, London and New York.

Johnson, Gregory A. 1973. Local Exchange and Early State Development in Southwestern Iran. *Museum of Anthropology, University of Michigan, Anthropological Papers* 51.

Joralemon, Peter David.
    1971. A Study of Olmec Iconography. *Studies of Pre-Columbian Art and Archaeology* 7. Dumbarton Oaks, Washington, D.C.
    1976. The Olmec Dragon: A Study in Pre-Columbian Iconography. In *Origins of Religious Art and Iconography in Pre-classic Mesoamerica,* ed. H. B. Nicholson, pp. 27–71. UCLA Latin American Center, Los Angeles.

Keatinge, Richard W.
    1977. Religious Forms and Secular Functions: The Expansion of State Bureaucracies as Reflected in Prehistoric Architecture on the Peruvian North Coast. In Anthropology and the Climate of Opinion, ed. S. A. Freed. *Annals of the New York Academy of Sciences* 293:229–45.

1978. The Pacatnamu Textiles. *Archaeology* 31(2):30–41.

1980. The Chimu Empire in a Regional Perspective: Cultural Antecedents and Continuities. In *Chan Chan: The Desert City and Its Hinterland,* ed. M. E. Moseley and K. C. Day. University of New Mexico Press, Albuquerque, in press.

King. T. F. 1978. Don't That Beat the Band? Nonegalitarian Political Organization in Prehistoric Central California. In *Social Archaeology: Beyond Subsistence and Dating,* ed. Charles L. Redman, pp. 225–48. Academic Press, New York.

Kosok, Paul. 1965. *Life, Land and Water in Ancient Peru.* Long Island University Press, New York.

Kubler, George.

1971. Commentary on: Early Architecture and Sculpture in Mesoamerica. In *Observations on the Emergence of Civilization in Mesoamerica,* ed. Robert F. Heizer and John A. Graham. *Contributions of the University of California Archaeological Research Facility* 11:155–67. Berkeley.

1973. Science and Humanism Among Americanists. In *The Iconography of Middle American Sculpture,* pp. 163–7. Metropolitan Museum of Art, New York.

Kutscher, Gerdt. 1950. Iconographic Studies as an Aid in the Reconstruction of Early Chimu Civilization. *Transactions of the New York Academy of Sciences, Series II,* 12(6):194–203.

LaBarre, Weston. 1971. Materials for a History of Studies of Crisis Cults: A Bibliographic Essay. *Current Anthropology* 12(1):3–44.

La Gory, Mark. 1975. An Ecological Analysis of Leadership Strength in Native South America. *The Western Canadian Journal of Anthropology* 5:73–87.

Lanning, Edward P. 1967. *Peru Before the Incas.* Prentice-Hall, Englewood Cliffs, N.J.

Larco Hoyle, Rafael.

1938. *Los Mochicas.* Lima (no publisher given).

1941. *Los Cupisniques.* Casa Editoral "La Cronica" y "Variedades," Lima.

1945a. *Los Cupisniques.* Sociedad Geográfica Americana, Buenos Aires.

1945b. *Los Mochicas.* Sociedad Geográfica Americana, Buenos Aires.

1948. *Cronología arqueologica del norte del Perú.* Sociedad Geográfica Americana, Buenos Aires.

Lathrop, Donald W.

1971. The Tropical Forest and the Cultural Context of Chavín. In *Dumbarton Oaks Conference on Chavin,* ed. Elizabeth P. Benson, pp. 73–100. Dumbarton Oaks, Washington, D.C.

1973a. The Antiquity and Importance of Long Distance Trade Relationships in the Moist Tropics of Pre-Columbian South America. *World Archaeology* 5:170–86.

1973b. Gifts of the Cayman: Some Thoughts on the Subsistence Basis of Chavín. In *Variation in Anthropology; Essays in Honor of John C. McGregor,* ed. D. Lathrop and J. Douglas, pp. 91–102. Illinois Archaeological Survey, Urbana.

1977. Our Father the Cayman, Our Mother the Gourd: Spinden Revisited, or a Unitary Model for the Emergence of Agriculture in the New World. In *Origins of Agriculture,* ed. C. A. Reed, pp. 713–51. Mouton, The Hague.

Leach, Edmund R.

1961. *Rethinking Anthropology.* Athlone Press, London.

1962. Pulleyar and the Lord Buddha: An Aspect of Religious Syncretism in Ceylon. *Psychoanalysis and the Psychoanalytic Review* 49:80–102.

1973. Concluding Address. In *The Explanation of Culture Change; Models in Prehistory,* ed. Colin Renfrew, pp. 761–71. Duckworth, London.

Lee, Richard B.

1972. The Intensification of Social Life Among the !Kung Bushman. In *Population Growth: Anthropological Implications,* ed. Brian Spooner, pp. 343–50. MIT Press, Cambridge.

1980. Lactation, Ovulation, Infanticide and Women's Work: A Study of Hunter-Gatherer Population Regulation. In *Biosocial Mechanisms of Population Regulation,* ed. Mark N. Cohen, Roy Malpass, and Harold Klein, pp. 321–48. Yale University Press, New Haven.

Lenski, Gerhard E. 1966. *Power and Privilege: A Theory of Social Stratification.* New York: McGraw-Hill.

Leone, Mark P.

1972. Issues in Anthropological Archaeology. In *Contemporary Archaeology: A Guide to Theory and Contributions,* ed. Mark P. Leone, pp. 14–27. Southern Illinois University Press, Carbondale.

1973. Archaeology as the Science of Technology: Mormon Town Plans and Fences. In *Research and Theory in Current Archaeology,* ed. Charles Redman, pp. 125–50. Wiley, New York.

Leon-Portilla, Miguel. 1963. *Aztec Thought and Culture.* University of Oklahoma Press, Norman.

Lessa, William A. and Evon Z. Vogt (eds.). 1958. *Reader in Comparative Religion: An Anthropological Approach.* Row, Peterson, Evanston, Ill.

Lewis, Herbert S. 1978. Warfare and the Origin of the State: Another Formulation. Paper presented to the Post-Plenary Session: The Study of the State; Tenth International Congress of Anthropological and Ethnological Sciences, New Delhi, India, December 21, 1978.

Lothrop, Samuel K. 1937. Cocle, an Archaeological Study of Central Panama; Part 1, Historical Background, Excavations at Sitio Conte, Artifacts and Ornaments. *Memoirs of the Peabody Museum of Archaeology and Ethnology, Harvard University* 7.

Lowe, Gareth W.

1975. The Early Preclassic Barra Phase of Altamira, Chiapas. *Brigham Young University, Papers of the New World Archaeological Foundation* 38.

1977. The Mixe-Zoque as Competing Neighbors of the Early Lowland Maya. In *The Origins of Maya Civilization,* ed. Richard E. W. Adams, pp. 197–248. University of New Mexico Press, Albuquerque.

Lowe, Gareth W. and J. Alden Mason. 1965. Archaeological Survey of the Chiapas Coast, Highlands, and Upper Grijalva Basin. In *Handbook of Middle American Indians,* ed. Robert Wauchope, Vol. 2, Part 1, pp. 195–236.

Lumbreras, Luis G.

1971. Towards a Re-evaluation of Chavín. In *Dumbarton Oaks Conference on Chavín,* ed. Elizabeth P. Benson, pp. 1–28. Dumbarton Oaks, Washington, D.C.

1972. Los Estudios Sobre Chavín. *Revista del Museo Nacional* 38:73–92.

1974a. Informe de labores del Proyecto Chavín. *Arqueológicas* 15:37–55.

1974b. *The Peoples and Cultures of Ancient Peru,* transl. Betty J. Meggers. Smithsonian Institution Press, Washington, D.C.

1977. Excavaciones en el Templo Antiguo de Chavín (Sector R); informe de la sexta campaña. *Ñawpa Pacha* 15:1–38.

Lumbreras, Luis G. and Hernan Amat Olazábal. 1969. Informe preliminar sobre las galarías interiores de Chavín (primer temporada de trabajos). *Revista del Museo Nacional* 34:143–97.

Lyon, Patricia J. 1978. Female Supernaturals in Ancient Peru. *Ñawpa Pacha* 16:95–140.

McDonald, Andrew J. 1977. Two Middle Preclassic Engraved Monuments at Tzutzuculi on the Chiapas Coast of Mexico. *American Antiquity* 42(4): 560–6.

MacNeish, Richard S.
    1958. Preliminary Archaeological Investigations in the Sierra de Tamaulipas, Mexico. *American Philosophical Society, Proceedings* 48, Part 6.
    1964. Ancient Mesoamerican Civilization. *Science* 143:531–7.
    1967. An Interdisciplinary Approach to an Archaeological Problem. In *The Prehistory of the Tehuacan Valley, Vol. 1, Environment and Subsistence*, ed. Douglas S. Byers, pp. 14–24. University of Texas Press, Austin.
    1971a. Early Man in the Andes. *Scientific American* 224(4):36–46.
    1971b. Speculations About How and Why Food Production and Village Life Developed in the Tehuacán Valley, Mexico. *Archaeology* 24(4): 307–15.
    1976. *The Science of Archaeology?* McMaster University, Hamilton, Ontario.
    1978. *The Science of Archaeology?* Duxbury Press, North Scituate, Mass.

MacNeish, Richard S., Melvin L. Fowler, Ángel García Cook, Frederick A. Peterson, Antoinette Nelkin-Terner, and James A. Neely. 1975. *Excavations and Reconnaissance. Vol. 5, The Prehistory of the Tehuacán Valley*, University of Texas Press, Austin.

MacNeish, Richard S., Antoinette Nelkin-Terner, and Angel Garcia Cook. 1970. Second Annual Report of the Ayacucho Archaeological–Botanical Project. R. S. Peabody Foundation for Archaeology, Andover, Mass.

MacNeish, Richard S., Thomas C. Patterson, and David L. Browman. 1975. The Central Peruvian Prehistoric Interaction Sphere. *Papers of the R. S. Peabody Foundation for Archaeology* 7, Andover, Mass.

MacNeish, Richard S., Frederick A. Peterson, and Kent V. Flannery. 1970. *Ceramics. Vol. 3, The Prehistory of the Tehuacán Valley*, University of Texas Press, Austin.

Malinowski, Bronislaw. 1922. *Argonauts of the Western Pacific*. Routledge, London.

Malo, David. 1951. Hawaiian Antiquities, 2d. ed. *Bernice Pahau Bishop Museum, Special Publications* 2.

Marcus, Joyce.
    1976. *Emblem and State in the Classic Maya Lowlands: An Epigraphic Approach to Territorial Organization*. Dumbarton Oaks, Trustees for Harvard University, Washington, D.C.
    1978. Archaeology and Religion: A Comparison of the Zapotec and Maya. *World Archaeology* 10:172–91.

Maruyama, Magoroh. 1963. The Second Cybernetics: Deviation Amplifying Mutual Causal Processes. *American Scientist* 51:164–79.

Matsuzawa, Tsugio. 1978. The Formative Site of Las Haldas, Peru: Architecture, Chronology and Economy. *American Antiquity* 43:652–73.

Meggers, Betty. 1954. Environmental Limitation on the Development of Culture. *American Anthropologist* 56:801–24.

Mendelsohn, Isaac. 1949. *Slavery in the Ancient Near East*. Oxford University Press, New York.

Menzel, Dorothy, John H. Rowe, and Lawrence E. Dawson. 1964. The Paracas Pottery of Ica; A Study in Style and Time. *University of California Publications in American Archaeology and Ethnology* 50.
Milisauskas, Sarunas. 1978. *European Prehistory*. Academic Press, New York.
Millon, René F.
  1967. Extensión y población de las ciudad de Teotihuacán en sus diferentes periodos: un calculo provisional. In *Teotihuacán, Onceava Mesa Redonda*, pp. 57–78. Sociedad Mexicana de Antropología, México, D. F.
  1973. *Urbanization at Teotihuacán, Mexico, Vol. 1, The Teotihuacán Map, Part 1: Text*. University of Texas Press, Austin.
  1976. Social Relations in Ancient Teotihuacán. In *The Valley of Mexico: Studies in Pre-Hispanic Ecology and Society*, ed. Eric R. Wolf, pp. 205–48. University of New Mexico Press, Albuquerque.
Millon, René F., R. Bruce Drewitt, and George L. Cowgill. 1973. *Urbanization at Teotihuacán, Mexico, Vol. 1, The Teotihuacan Map, Part 2: Map*. University of Texas Press, Austin.
Morris, Donald R. 1965. *The Washing of the Spears*. Simon & Schuster, New York.
Moseley, Michael E.
  1975. *The Maritime Foundations of Andean Civilization*. Cummings, Menlo Park, California.
  1978. The Evolution of Andean Civilization. In *Ancient Native Americans*, ed. Jesse D. Jennings, pp. 491–541. Freeman, San Francisco.
Moseley, Michael E. and Luis Watanabe. 1974. The Adobe Sculpture of Huaca de los Reyes. *Archaeology* 27(3):154–61.
Moseley, Michael E. and Gordon R. Willey. 1973. Aspero, Peru: A Reexamination of the Site and Its Implications. *American Antiquity* 38:452–67.
Murra, John V.
  1972. El "control vertical" de un máximo de pisos ecologicos en la economía de las sociedades andinas. In Iñigo Ortíz de Zúñiga, *Visita de la Provincia de Leon de Huanuco (1562)*, Vol. 2:429–76. Universidad Nacional Hermilio Valdizán, Huánuco, Peru.
  1975. El tráfico de *mulla* en la costa del Pacífico. In *Formaciones económicas y politicas del mundo andino*, J. V. Murra, pp. 255–67. Instituto de Estudios Peruanos, Lima.
Navarrete, Carlos.
  1971. Algunas piezas Olmecas de Chiapas y Guatemala. *Anales de Antropología* 8:69–82.
  1974. The Olmec Rock Carvings at Pijijiapan, Chiapas, Mexico and Other Olmec Pieces from Chiapas and Guatemala. *Brigham Young University, Papers of the New World Archaeological Foundation* 35.
Netherly, Patricia J. 1977. *Local Level Lords on the North Coast of Peru*. Unpublished Ph.D. dissertation, Department of Anthropology, Cornell University.
Netting, Robert McC. 1972. Sacred Power and Centralization: Aspects of Political Adaptation in Africa. In *Population Growth: Anthropological Implications,* ed. Brian Spooner, pp. 219–44. MIT Press, Cambridge, Mass.
Nicholson, Henry B.
  1971. Religion in Prehispanic Central Mexico. In *Handbook of Middle American Indians*, ed. Robert Wauchope, Vol. 2, pp. 395–451. University of Texas Press, Austin.
  1976. Preclassic Mesoamerican Iconography from the Perspective of the

Postclassic: Problems in Interpretational Analysis. In *Origins of Religious Art and Iconography in Preclassic Mesoamerica*, ed. Henry B. Nicholson, pp. 157–75. UCLA Latin American Center, Los Angeles.

Niederberger, C. 1976. Zohapilco. *Colección Científica, Departamento de Prehistoria*, No. 30. México, D. F.

Norman, V. Garth.
1973. Izapa Sculpture; Part 1: Album. *Brigham Young University, Papers of the New World Archaeological Foundation* 30.
1976. Izapa Sculpture; Part 2: Text. *Brigham Young University, Papers of the New World Archaeological Foundation* 30.

Oberg, Kalervo. 1955. Types of Social Structure Among the Lowland Tribes of South and Central America. *American Anthropologist* 57:472–87.

Odum, Eugene P. 1971. *Fundamentals of Ecology*. 3d ed. Saunders, Philadelphia.

Parsons, Lee A. 1967. Bilbao, Guatemala, Vol. 1. *Milwaukee Public Museum Publications in Anthropology* 11.

Parsons, Lee A. and Barbara J. Price. 1971. Mesoamerican Trade and Its Role in the Emergence of Civilization. In Observations on the Emergence of Civilization in Mesoamerica, ed. Robert F. Heizer and John A. Graham. *Contributions of the University of California Archaeological Research Facility* 11:169–95. Berkeley.

Parsons, Talcott. 1956. Introduction. In *The Sociology of Religion*, Max Weber, pp. xix–lxvii. Beacon Press, Boston.

Patterson, Thomas C.
1971a. Central Peru: Its Population and Economy. *Archaeology* 24(4): 316–21.
1971b. Chavín: An Interpretation of Its Spread and Influence. In *Dumbarton Oaks Conference on Chavin*, ed. Elizabeth P. Benson, pp. 29–48. Dumbarton Oaks, Washington, D.C.

Patterson, Thomas C., and Michael E. Moseley. 1968. Late Preceramic and Early Ceramic Cultures on the Central Coast of Peru. *Ñawpa Pacha* 6:115–33.

Paulsen, Allison C. 1974. The Thorny Oyster and the Voice of God; Spondylus and Strombus in Andean Prehistory. *American Antiquity* 39:597–607.

Peebles, Christopher and S. Kus. 1977. Some Archaeological Correlates of Ranked Societies. *American Antiquity* 42(3):421–48.

Piddocke, Stuart. 1965. The Potlatch System of the Southern Kwakiutl: A New Perspective. *Southwestern Journal of Anthropology* 21:244–64.

Polanyi, Karl. 1945. *Origins of Our Time; The Great Transformation*. Victor Gollancz, London.

Ponce-Sanquines, Carlos. 1971. *Las culturas Wankarami y Chiripa y su relacion con Tiwanaka*. Academia Nacional Ciencia de Bolivia, La Paz.

Porter, Muriel.
1953. Tlatilco and the Preclassic Cultures of the New World. *Viking Publications in Anthropology* 19.
1956. Excavations at Chupicuaro, Guanajuato, Mexico. *American Philosophical Society, Transactions* 46, Part 5.

Pozorski, Thomas G.
1975. El complejo Caballo Muerto y los frisos de barro de la Huaca de los Reyes. *Revista del Museo Nacional* 51:211–52.
1976. Caballo Muerto: A Complex of Early Ceramic Sites in the Moche Valley, Peru. Unpublished Ph.D. dissertation, University of Texas, Austin.

Prem, Hanns J. 1971. Calendrics and Writing in Mesoamerica. In Observations on the Emergence of Civilization in Mesoamerica, ed. Robert F. Heizer and John A. Graham. *Contributions of the University of California Archaeological Research Facility* 11:112–32. Berkeley.

Price, Barbara J.
   1976. A Chronological Framework for Cultural Development in Mesoamerica. In *The Valley of Mexico: Studies in Pre-Hispanic Ecology and Society,* ed. Eric R. Wolf, pp. 13–22. University of New Mexico Press, Albuquerque.
   1978. Secondary State Formation: An Explanatory Model. In *Origins of the State: The Anthropology of Political Evolution,* ed. Ronald Cohen and Elman R. Service, pp. 161–86. Institute for the Study of Human Issues, Philadelphia.

Proskouriakoff, Tatiana.
   1960. Historical Implications of a Pattern of Dates at Piedras Negas, Guatemala. *American Antiquity* 25:454–75.
   1971. Early Architecture and Sculpture in Mesoamerica. In Observations on the Emergence of Civilization in Mesoamerica, ed. Robert F. Heizer and John A. Graham. *Contributions of the University of California Archaeological Research Facility* 11:141–56. Berkeley.

Puleston, Dennis E. and E. W. Callender, Jr. 1967. Defensive Earthworks at Tikal. *Expedition* 9(2):40–8.

Quirarte, Jacinto.
   1976. The Relations of Izapan-Style Art to Olmec and Maya Art: A Review. In *Origins of Religious Art and Iconography in Preclassic Mesoamerica,* ed. Henry B. Nicholson, pp. 73–86. UCLA Latin American Center, Los Angeles.
   1977. Early Art Styles of Mesoamerica and Early Classic Maya Art. In *The Origins of Maya Civilization,* ed. Richard E. W. Adams, pp. 249–83. University of New Mexico Press, Albuquerque.

Rands, Robert L. and Robert E. Smith. 1965. Pottery of the Guatemalan Highlands. In *Handbook of Middle American Indians,* Vol. 2, Part 1, pp. 95–145. University of Texas Press, Austin.

Rappaport, Roy A.
   1968. *Pigs for the Ancestors.* Yale University Press, New Haven.
   1971. The Sacred in Human Evolution. *Annual Review of Ecology and Systematics* 2:23–44.

Rathje, William.
   1970. Socio-political Implications of Lowland Maya Burials: Methodology and Tentative Hypotheses. *World Archaeology* 1(3):359–74.
   1971a. *Lowland Classic Maya Socio-political Organization: Degree and Form through Space and Time.* Unpublished Ph.D. dissertation, Harvard University.
   1971b. The Origin and Development of Lowland Classic Maya Civilization. *American Antiquity* 36(3):275–85.

Ravines, Rogger. 1975. Garagay: un viejo templo en los Andes. *Revista del Instituto Nacional de Cultura,* Textual 10:6–12.

Ravines, Rogger and William H. Isbell. 1975. Garagay: sitio temprano en el Valle de Lima. *Revista del Museo Nacional* 51:253–72.

Redman, Charles L. 1978. *The Rise of Civilization.* Freeman, San Francisco.

Reed, Charles A. 1977. Introduction. In *Origins of Agriculture,* ed. Charles A. Reed, pp. 1–5. Mouton, The Hague.

Renfrew, Colin.
   1973. Monuments, Mobilization and Social Organization in Neolithic
      Wessex. In *The Explanation of Culture Change: Models in Prehistory*, ed.
      Colin Renfrew, pp. 539–58. University of Pittsburgh Press, Pittsburgh.
   1974. Beyond a Subsistence Economy: The Evolution of Social Organiza-
      tion in Prehistoric Europe. In Reconstructing Complex Societies, an
      Archaeological Colloquium, ed. Charlotte B. Moore. *Bulletin of the
      American Schools of Oriental Research, Supplement*, 20:69–88.
   1976. *Before Civilization*. Penguin Books, Harmondsworth.
Rice, Don S. 1976. Middle Preclassic Maya Settlement in the Central Maya
   Lowlands. *Journal of Field Archaeology* 3(4):425–45.
Ricketson, Oliver G. and Edith B. Ricketson. 1937. Uaxactun, Guatemala:
   Group E, 1926–1931. *Carnegie Institution of Washington, Publication 477.*
   Washington, D.C.
Roe, Peter G. 1974. A Further Exploration of the Rowe Chavín Seriation
   and Its Implications for North Central Coast Chronology. *Studies in
   Precolumbian Art and Archaeology* 13. Dumbarton Oaks, Washington,
   D.C.
Rosas La Noire, Hermilio. 1976. Investigaciones arqueológicas en la cuenca
   del Chotano, Cajamarca. *Actas del XLI Congreso Internacional de America-
   nistas* 3:564–78. Mexico, D. F.
Rosas La Noire, Hermilio and Ruth Shady Solis. 1970. *Pacopampa: un centro
   Formativo en la sierra nor-peruana.* Seminario de Historia Rural Andina,
   Universidad Nacional Mayor de San Marcos, Lima.
Rostworowski de Diez Canseco, María. 1977. Breve ensayo sobre el Señorío
   de Ychma. In *Etnía y Sociedad*, María Rostworowski de Diez Canseco,
   pp. 197–210. Instituto de Estudios Peruanos, Lima.
Rowe, John H.
   1946. Inca Culture at the Time of the Spanish Conquest. In Handbook
      of South American Indians, Vol. 2, The Andean Civilizations, ed. Ju-
      lian H. Steward, *Smithsonian Institution Bureau of American Ethnology,
      Bulletin* 143:183–330.
   1962. *Chavín Art: An Inquiry into Its Form and Meaning.* New York: The
      Museum of Primitive Art.
   1967. Form and Meaning in Chavín Art. In *Peruvian Archaeology; Selected
      Readings*, ed. John H. Rowe and D. Menzel, pp. 72–103. Peek Publica-
      tions, Palo Alto.
Rowe, John H. and Dorothy Menzel. 1967. Introduction. In *Peruvian Archaeology: Selected Readings*, ed. John H. Rowe and Dorothy Menzel.
   Peek Publications, Palo Alto.
Roys, Ralph L. 1967. *The Book of Chilam Balam of Chumayel.* University of
   Oklahoma Press, Norman. (Originally published in 1933.)
Sahagún, Fray Bernadino de. 1959. *Florentine Codex, Book 9, The Merchants*,
   transl. Charles E. Dibble and Arthur J. O. Anderson. School of American Research, Santa Fe.
Sahlins, Marshall D.
   1958. *Social Stratification in Polynesia.* University of Washington Press,
      Seattle.
   1968. *Tribesmen.* Prentice-Hall, Englewood Cliffs, N.J.
   1976. *Culture and Practical Reason.* University of Chicago Press, Chicago.
Sahlins, Marshall D. and E. Service (ed.). 1960. *Evolution of Culture.* University of Michigan Press, Ann Arbor.

Sanders, William T.
1968. Hydraulic Agriculture, Economic Symbiosis, and the Evolution of States in Central Mexico. In *Anthropological Archaeology in the Americas,* ed. Betty Meggers, pp. 88–107. Anthropological Society of Washington, Washington, D.C.
1974. Chiefdom to State: Political Evolution at Kaminaljuyu, Guatemala. In Reconstructing Complex Societies, An Archaeological Colloquium, ed. Charlotte B. Moore. *Bulletin of the American Schools of Oriental Research, Supplement,* 20:97–113.
1977. Environmental Heterogeneity and the Evolution of Lowland Maya Civilization. In *The Origins of Maya Civilization,* ed. Richard E. W. Adams, pp. 287–97. University of New Mexico Press, Albuquerque.
Sanders, William T., Anton Kovar, Thomas Charlton, and Richard A. Diehl. 1970. The Natural Environment, Contemporary Occupation and 16th Century Population of the Valley. *Pennsylvania State University, Department of Anthropology, Occasional Papers in Anthropology* 3.
Sanders, William T. and Joseph Marino. 1970. *New World Prehistory: Archaeology of the Americas.* Prentice-Hall, Englewood Cliffs, N.J.
Sanders, William T. and J. W. Michels (ed.). 1977. *Teotihuacán and Kaminaljuyu: A study in Prehistoric Culture Contact.* Pennsylvania State University Press, University Park.
Sanders, William T. and Barbara J. Price. 1968. *Mesoamerica, The Evolution of a Civilization.* Random House, New York.
Sanders, William T. and David Webster. 1978. Unilinealism, Multilinealism, and the Evolution of Complex Societies. In *Social Archaeology: Beyond Subsistence and Dating,* ed. Charles Redman, Mary Jane Berman, Edward Curtin, William Langhorne, Jr., Nina Versaggi, and Jeffrey Wanser, pp. 249–302. Academic Press, New York.
Sansom, George. 1958. *A History of Japan to 1334.* Stanford University Press, Stanford.
Saxe, Arthur A. 1977. On the Origin of Evolutionary Processes: State Formation in the Sandwich Islands. In *Explanation of Prehistoric Change,* ed. James N. Hill, pp. 105–51. University of New Mexico Press, Albuquerque.
Schneider, Harold K. 1974. *Economic Man: The Anthropology of Economics.* Free Press, New York.
Schoeninger, Margaret J. 1979. Social Stratification in an Archaeological Population. Paper presented at the 78th Annual Meeting of the American Anthropological Association, Cincinnati.
Sereno, Renzo. 1968. *The Rulers.* Harper & Row, New York.
Service, Elman R.
1962. *Primitive Social Organization, An Evolutionary Perspective.* Random House, New York.
1971. *Primitive Social Organization, An Evolutionary Perspective.* 2d ed. Random House, New York.
1975. *Origins of the State and Civilization: The Process of Cultural Evolution.* Norton, New York.
1978. Classical and Modern Theories of the Origins of Government. In *Origins of the State: The Anthropology of Political Evolution,* ed. Ronald Cohen and Elman R. Service, pp. 21–34. Institute for the Study of Human Issues, Philadelphia.

Sharer, Robert J.
   1974. The Prehistory of the Southeastern Maya Periphery. *Current Anthropology* 15:165–87.
   1978. *The Prehistory of Chalchuapa, El Salvador, Vol. 3, Pottery and Conclusions.* University of Pennsylvania Press, Philadelphia.
Sheets, Payson D. 1979. Maya Recovery from Volcanic Disasters: Ilopango and Cerén. *Archaeology* 32(3):32–42.
Shimada, Izumi. 1976. *Socioeconomic Organization at Moche V, Pampa Grande, Peru: Prelude to a Major Transformation to Come.* Unpublished Ph.D. dissertation, University of Arizona.
Shook, Edwin M. 1971. Inventory of Some Pre-Classic Traits in the Highlands and Pacific Guatemala and Adjacent Areas. In Observations on the Emergence of Civilization in Mesoamerica, ed. Robert F. Heizer and John A. Graham. *Contributions of the University of California Archaeological Research Facility* 11:70–7. Berkeley.
Shook, Edwin M. and A. V. Kidder. 1952. Mound E-III-3, Kaminaljuyu, Guatemala. *Carnegie Institution of Washington, Publication* 596 (Contribution 53). Washington, D.C.
Sisson, Edward B.
   1973. First Annual Report of the Coxcatlan Project. R. S. Peabody Foundation for Archaeology, Andover, Mass.
   1974. Second Annual Report of the Coxcatlan Project. R. S. Peabody Foundation for Archaeology, Andover, Mass.
Smith Carol A. 1976. Exchange Systems and the Spatial Distribution of Elites: The Organization of Stratification in Agrarian Societies. In *Regional Analysis, Vol. 2, Social Systems*, ed. Carol A. Smith, pp. 309–74. Academic Press, New York.
Sokal, Robert R. and Peter H. A. Sneath. 1963. *Principles of Numerical Taxonomy.* Freeman, San Francisco.
Spence, Michael W.
   1967. The Obsidian Industry of Teotihuacán. *American Antiquity* 34:507–14.
   1973. The Development of the Classic Period Teotihuacán Obsidian Production System. Paper presented at the 38th Annual Meeting of the Society for American Archaeology, San Francisco.
Spencer, Charles. 1977. Irrigation and Society in Formative Tehuacán. Unpublished manuscript, University of Michigan.
Spencer, Herbert
   1882. *The Principles of Sociology.* Vol. 2. Appleton, New York.
   1967. *The Evolution of Society; Selections from Herbert Spencer's Principles of Sociology*, ed. Robert L. Carneiro. University of Chicago Press, Chicago.
Steponaitis, Vincas P. 1978. Location Theory and Complex Chiefdoms: A Mississippian Example. In *Mississippian Settlement Patterns*, ed. Bruce D. Smith, pp. 417–53. Academic Press, New York.
Steward, Julian H.
   1948a. Preface. In Handbook of South American Indians, Vol. 4, The Circum-Caribbean Tribes, ed. Julian H. Steward. *Smithsonian Institution, Bureau of American Ethnology, Bulletin* 143:xv–xvii.
   1948b. The Circum-Caribbean Tribes: An Introduction. In Handbook of South American Indians, Vol. 4, The Circum-Caribbean Tribes, ed. Julian H. Steward. *Smithsonian Institution, Bureau of American Ethnology, Bulletin* 143:1–41.
   1955. *Theory of Culture Change.* University of Illinois Press, Urbana.

Steward, Julian H. (ed.).
  1948. Handbook of South American Indians; Vol. 4, The Circum-Caribbean Tribes. *Smithsonian Institution, Bureau of American Ethnology, Bulletin* 143.
Steward, Julian H., and Louis C. Faron. 1959. *The Native Peoples of South America.* McGraw-Hill, New York.
Strong, William D., and John M. Corbett. 1943. A Ceramic Sequence at Pachacamac. In Archaeological Studies in Peru 1941–1942, ed. William D. Strong, Gordon R. Willey, and John M. Corbett. *Columbia University Studies in Archaeology and Ethnology* 1(2):27–122.
Sturtevant, William C. 1961. Taino Agriculture. In The Evolution of Horticultural Systems in Native South America, Causes and Consequences, ed. Johannes Wilbert. *Antropologica, Supplement Publication* 2:69–82. Sociedad de Ciencias Naturales La Salle, Caracas
Sussman, Robert W. 1972. Child Transport, Family Size, and Increase in Human Population During the Neolithic. *Current Anthropology* 13:258–59.
Suttles, Wayne. 1960. Affinal Ties, Subsistence and Prestige Among the Coast Salish. *American Anthropologist* 62:296–305.
Tacitus. 1970. *The Agricola and the Germania,* transl. H. Mattingly. Penguin Books, Harmondsworth.
Taylor, Donna. n.d. A Measure of Centralization. Unpublished manuscript.
Tello, Julio C.
  1922. *Introducción a la historia antigua del Perú.* Lima.
  1923. Wira-Kocha. *Inca* 1(1):93–326. 1(1):583–606. Lima.
  1943. Discovery of the Chavín Culture in Peru. *American Antiquity* 9:135–60.
  1956. Arqueología del Valle de Casma. *Universidad Nacional Mayor de San Marcos, Lima, Publicación Antropológica del Archivo "Julio C. Tello"* 1.
  1960. Chavín: cultura matriz de la civilización andina. (Primer Parte.) *Universidad Nacional Mayor de San Marcos, Lima, Publicación Antropológica del Archivo "Julio C. Tello"* 2.
Thompson, Donald. 1964. Formative Period Architecture in the Casma Valley, Peru. *Actas y Memorias del XXXV Congreso Internacional de Americanistas* 1:205–21. Mexico, D.F.
Thompson, J. Eric S. 1973. Maya Rulers of the Classic Period and the Divine Right of Kings. In *The Iconography of Middle American Sculpture,* pp. 52–71. Metropolitan Museum of Art, New York.
Thurnwald, Richard. 1932. *Economics in Primitive Communities.* Oxford University Press, London.
Tolstoy, Paul. 1975. Settlement and Population Trends in the Basin of Mexico. Unpublished manuscript, Queens College of the State University of New York.
Topic, Theresa. 1977. *Excavations at Moche, Peru.* Unpublished Ph.D. dissertation, Harvard University.
Tozzer, Alfred M. (ed. trans.). 1941. Landa's Relación de las Cosas de Yucatán. *Harvard University, Peabody Museum of Archaeology and Ethnology, Papers* 18.
Trigger, Bruce G. 1978. *Time and Traditions.* Columbia University Press, New York.
Trimborn, Hermann. 1949. *Senorio y barbarie en el Valle del Cauca.* Translated from the German by Jose María Gimeno Capella. Consejo Superior de Investigaciones Científicas, Instituto Gonzálo Fernández de Oviedo, Madrid.

Turnbull, Colin. 1968. The Importance of Flux in Two Hunting Societies. In *Man the Hunter*, ed. Richard B. Lee and Irving DeVore, pp. 133–7. Aldine, Chicago.

Uhle, Max. 1903. *Pachacamac. Report of the William Pepper Peruvian Expedition of 1896*. Department of Archaeology, University of Pennsylvania, Philadelphia.

Voorhies, Barbara. 1976. The Cantuto People: An Archaic Period Society of the Chiapas Littoral, Mexico. *Brigham Young University, Papers of the New World Archaeological Foundation* 41.

Wach, Joachim. 1944. *The Sociology of Religion*. University of Chicago Press, Chicago.

Wallace, Anthony F. C.
  1956. Revitalization Movements. *American Anthropologist* 58:264–81.
  1966. *Religion: An Anthropological View*. Random House, New York.

Walter, Eugene V. 1969. *Terror and Resistance: A Study of Political Violence*. Oxford University Press, New York.

Weaver, Muriel Porter. 1972. *The Aztecs, Maya, and Their Predecessors*. Seminar Press, New York.

Webb, Malcolm C.
  1965. The Abolition of the Taboo System in Hawaii. *Journal of the Polynesia Society* 74:21–39.
  1973. The Peten Maya Decline Viewed in the Perspective of State Formation. In *The Classic Maya Collapse*, ed. T. Patrick Culbert, pp. 367–404. University of New Mexico Press, Albuquerque.
  1974. Exchange Networks: Prehistory. *Annual Review of Anthropology* 3:357–83.
  1975. The Flag Follows Trade: An Essay on the Necessary Interaction of Military and Commercial Factors in State Formation. In *Ancient Civilization and Trade*, ed. C. C. Lamberg-Karlovsky and Jeremy A. Sabloff, pp. 155–210. University of New Mexico Press, Albuquerque.

Weber, Max.
  1930. *The Protestant Ethic and the Spirit of Capitalism*, transl. Talcott Parsons, Allen & Unwin, London.
  1956. *The Sociology of Religion*, transl. Ephraim Fischoff. Boston: Beacon Press.
  1968. *Max Weber on Charisma and Institution Building; Selected Papers*, ed. S. N. Eisenstadt. University of Chicago Press, Chicago.

Webster, David.
  1975. Warfare and the Evolution of the State: A Reconsideration. *American Antiquity* 40:464–70.
  1977. Warfare and the Evolution of Maya Civilization. In *The Origins of Maya Civilization*, ed. Richard E. W. Adams, pp. 335–72. University of New Mexico Press, Albuquerque.

Weiner, Annette B. 1976. *Women of Value, Men of Renown: New Perspectives in Trobriand Exchange*. University of Texas Press, Austin.

Weiss, K. M. 1978. Archaeological Approaches to Population Inference. *American Antiquity* 43:733–76.

Wellhausen, Julius. 1884–99. *Skizzen und Vorarbeiten*, Vol. 3. Reimer, Berlin.

Wetherington, Ronald K. (ed.). 1978. *The Ceramics of Kaminaljuyu, Guatemala*. Pennsylvania State University Press, University Park.

Wheatley, Paul. 1971. *The Pivot of the Four Quarters: A Preliminary Enquiry Into the Origins and Character of the Ancient Chinese City*. Aldine, Chicago.

White, Leslie A.
  1949. *The Science of Culture*. Grove Press, New York.
  1959. *The Evolution of Culture*. McGraw-Hill, New York.
Wicke, Charles R. 1971. *Olmec: An Early Art Style of Precolumbian Mexico*. University of Arizona Press, Tucson.
Wilkerson, Jeffrey. 1976. Report to the National Geographic Society on the 1976 Season. Florida State Museum, Gainesville.
Willey, Gordon R.
  1948. Functional Analysis of "Horizon Styles" in Peruvian Archeology. In A Reappraisal of Peruvian Archaeology, assembled by W. C. Bennett. *Memoirs of the Society for American Archaeology* 13(4):8–15.
  1951. The Chavín Problem: A Review and Critique. *Southwestern Journal of Anthropology* 7:103–44.
  1953. Prehistoric Settlement Patterns in the Virú Valley. *Smithsonian Institution, Bureau of American Ethnology, Bulletin* 155.
  1962. The Early Great Styles and the Rise of Pre-Columbian Civilizations. *American Anthropologist* 64:1–14.
  1976. Mesoamerican Civilization and the Idea of Transcendence. *Antiquity* 50:205–15.
  1977a. The Rise of Classic Maya Civilization: A Pasión Valley Perspective. In *The Origins of Maya Civilization*, ed. Richard E. W. Adams, pp. 133–57. University of New Mexico Press, Albuquerque.
  1977b. The Rise of Maya Civilization: A Summary View. In *The Origins of Maya Civilization*, ed. Richard E. W. Adams, pp. 383–423. University of New Mexico Press, Albuquerque.
Willey, Gordon R. and John M. Corbett. 1954. Early Ancón and Early Supe Culture. *Columbia University Studies in Archaeology and Ethnology* 3.
Willey, Gordon and P. Phillips. 1962. *Method and Theory in American Archaeology*. University of Chicago Press, Chicago.
Willey, Gordon R., and Demitri B. Shimkin. 1973. The Maya Collapse: A Summary View. In *The Classic Maya Collapse*, ed. R. Patrick Culbert, pp. 457–501. University of New Mexico Press, Albuquerque.
Williams, Leon, Carlos.
  1971. Centros ceremoniales tempranos en el Valle de Chillón, Rimac, y Lurin. *Apuntes Arqueológicos* 1:1–4.
  1972. La difusión de los pozos ceremoniales en la costa peruana. *Apuntes Arqueológicos* 2:1–9.
Williamson, Robert W. 1924. *The Social and Political Systems of Central Polynesia*. 3 Vols. Cambridge University Press, London.
Wilson, David J.
  1981. Of Maize and Men: A Critique of the Maritime Hypothesis of State Origins on the Coast of Peru. *American Anthropologist* 83:93–120.
Winter, Marcus.
  1974. Residence Patterns at Monte Alban. *Science* 186:982–7.
  1976. The Archaeological Household Cluster in the Valley of Oaxaca. In *The Early Mesoamerican Village*, ed. Kent V. Flannery, pp. 25–30. Academic Press, New York.
Winter, Marcus and Jane W. Pires-Ferreira. 1976. Distribution of Obsidian Among Households in Two Oaxacan Villages. In *The Early Mesoamerican Village*, ed. Kent V. Flannery, pp. 306–10. Academic Press, New York.
Wittfogel, Karl. 1957. *Oriental Despotism*. Yale University Press, New Haven.

Wobst, H. M.
  1974. Boundary Conditions for Paleolithic Social Systems: A Simulation
    Approach. *American Antiquity* 39:147–77.
  1975. The Demography of Finite Populations and the Origin of the In-
    cest Taboo. *American Antiquity* 40:75–81.
  1976. Locational Relationships in Paleolithic Society. *Journal of Human
    Evolution* 4:49–58.
Wolf, Eric R. 1951. The Social Organization of Mecca and the Origins of
    Islam. *Southwestern Journal of Anthropology* 7:329–56.
Woodbury, Richard and James A. Neely. 1972. Water Control Systems of
    the Tehuacán Valley. In *The Prehistory of the Tehuacan Valley, Vol. 4,
    Chronology and Irrigation,* ed. Frederick Johnson, pp. 81–153. Univer-
    sity of Texas Press, Austin.
Wright, Henry T. 1977. Recent Research on the Origin of the State. In
    Annual Review of Anthropology 6:379–97.
Wright, Henry T. and Gregory A. Johnson. 1975. Population, Exchange,
    and Early State Formation in Southwestern Iran. *American Anthropolo-
    gist* 77:267–89.
Wright, Henry T. and Melinda Zeder. 1977. The Simulation of a Linear
    Exchange System Under Equilibrium Conditions. In *Exchange Systems
    in Prehistory,* ed. Timothy Earle and J. E. Erickson, pp. 233–54. Aca-
    demic Press, New York.
Yoffee, Norman. 1979. The Decline and Rise of Mesopotamian Civiliza-
    tion: An Ethnoarchaeological Perspective on the Evolution of Social
    Complexity. *American Antiquity* 44:5–34.

Index